INTERSECTIONS
Faith, Church, and the Academy

Mark E. Hanshaw and Timothy S. Moore
General Editors

HIGHER EDUCATION & MINISTRY
General Board of Higher Education and Ministry
THE UNITED METHODIST CHURCH

Intersections: Faith, Church, and the Academy

The General Board of Higher Education and Ministry leads and serves The United Methodist Church in the recruitment, preparation, nurture, education, and support of Christian leaders—lay and clergy—for the work of making disciples of Jesus Christ for the transformation of the world. The General Board of Higher Education and Ministry of The United Methodist Church serves as an advocate for the intellectual life of the church. The Board's mission embodies the Wesleyan tradition of commitment to the education of laypersons and ordained persons by providing access to higher education for all persons.

Contents

Preface

From the early days of John Wesley's work—tending the needs of the most marginal residents of eighteenth-century London—to the present day, the Methodist movement's central concern has been the question of what it means to be in relationship with a diverse and divided world. Indeed, while his language may appear somewhat archaic, we see Wesley striving to make sense of the good works undertaken by members of other faiths. In contrast to the failings of his own Christian community, he commented on the character of other faith traditions in a sermon delivered late in his career:

> But with Heathens, Mahometans, and Jews we have at present nothing to do; only we may wish that their lives did not shame many of us that are called Christians. We have not much more to do with the members of the Church of Rome. But we cannot doubt, that many of them, like the excellent Archbishop of Cambray, still retain (notwithstanding many mistakes) that faith that worketh by love. And how many of the Protestants enjoy this, whether members of the Church of England, or of other congregations?[1]

The question of what it means for Methodists to be aware of and engaged with individuals of differing cultural backgrounds and religious beliefs has loomed ever larger in the days since John Wesley. We now live in a global society, where people of highly varied backgrounds and life experiences work, live, and function side by side. For many of the present generation, the homogeneity of the English countryside, once known by Wesley, must seem little more than a historic relic.

Expanded cultural diversity can bring many benefits to a community. At the same time, it may also serve as a source of social anxiety and, potentially, conflict. Even as diverse friendships and partnerships across the globe help break down the ethnic and religious barriers that once separated communities and peoples, we are witness to ongoing atrocities. Recent global events, ranging from the mass migrations of peoples under siege to political battles that have divided nations and regions over issues of religion and ethnicity, continually remind us that the work of bridging cultural divisions is far from over.

These shifts in our global demographic landscape have given new importance to the questions that Methodists have wrestled with from the beginning. Frequently, individuals look to the church and its institutions for guidance on how to understand and respond to this social and cultural landscape. As renowned scholar John Hick observed more than three decades ago:

> Christians have always lived, consciously or unconsciously, in a religiously plural world. In some places and periods they have been acutely aware of other religious traditions living and growing alongside their own. But in Western Christianity this pluralistic consciousness has only fully emerged during the lifetimes of people now living. Prior to that, religions such as Hinduism and Buddhism, Judaism and Islam, were generally seen as strange and dark residues of paganism, utterly inferior to Christianity and proper targets of the churches' missionary zeal. Today, however, we have all become conscious, in varying degrees, that our Christian history is one of a number of variant streams of religious life, each with its own distinctive forms of experience, thought and spirituality. And accordingly

> we have come to accept the need to re-understand our own
> faith, not as the one and only, but as one of several.[2]

It would seem that Hick's words are only more relevant in the complex world that has emerged in the decades since he put pen to paper.

Among the groups most desirous of direction and insight regarding our place in a diverse world may be those who have just begun laying the foundations for their own futures. Our youth—from school-aged students still struggling to comprehend the size and complexity of our global community to college students weighing a daunting array of educational pathways within a rapidly changing social environment—are left asking what sort of world they will inherit.

Within this global climate of uncertainty and disorientation, our United Methodist–related colleges and universities can and must play a central role in helping students better understand the parameters of the social struggles unfolding before us. At the same time, our colleges and universities have the opportunity to do more than facilitate understanding. These vital educational institutions can provide the environment and opening necessary to turn inquisitive students into active community leaders. And indeed, many United Methodist colleges and universities have taken up this challenge.

In 1988, the General Conference of The United Methodist Church adopted a widely cited resolution on interfaith relations. That resolution has been reaffirmed and amended by four subsequent General Conference gatherings. Entitled "Called to Be Neighbors and Witnesses: Guidelines for Interreligious Relationships," the resolution calls upon members of the church to promote "mutual understanding, cooperation and transformation" through purposeful engagement with individuals of differing faiths.[3] During the period since the passage of the original version of this resolution, innovative and inspired interfaith engagement arising from within the United Methodist community has taken place on college campuses.

This volume seeks to provide a glimpse at some of that innovation and inspired engagement. While crafted to serve the needs of a diverse array of individuals from clergy to academic administrators and from lay parishioners to faculty, the most important audience for this volume may be students at our United Methodist–related schools. These students will be best positioned to reshape our world in ways that respond to the increased diversity within our individual communities.

Intersections: Faith, Church, and the Academy was conceived as an interfaith resource. It has been designed to provide insight into both the history of the involvement of Methodism in the interfaith movement and the issues that may shape the future of this field of engagement. More important, this volume seeks to underscore some of the efforts taking place on college and university campuses and chaplaincy ministries aimed at building bridges between diverse groups of advantaged and disadvantaged populations. It is meant to provide a platform from which we can learn the experiences and innovations of our peers. It is further meant to inspire future opportunities for Methodist institutions to play key roles in preparing individuals to be the intercultural leaders of the present and future.

In this volume, readers will find an array of chapters written by scholars, chaplains, university administrators, and clergy. The chapters seek to shed light on projects, programs, research, and experiences that are shaping lives and perspectives.

The opening chapter includes the voice of one who has greatly influenced interfaith efforts around the globe. S. Wesley Ariarajah, the former deputy general secretary of the World Council of Churches and broadly published scholar, opens this volume with a rich reflection on Methodists' efforts to contribute to the global interfaith movement. His chapter reaches back to the origins of the interfaith movement and traces the history forward into the modern era. He lays a useful and intriguing foundation for understanding other contributions to this volume.

In the second chapter, Timothy S. Moore, director of donor development at Union Presbyterian Seminary and coeditor of this volume, wrestles with a patient and persistent commitment embedded in the foundations of United Methodist–related higher education. That commitment is to hold in positive tension both learning and piety. The joint presence of learning and faith in these academic institutions generates the possibility that this tension will impact the culture, climate, and curricula at these schools, making distinct the kind of education received at church-related institutions. Less theoretical than practical, Moore's essay examines a constructive benefit that such a tension may offer when taken seriously by outlining an education program implemented at one United Methodist–related school.

In chapter 3, Eva Semien Baham, assistant professor of history at Dillard University, addresses a core question. She seeks to consider how faith may become active without being dominated by religious particularism. Baham answers this question by outlining the historical and cultural backgrounds of New Orleans. From this context, she traces the blurring of religious boundaries by religious groups to work together on behalf of African Americans. New Orleans's religious and social diversity illustrates an intricately delicate dance of good intentions in a highly charged environment. In her chapter, Baham asserts that effective aid necessitated interfaith cooperation to benefit the city's African American population. Concentrating on her own institution's founding, Baham examines that institution's establishment as a collective advantage emergent from both interracial and interfaith cooperation.

In chapter 4, Kent Andersen, director of the Hess Center for Leadership and Service at Birmingham-Southern College, offers a personal reflection on the perspective-changing impact of his own participation in service-learning projects initiated through the chaplain's office in the college he serves. As an individual embracing no defined faith perspective, Andersen reflects on the impact of service-learning experiences organized in connection with San Francisco's Glide Memorial United Methodist Church, a "radically inclusive" community. As he observes, the experiences proved powerfully thought-provoking, prompting him to rethink his own faith perspective. Further, the chapter focuses attention on the important place of service-learning on the college campus.

In chapter 5, Chad Pevateaux, assistant professor at Texas Wesleyan University, draws upon the biblical story of Job as a metaphor to discuss methods that he employs in specific courses to encourage students to objectively consider the relationships that bind varying religious systems. Pevateaux draws parallels between the suffering of Job and the many tragedies that have become the backdrop of life for modern students. Further, he reminds us of the fact that so many of these tragedies have some religious dimension. In light of these tragedies, he argues that helping students to develop an interfaith perspective can be critical to providing the resources necessary to overcome the uncertainty and fear that naturally arise when one confronts such tragedy. Further, he argues that students can find security in understanding.

In chapter 6, Nathan Eric Dickman, associate professor at Young Harris College, offers a call, rooted in his own teaching experience, for the employment of a methodology of teaching courses in religion that is rooted in radically open inquiry and the cultivation of interreligious literacy. Dickman observes that religious affiliation in modern America has come to be approached frequently through the lens of a consumerist perspective, even though religious literacy appears to be in decline. He makes the persuasive argument that United Methodist colleges and universities should broadly embrace the strategy of encouraging open questioning in religious studies courses. Such open questioning, while sometimes uncomfortable, is a central ingredient in promoting expanded religious and interreligious literacy, he concludes.

In chapter 7, Hans Gustafson, associate director of the Jay Phillips Center for Interfaith Learning at University of St. Thomas, explores an intentional effort by his university to encourage faculty to add interreligious community engagement (i.e., service-learning) to their course pedagogy. In his chapter, he describes the essentials for course design and implementation; shares key readings, student learning outcomes, and types of community partners; and offers strategies for student assessment. Vitally, Gustafson provides the background context to his theory and practice behind college-level, course-based community engagement attuned to intentional "interreligious" course-based community engagement.

In chapter 8, Diane R. Wiener, director of the Disability Cultural Center at Syracuse University, and Jikyo Bonnie Shoultz, chaplain at the Buddhist Campus Ministry at Syracuse University, discuss the university's implementation of a unique model for interfaith conversations, called the Interfaith Dialogue Dinner Series at Syracuse University. Using a combination of personal narratives, academic elements, and excerpts from informal conversations and interviews, Wiener and Shoultz reflect on the impact of the event series on people's lives; experiences of faith, secularism, and community; and relationships formed, both on and off-campus.

In chapter 9, Gladys Childs, an associate professor at Texas Wesleyan University, and Dennis Hall, vice president of student affairs at Texas Wesleyan, introduce mindfulness as a key methodological commitment and strategy for governing decisions and conversations on the university campus. The authors consider mindfulness to be a key component when designing initiatives, experiences, and extra- or cocurricular activities. They recognize mindfulness as the potential thread that sews together an often-disjointed collegiate experience. Specifically, throughout their chapter, Childs and Hall overlay this commitment to mindfulness onto their outline of the challenges associated with their naïveté of other religious perspectives, the allotment of resources and space, the celebration of diverse holy days, and the multifaceted nature of student need.

In chapter 10, Nicholas Rademacher, associate professor of religious studies at Cabrini University, attends to the dual and, at times, competing interests of faith-based institutions of higher education to preserve and enhance their specific religious identity while taking seriously the increasing religious diversity of the student body, staff, and faculty. In his chapter, Rademacher shares the responses to this challenge undertaken by his institution, recounting several university-wide initiatives and personal approaches employed to address the matter of dual interests.

In chapter 11, Aaron Twitchell, chaplain and instructor at the Pennington School in Pennington, New Jersey, argues for intentionality in the training and supervision of chaplains assigned to boarding schools and other residential settings. More specific, Twitchell offers insights gained from his experiences on the campus to frame his position that contemporary chaplaincy—with its many cultural, religious, and emotional nuances—requires extensive training in a clinical setting; ongoing support; education; and training by clinical supervisors and colleagues; participation in a local community of clinical chaplains; and, ideally, board certification in clinical chaplaincy to be effective. Throughout his chapter, he proffers that these requirements ought to be the minimum benchmarks for a robust and relevant school chaplaincy and interfaith ministry.

In chapter 12, founder and president of the Interfaith Youth Core, Eboo Patel, and his colleague, Carolyn Roncolato, look to the history of The United Methodist Church to argue that interfaith engagement is central to the vision of the denomination. Drawing upon the Social Principles, Patel and Roncolato identify broad alignment between asserted United Methodist priorities and the work of contemporary interfaith leaders. As individuals who have devoted their careers to the task of expanding interfaith engagement upon college and university campuses, Patel and Roncolato identify the United Methodist tradition as one that has "prioritized interfaith cooperation" and laid a foundation for future leadership in interfaith cooperation and relationship.

In chapter 13, John A. Tures, professor of political science at La-Grange College, challenges general assumptions related to the connection between religion and war. Referencing major conflicts involving two or more nation-states taking place over the period between the middle of the seventeenth century and the end of the twentieth century, Tures seeks to differentiate those that were prompted due to religious disagreement or dispute from those that stemmed from other motivations. Based on his data, Tures concludes that wars have been motivated by factors including claims to land and the desire to capture resources much more frequently than by religious concerns. This analysis, he suggests, may help to eradicate the common myth that religion serves as the greatest factor prompting war.

In the final chapter, Mark E. Hanshaw, coeditor of this volume and, at the time of this writing, a dean at Texas Wesleyan University, analyzes results from research conducted on business leaders in the North Texas region, focused on interest in interfaith training. The research, conducted during 2016 and 2017, sought opinions from corporate leaders and executives from a diverse array of industries on the topic of the utility of educational programming pertaining to interfaith issues. The research shows a significant interest on the part of those surveyed in having available new forms of interfaith training to support corporate and business operations. The chapter ends with consideration of the lessons that may be drawn from this research.

Taken as a whole, this book seeks to challenge its readers to identify ways they can prompt interfaith engagements within their own communities. It provides insight regarding specific interfaith educational strategies and trends. Further, the volume serves to challenge its readers to actively cultivate opportunities to interact with and learn from individuals of varied religious and cultural perspectives. It is our assertion that only through such open engagement can greater understanding be fostered. On this point, the words of the great Indian social activist Mohandas K. Gandhi ring true.

> It has been my experience that I am always true from my point of view, but am often wrong from the point of view of my honest critics. I know that we are both right from our respective points of view. And this knowledge saves me from attributing motives to my opponents or critics. The seven blind men who gave seven different descriptions of the elephant were all right from their respective points of view, and wrong from the point of view of one another, and right and wrong from the point of view of the man who knew the elephant. I very much like this doctrine of the manyness of reality. It is this doctrine that has taught me to judge a Mussulman from his

own standpoint and a Christian from his. Formerly I used to resent the ignorance of my opponents. Today I can love them because I am gifted with the eye to see myself as others see them and vice versa.[4]

Again, it is our hope that this resource serves to inform and enlighten. It is also our hope that it prompts action. From colleges to congregations, individuals are seeking new approaches aimed at overcoming societal division and resentments. Some working strategies designed to prompt increased cross-cultural engagements are incorporated within this volume. However, if it serves its purpose, this text is more than merely a repository of ideas, but is, instead, the beginning of a broad conversation and a call to honest engagement with and in the world. Finally, we extend our thanks to all of those who contributed to this important volume.

Mark E. Hanshaw and Timothy S. Moore

Notes

1 John Wesley, Sermon 106, "On Faith," April 9, 1788, in *The Sermons of John Wesley,* Thomas Jackson, ed., Global Ministries: The United Methodist Church, https://www.umcmission.org/Find-Resources/John-Wesley-Sermons/Sermon-106-On-Faith.

2 John Hick, *God Has Many Names* (Philadelphia: Westminster John Knox Press, 1982), 7.

3 "Called to Be Neighbors and Witnesses: Guidelines for Interreligious Relationships," Resolution #3141, in *The Book of Resolutions of The United Methodist Church: 2012* (Nashville: United Methodist Publishing House, 2012).

4 M. K. Gandhi, *Young India*, Jan. 21, 1926.

HISTORICAL
INTERSECTIONS

The Interfaith Movement and Methodism

S. Wesley Ariarajah

Humankind has always lived in a religiously plural world, and there have been periods of history when mutual rivalry and conflict or harmony and mutual respect have marked their life together. However, it is customary to point to the Parliament of the World's Religions, in Chicago, USA, in 1893, as the beginning of the modern global interfaith movement, where a conscious effort was made to bring representatives of some of the major religious traditions of the world together to promote peace and harmony among them and in the world. The parliament was held in conjunction with the World Columbian Exhibition to mark the anniversary of the "discovery" of America by Christopher Columbus and was concerned primarily with promoting trade and industry.

However, one of the organizers of the exhibition, Charles Carroll Bonney, a distinguished lawyer, came up with the idea that the exposition must be accompanied by a series of world congresses on the major areas of human intellectual activity. Bonney felt that it should also include a parliament of the world's religions in the belief that "when the religious faiths of the world recognize each other as brothers, children of the one Father whom all profess to love and serve, then and not till then, will the nations of the world yield to the Spirit of concord and learn war no more."[1]

The concept of a parliament of the world's religions was made a reality; more than four thousand people attended the opening ceremony. Among the religious leaders that made a significant impact on the parliament were the Buddhist priest Anagarika Damapala of Sri Lanka, the founder of the Mahabodi Society (1864–1933); and Swami Vivekananda (1863–1902), disciple of Sri Ramakrishna, who began the process of popularizing the Vedantic philosophy and setting up of Vedantic centers in the Western Hemisphere. Marcus Braybrooke, in his detailed account of the parliament, points out that there was also much discussion on the relationship of religions to each other. One of the most popular presentations on this issue was made by Swami Vivekananda, challenging the exclusiveness and narrow-mindedness of missionaries in India and calling for the unity of all religious traditions. There were also some discussions on very practical topics, such as social reform in India, what Judaism has done for women, and crime and its remedy.

Although the parliament was considered a resounding success, there was no immediate follow-up, and it took many decades for more institutional expressions of interfaith movement to materialize at the global level. Among the notable ones to emerge was the International Association for Religious Freedom (IARF), dating back to 1900, dealing mainly with issues of religious freedom; and the World Congress of Faiths (1936), which made serious attempts to follow up the intentions and the spirit of the parliament. Other significant organizations that followed include the Temple of Understanding (1960), with primary emphasis on the spiritual unity among religions; and the World Conference on Religion and Peace (WCRP). The WCRP, which had its first assembly in Kyoto, Japan, in 1970, was deeply committed to global peace and nuclear disarmament. Now renamed Religions for Peace, today it is a well-organized global interfaith organization with regional and national chapters and with regular assemblies every three years. It also plays a significant role at the United Nations as an NGO.

The year 1993 was the centennial of the first parliament held in Chicago, and the religious leaders in Chicago moved to mark the centenary with a second Parliament of World's Religions, meeting again in Chicago. Most of the religious traditions of the world were well represented at this parliament, where, in addition to many other engagements, the religious representatives hammered out a document titled *Towards a Global Ethic,* which called on all religious communities to commit themselves to basic values such as nonviolence, a just economic order, tolerance and truthfulness, and gender equality. Although there was disagreement among them on how these values might be interpreted and practiced in different contexts and cultures, the agreement itself was seen as a big step forward. Nearly thirty thousand people attended the closing open-air ceremony, at which the main speaker was the Dalai Lama.

Although this second parliament was also a success, the decision was made not to make it into yet another international interfaith organization but to call such parliaments every four to five years in different parts of the world. Following up on this decision, subsequent parliaments have been held in Cape Town (1999), Barcelona (2004), Melbourne (2009), and Salt Lake City (2015).

Other significant interfaith organizations today include the International Peace Council, United Religions Initiative, Youth Core, Elijah Interfaith Institute, and many others that function at regional and national levels. Although most of the interfaith movements originally had Christian initiative and leadership, today a significant number of initiatives comes also from other faith groups and leaders. Wilfred Cantwell Smith marveled at this development with the memorable statement, "The world has gone irreversibly interfaith!"[2]

Having had this general overview of the development of interfaith engagements at the global level, I wish to turn now, first to the

Christian struggles to come to terms with religious plurality and dialogue, and then to the contribution Methodism and Methodist theology can make to this vital concern.

The Christian Struggle with Religious Plurality

As a religion that grew out of Judaism, Christianity from its beginning had to struggle with the question of its relationship to Judaism. When it moved into the Greco-Roman world, it had to come to terms with Greek philosophy and the Greek and Roman religious traditions. A study of the early history of the church would show that some of the early Christian theologians also had to deal with the question of Christian relationship to other religions. However, a more organized attempt to look at the relationship of the gospel to other religions can be traced from the time of the first World Missionary Conference held in Edinburgh, Scotland, in 1910, which is also commonly considered the beginning of the modern ecumenical movement.

John R. Mott, a Methodist layman from the United States, and some of his friends were the initiators of the idea of calling a conference of all the Protestant mission agencies and societies to Edinburgh so that the human and financial resources could be meaningfully deployed in mission work. Mott believed that if the missionary agencies and societies would pool their resources, do a deep study of the issues faced in the mission fields, and develop a common strategy, it would be possible to evangelize the whole world in that generation. Since Europe and the Americas were already considered "Christian" continents, the main focus was on Asia and Africa, much of which were under colonial rule.

Mott succeeded in persuading most of the mission agencies and societies to participate. There were twelve hundred official delegates, mainly from Europe and North America (seventeen from Asia and none from Africa). The conference organized its work into eight commissions on subjects related to the missionary task. It is not my intention here to give the details of the conference itself or the work of all the commissions, but to highlight the work of Commission IV on "the missionary message in relation to the non-Christian world." Although it was intended to work on how the missionary message could be shaped so that it would be easily received by peoples of other religious traditions, in reality, the work of Commission IV turned out to be the beginning of serious questioning of the commonly held assumptions about other religious traditions in missionary work.

This happened because the leaders of Commission IV decided to send an advanced questionnaire to missionaries working in the field about their attitudes toward other religions and appropriate ways to approach them. The commission was surprised to receive more than two hundred sets of answers, some of considerable length. Most of the answers, especially those of the missionaries working in the Hindu context, challenged many of the traditional assumptions about other religions that undergirded the missionary task. Almost all the replies emphasized that Christians "should possess, and not merely assume," a sympathetic attitude toward Hinduism. They also called for pro-longed and patient study of Hinduism so that such sympathy may be "based upon knowledge and . . . not be the child of emotion or imagination." In the commission's view, "more harm has been done in India than in any other country by missionaries that have lacked the wisdom to appreciate the nobler side of the religion which they have labored so indefatigably to supplant."[3]

F. W. Steinthal, for instance, claimed in his response that knowl-edge of Hinduism should go well beyond familiarity with its history, ritual, philosophy, and so on, to the point of grasping, as far as one is able, the "real life" that throbs within:

> Below the strange forms and hardly intelligible language, lies life, the spiritual life of human souls, needing God, seeking God, laying hold of God, so far as they have found Him. Until we have at least reached so far that under the ceremonies and doctrines we have found the religious life of the people, and at least to some extent have begun to understand this life, we do not know what Hinduism really is, and are missing the essential connection with the people's religious life.[4]

J. N. Farquhar, one of the early missionaries, well known for his volume *The Crown of Hinduism*, where he advocated what is known as the "fulfillment theory" of seeing Christ as fulfilling the longings of Hinduism, said that undue criticism of Hinduism must be stopped. He argued, in a forty-three-page response to the commission's question- naire, that "Christ's own attitude to Judaism ought to be our attitude to other faiths, even if the gap be far greater and the historical con- nection absent."[5]

In summing up the commission's findings on Christian message to the whole Missionary Conference, the commission reiterated its conviction that the Christian attitude toward Hinduism, notwithstand- ing the elements that the Christian must reject, should be one of understanding and sympathy. It said that the Christian should seek the noble elements in non-Christian religions and use them as steps to higher things, for Hinduism in its higher forms "plainly manifest the working of the Holy Spirit." The "merely iconoclastic attitude," the commission said, was condemned by the majority of its correspon- dents as "radically unwise and unjust."[6]

Further, the findings held that the challenge to explore fully the nature of the inner life of the soul in God can be seen as the most important impact of the Christian encounter with Hinduism:

> It may be that here there will be the richest result of it all, that whether through the Christianized mind of India or through the mind of the missionary stirred to its depths by contact with the Indian mind, we shall discover new and wonderful things in the ancient revelation which have been hidden in part from the just and faithful of the Western world.[7]

I have dealt with the work of Commission IV at the 1910 World Missionary Conference mainly to indicate that although the concept of dialogue arose at a later stage, there were, already in 1910, strong feelings about the need to rethink Christian relationship to other re- ligions. However, the rest of the Missionary Conference was domi- nated by leaders who were determined to evangelize the world in that generation. The *Report of Commission IV* remained at the margins of the conference's interest.[8]

Further Advances in the Second Missionary Conference

The success of the Edinburgh conference resulted in the missionary movement's decision that World Missionary Conferences should be held periodically, ideally every ten years. However, the second conference was held only in 1928 at the Mount of Olives, Jerusalem. By this time the views held by Commission IV had received some currency; comparative study of religions had begun to make its impact in the academic world; and there was general concern among Christians on the rise of secularism, both in the West and the East, affecting all religions.

In the United States, W. E. Hocking, professor at Harvard University, began to advocate the view that it is not other religions but secularism that is a danger to the Christian faith. But he went further to argue that the universal spread of secular philosophy required a new alignment of religious forces with whatever was of true substance of religion everywhere. He began to use the phrase "world religion" in an all-embracing way, to include the different systems and names that in his view were not separate, for they "merged in the universal human faith in the Divine Being."[9] Further, one of the main speakers of the Jerusalem conference, Nicol Macnicol, argued that one should mainly look at the "values" advocated by other religions that can enrich the Christian faith.

All this meant that while at Edinburgh the advocacy to rethink the Christian attitude to other religions stayed in the margins, at Jerusalem this call found a central place. The challenge to respect other religions and to respond to the "values" found in them was well received. The Jerusalem report said, "On our part we repudiate any symptoms of religious imperialism that would desire to impose beliefs and practices on others in order to manage their souls in their supposed interest. We obey God who respects our wills and we desire to respect those of others."[10]

The report went even further to exemplify the "noble qualities" in non-Christian "persons and systems" as the proof that God has "not left Himself without witness" among any people. It went on to illustrate such noble qualities, without any attempt to evaluate their spiritual value either to the adherents of other faiths or to Christians:

> We recognize as part of the one Truth that sense of majesty of God and the consequent reverence in worship, which are conspicuous in Islam, the deep sympathy for the world's sorrow and unselfish search for the way of escape, which are at the heart of Buddhism; the desire for contact with Ultimate Reality conceived as spiritual, which is prominent in Hinduism; the belief in the moral order of the universe and consequent insistence on moral conduct, which are inculcated by Confucianism; the disinterested pursuit of truth and human welfare which is often found in those who stand for secular civilization but do not accept Christ as their Lord and Saviour.[11]

There is no need to point out that this very expansive approach to other religious traditions did not sit well with much of the leadership of the missionary movement, especially in Europe. But the most controversial part of the message, in the discussions after the conference, was its call to other religions, under the influence of Hocking, to join hands with Christians in the struggle against secularism. To keep secularism and materialism at bay, it called upon the non-Christian religions "to hold fast to faith in the unseen and the eternal in face of the growing materialism of the world; to cooperate with us against all the evils of secularism."[12]

The last part of the Jerusalem report reaffirmed some of the traditional convictions about Christ and the gospel message and the need to take it to the world. But many within the missionary movement felt that the Jerusalem conference had compromised the need and the urgency of the evangelistic calling of the church. After the conference was over, its perspectives on other religions became a full-blown controversy. It had set the stage for the need for a clear, concise, and well-considered Christian position in relation to people of other faiths and a convincing theological rationale for Christian missions directed at them. This is what the third World Missionary Conference in Tambaram, near Madras, set out to do in 1938.

Reclaiming the Missionary Mandate

Fearing that the very concept and practice of mission were under threat, leaders of the missionary movement called on one of the well-known Dutch missiologists of that time, Hendrik Kraemer, to come out with a preparatory volume for the third World Missionary Conference that would spell out the biblical-theological rationale for mission, which would also, of necessity, make a theological evaluation of other religious traditions. Kraemer was considered the best person to do it because, apart from being a good theologian and missiologist, he had served for many years as a missionary among Muslims in Egypt and in Java, Indonesia, and had built up friendly and dialogical relationships with them.

It is beyond the scope of this essay to discuss the contents of the more-than-two-hundred-page volume *The Christian Message in a Non-Christian World*, which Kraemer wrote as the preparatory volume, or to analyze his presentation of the beliefs of other religious traditions. However, it is important to briefly state the theological rationale he gave for Christian missions and the controversy it created.

Building on the theology of Karl Barth, Kraemer insisted that God, as a wholly transcendent Reality, cannot be known or grasped by human beings. God can be known only through God's own self-revelation, and this revelation took place in the history of Israel and culminated in Jesus Christ. To this he added the concept of "biblical realism," by which he meant that the Bible is realistic about the human condition. As "fallen" beings that rebelled against God, all humans have lost their capacity to relate to God through their own efforts. This meant that all religious efforts to know and reach God, however spiritual, noble, and genuine they might be, are vain attempts.

But God, in God's love and grace, has revealed Godself to human beings in Jesus Christ. However, the only way to discern and apprehend this revelation is by responding to it in faith. Kraemer maintained that

> revelation in its proper sense is when it is by its very nature inaccessible and *remains so, even when it is revealed*. The necessary correlate to the concept of revelation is therefore faith. It lies in the very nature of revelation that the only organ for apprehending it is faith; and for the same reason faith, in the strictly religious sense, can only be appropriately defined as at the same time a divine gift and a human act.[13]

Much more can and needs to be said on Kraemer's theology, but the main lines are clear. All religious efforts, including that of Christianity as a religion, are vain in that they are all part of the human rebellion against God. God has come to the rescue by offering God's self-revelation in Christ, but this revelation can be grasped only through the response of faith. This means that all human beings should be given the opportunity to hear the gospel of God's self-revelation in Christ and be challenged to respond to it in faith. Christians have no choice but to proclaim the gospel message to all.

Based on this, Kraemer also advocated another position that there is "discontinuity" between religions and the gospel message. The gospel cannot be seen as fulfillment of other religions or as something that can be built on the "values" in other religious traditions. Rather, it presents a challenge to all human beings to say yes or no—a challenge to respond in faith to the gospel. Kraemer was clear that this does not mean that we should denigrate other religions, refrain from appreciating the high spiritual values they uphold, or hold back on developing close and friendly relationship with them. Yet, it is incumbent on us to present the challenge of the gospel to them and invite them to faith in Jesus Christ.

To the leaders of the missionary movement, especially from the Western Hemisphere, Kraemer appeared to have put the missionary mandate back on the rails. But many Asian leaders and missionaries in Asia challenged Kraemer's portrayal of other religions, his under-standing of the human condition, his restrictive interpretation of rev-elation, and his insistence on discontinuity between the gospel and religious traditions. It broke out into full-blown controversy in Tam-baram and continued after the event as the "Tambaram controversy," which eventually led to some of the breakthroughs in Christian under-standing of other religions.[14]

Post-Tambaram Developments

After the Tambaram meeting most of the Western churches got em-broiled in the Second World War. The Tambaram controversy, however, continued in Asia. The end of the war also led to other developments in Asia that impacted the future of Christian relationships to other religions. The national independence of India in 1947, followed by the end of colonial rule in other parts of the world, the Communist Revolution in China in 1949, the Korean War, the rise of nationalism, and the resurgence of Asian religions that had been liberated from co-lonial subjugation, among other events, created a whole new reality, which also called on churches to rethink their relationship to people of other religious traditions.

In the meantime, the devastation brought about by the war in Europe, the urgency to respond to the needs of millions of refugees, the challenge to work on reconciliation among nations that had been at war, among other pressing needs, precipitated the formation of the World Council of Churches (WCC) in 1948. The missionary movement had also, by then, been institutionalized into the International Mis-sionary Council (IMC). When the churches were ready to return to the mission question, they realized the importance of taking up the Tam-baram controversy. It was decided that the WCC and IMC would co-sponsor a study process in the churches, led by study centers around the world, on the "Word of God and Living Faiths of Men [sic]."

An important consultation was held in Kandy, Sri Lanka, in 1967, to draw together the findings of the study process. At this consul-tation the theological hard line taken by Barth–Kraemer theology toward other faiths was deeply questioned. God's equal concern for all of humankind in creation, providence, and salvation was emphasized, and the concept of "dialogue" as a more appropriate way to relate to people of other religious traditions was developed.[15]

The impetus provided by this consultation led the fourth assembly of the WCC in Uppsala, Sweden, in 1968 to confirm the concept of "dialogue." This affirmation led to the creation of the WCC's "Sub-unit for Dialogue with People of Living Faiths and Ideologies" (DFI) in 1971. Interestingly, about the same time, the Roman Catholic Church had also called the Second Vatican Council to respond to the new challenges faced by the Church. One of the areas that came up for close scrutiny was the Church's relationship to other religious traditions. The council made an important promulgation known as the Declaration on the Relationship of the Church to Non-Christian Religions (*Nostra Aetate*). This process also led to the institutionalization of a dialogue program within the Roman Catholic Church, called the "Vatican Secretariat for Non-Christian Religions." It was later upgraded and renamed the Pontifical Council for Interreligious Dialogue.

Dimensions of Christian Engagement with Other Religions

In spite of the institutionalization of interfaith dialogue within the ecumenical movement and the Roman Catholic Church, there were many struggles before it became acceptable to the churches. Today many Methodist churches around the world have developed guidelines for interfaith dialogue and have set up interfaith dialogue programs and ministries. However, many who would accept dialogue as a necessary discipline to live in religiously plural societies refuse to accept the challenge it brings to the Christian theological understanding of other religions (theology of religions) and the implications it has for the way Christian faith itself has been understood and passed down through the centuries. Thus, there are four different dimensions to theological work in relation to other religious traditions.

First is the task of building positive interfaith relations between Christians and peoples of other religious traditions through interfaith dialogue. Here the emphasis is on building a "community of communities" that contributes to mutual understanding, mutual respect, and cooperation on matters of common interest to the whole community. But this can be easily done only when Christians are also enabled to see other religious traditions with a new theological perspective. This also means that they need to know what others believe and how their beliefs have shaped their spirituality, their histories, and their cultural practices.

The second task, following up on the first, is to do some serious rethinking of the Christian theology of religions. What theological sense can we make of the fact that peoples of other religious traditions pray, claim to have relationship with God, and have long and rich spiritual histories? Are the Christian positions taken through the centuries on other religions adequate for our day? If not, what theological assessment can we make of the spiritual life of others?

Third is to explore the challenges interfaith relations bring to the Christian faith itself. Does God listen to the prayers of a Muslim or a Hindu? If not, why not? If God does relate to people of other religious traditions, how does it impact our traditional understanding of God, our convictions about Christ, our understanding of salvation, and our concept of mission?

Fourth, we also need to find answers to concrete questions and issues that arise when Christians live in religiously plural societies: Can we pray together? What is our attitude toward interreligious marriages? Can Christians and other religious traditions work together on common problems faced by the community? How does one deal with fundamentalism and religious extremism? What is the nature of the religious education we need to give our children in an interfaith community? Today, even more issues have come on the interfaith agenda, such as: religion and violence, religion and culture, conversion and religious freedom, individual rights and rights of communities, rights of women and children within religious communities, religion and state, the place of religion in public discourse, and so on.

These pressing questions have led some within the Christian community to advocate that what is needed today is not confessional theologies but "public theology"—which is theological reflection related to the whole human community with theology at the service of the well-being of all, irrespective of religious labels. This requires different starting points and data for the theological task, different methodologies, and new partnerships in the theological work.

These are all issues and questions that need also to be addressed by the higher education ministries of the Methodist Church. There is a need for intense research, creative thinking, bold ventures, and new ways of understanding and practicing the faith, which also needs to be mediated to the congregations. In other words, at the higher education levels, Methodist scholarship needs to be helped to delve deeper into the teachings of other religious traditions and their own.

Here are some examples of questions I had placed before students:

- What contribution do the Hindu and Buddhist understandings on wealth, power, and renunciation make to the Christian understanding of the gospel and its application today?

- What is the place of Islamic spirituality within the Islamic tradition? How does it relate to contemporary expressions of Islam and its relationship to other religions?

- What lessons can Christian theology and practice learn from the understanding and approach to nature in Asian religious traditions, and how do we translate them toward common religious struggles to meet the ecological crisis?

These examples are given to highlight the concern that we need to move beyond a study of other religious traditions as such, to the level of engagement and exploration that would make religious traditions respond to some of the pressing questions of our day. This can be done within Methodism only in the institutions of higher learning. But are there resources within the Methodist tradition to help higher education ministries in this field?

Methodist Theological Resources

John Wesley was born on June 17, 1703 and passed away on March 2, 1791. His ministry and teachings were situated within the social, religious, cultural, and economic context of eighteenth-century Britain, partially extending into North America. It is also clear that the Puritan heritage he inherited and the Western theological tradition he acquired at Oxford shaped the broad outlines of his theology. Also of importance was his "heart-warming experience" on May 24, 1738.[16] The strength of John Wesley's theological heritage is one way he managed to integrate his many influences into a spiritual and theological movement that remains vibrant to this day.

Yet, Wesley was a man of his time and place, and like that of all great teachers and leaders, his contribution also needs to be reinterpreted for our day. In looking for Methodist resources, we need to discern what aspects of his theology need to be lifted up for our time. This is not an easy task because Methodism today is a global phenomenon, cutting across nations, cultures, and a variety of contexts—very different from the context he addressed.

I have found it useful to look at the Methodist, and especially the Wesleyan, heritage through two lenses. The first relates to theological methodology. What inspiration can we get for Methodist higher education from Wesley's theological methodology? The second relates to aspects of his theological work that can be elaborated and spelled out for our time, and in the context of this essay, to Christian understandings of and relationship to other religious traditions.

Theological Methodology

Since this discussion is familiar to many, I would like to summarize Wesley's theology in five points.

First, Wesley's theology is a "responsive theology." Although he stood within the broad outlines of the classical theological tradition of the church, he saw that the Christian faith comes alive only when it responds to the concrete socioeconomic and religious situations of men and women in a given place.

Second, his theology was for and about the people. At a time when theology was the preserve of the institutional church and the academy, Wesley brought it down to the level of the ordinary people. It is no surprise that while one has to read the *Institutes of the Christian Religion* to know John Calvin's theology, one has to read sermons, letters, journals, and hymns to learn Wesley's theology.

Third, while Wesley was deeply rooted in the Bible, his spiritual life was nurtured in Bible study groups at Oxford, and he looked upon his ministry as "spreading spiritual holiness over the land,"[17] he recognized the need for a cluster of teaching authorities for doing theology and exercising Christian discipleship. For him, the authority of the faith is to be found in the Bible, in tradition, in reason, and in experience. Standing within considerable parts of the Western tradition, which has been suspicious of reason and fearful of experience, and the Reformation tradition, which claimed "Scripture alone" as one of the three "alones," he remained faithful to the fourfold authority he found to be true.

Fourth, Wesley's theology was also an integrated theology. He affirmed the personal and the social, the experiential and the intellectual, the local and the universal, and the immediate and the eschatological. While remaining within the institutional church, he also built a renewal movement. He drew inspiration and resources from the early church theologians, from classical theology, from the theology of the Reformers, and from the Eastern Orthodox and Arminian traditions. He reminds me of the Hindu sages who developed the Vedic aphorism: "Let Truth come from all corners of the earth."

Lastly, he held deeply devotional faith and concrete expressions of discipleship together. For him, all theological reflections and faith convictions have to be at the service of enabling personal and social holiness and in fostering discipleship that is turned toward the world in meeting the needs of the people.

One of the temptations, especially at the higher educational levels, is to see theology only as an academic discipline. Without undermining the need for academic rigor, Wesley has redefined the purpose of the theological task and the methodology that would make it a fruitful exercise.

Theological Resources for Interfaith Engagement

Anyone seeking a "biblical basis" for interfaith dialogue will find that the New Testament has little to say about other religions and what our attitude to them should be. Jesus also did not deal specifically with the many religious traditions prevalent at his time. The only way one can use biblical material in the New Testament for interfaith dialogue is to highlight the implications of Jesus's teachings, especially in relation to one's neighbors, to our attitude and approach to our neighbors who live by other convictions.

A similar situation pertains to John Wesley's teachings. Wesley was not presented with the challenge of responding to the reality of other religious traditions, nor generally did he teach explicitly on what the Methodist attitude toward other faiths should be. However, living in multi-faith environments and constantly under pressure to relate to it, the Methodists have a responsibility to develop an adequate theology of religions, theological bases for our relationships, and a missiology that takes the contemporary realities seriously. This is a challenging task and needs to be undertaken at the level of higher education.

In search of brevity, I would highlight here only three of the theological perspectives in John Wesley's theology that need to be fully developed for an adequate Methodist theology for a religiously plural world.

To begin with, Wesley had an anthropology that lends itself to new ways of understanding the human predicament and the religious life of our neighbors. Although he subscribed to the view that human beings are sinners and God's grace alone can redeem them, he found it difficult to subscribe to the theory of total depravity as implied in classical theology and held by some of the Reformers. On the contrary, he held that God's law is written in the heart of every human being. Human conscience helps the person know what is right, even if it is not possible to fulfill the law as God requires without God's grace.[18] What is important here is that Wesley denied that conscience is "natural." In his view, it is "the supernatural gift of God above all his natural endowments."

The second is Wesley's concept of God's grace, which is available to all human beings— "free in all, and free for all." Although it is based on Wesley's Christological interpretation of the Johannine Prologue of the Word that existed from the beginning, which was "the true light, which enlighteneth everyone that comes into the world" (John 1:9 DRA), his insistence on the catholicity of God's grace provides new opportunities to rethink the relationship of God and world in a religiously plural context. In this regard, the concept of prevenient grace also holds many possibilities.

Third, and perhaps most important, Wesley did not hesitate to draw the implications of his teaching on the universality of God's grace to the issue of Christian missions, which is one of the main sticking points in interfaith relationships. The popular Christian claim that one has to preach the gospel to people of other faiths and challenge them to openly accept Jesus so that "they may not perish" is one of the major stumbling blocks to interfaith relations. For his part, Wesley believed that Christ works even in those who do not hear the gospel in this life. Such persons are judged, he held, according to their response to the universal grace of God. Wesley saw no contradiction between this view and his belief in justification by faith. Those who have not had the opportunity of hearing the gospel, yet have responded to prevenient grace, are, like the patriarchs, justified by faith in anticipation of the full revelation of Christ.[19]

There is no doubt that some would disagree with this rather selective presentation of Wesley's theology and would certainly be able to point to other parts of his theology to develop other points of view. Wesley's choice not to do "systematic theology" is a problem for some, while others see it as a blessing, because it is open to be developed in new and creative ways. Wesley's theology is contextual and cannot be reproduced as such for our time. Taking the words once spoken and making them speak again today, creatively, meaningfully, relevantly is the challenge that faces Methodist higher education.

Notes

1 Marcus Braybrooke, *Pilgrimage of Hope: One Hundred Years of Interfaith Dialogue* (London: SCM, 1992), 16.

2 For a reasonably exhaustive list of interfaith initiatives and organizations see GHFP, "Primary Interfaith Organizations," 2017, http://www.interfaith.directory/organizations.

3 World Missionary Conference, *Report of Commission IV: The Missionary Message in Relation to Non-Christian Religions* (Edinburgh and London: Oliphant; New York: Fleming H. Revell, 1910), 171; microfiche at https://archive.org/details/cihm_88498.

4 World Missionary Conference, 172.

5 World Missionary Conference, 173.

6 World Missionary Conference, 267.

7 World Missionary Conference, 256.

8 For a fuller discussion of the work of Commission IV, see S. Wesley Ariarajah, *Hindus and Christians: A Century of Protestant Ecumenical Thought* (Grand Rapids: Eerdmans, 1991).

9 Report of W. E. Hocking's contribution in International Missionary Council, *Report of the Jerusalem Meeting of the International Missionary Council March 24th–April 8th, 1928* (London: Oxford University Press, 1928), 369ff.

10 International Missionary Council, 484.

11 International Missionary Council, 491.

12 International Missionary Council, 491–92.

13 Hendrik Kraemer, *The Christian Message in a Non-Christian World* (London: Edinburgh House [for the IMC], 1938), 69.

14 To facilitate the discussions beyond the conference, Kraemer's position and the positions of those who opposed his views were put together into a volume that is a very valuable resource for the issues raised on the matter. W. Pater, ed., *The Authority of the Faith* (London: Oxford University Press, 1939).

15 The consultation in Kandy was organized by the Department of Studies of the WCC from February 27 through March 6, 1967. It brought together Protestants, Orthodox, and Roman Catholic theologians who had been involved in exploring the question of Christian relations to people of other religions. Among those who presented the main papers were Kenneth Crag (specialized in Christian–Muslim relations), Lynn A. de Silva (Christian–Buddhist relations), and J. Blauw (missiologist).

16 See "I Felt My Heart Strangely Warmed," from *Journal of John Wesley*, Christian Classics Ethereal Library, accessed November 6, 2017, http://www.ccel.org/ccel/wesley/journal.vi.ii.xvi.html.

17 "Minutes of Several Conversations" Q.3, in *The Works of John Wesley*, ed. T. Jackson (New York: Baker, 1978), 8:299.

18 John Wesley, *The Works of the Rev. John Wesley*, 14 vols. (London: Wesleyan Methodist Book Room, 1829–1831; repr., Grand Rapids, MI: Baker Book House, 1978). Citations are to the Baker edition.

19 Wesley, 7:188; cf. 6:206.

Annotations on Chapter 3

Intersection, Difference, and Deference

Timothy S. Moore

The Methodist movement in America officially organized as a church body in December 1784 at what has been termed "the Christmas Conference." Preeminently, that conference established a distinctive ecclesial body. In addition, the conference adopted organizational structures and subscribed to common doctrine. It confirmed the leadership of Thomas Coke and conferred leadership on Francis Asbury. Among these seminal tasks from that conference stands a smaller yet vital act. This smaller sub-narrative is the story of a college's founding.

Early in the Methodist movement, Kingswood School had been established in England. The establishment of that school marked the first in a string of Methodist learning institutions, bolstering within Methodism that persisting link between vibrant faith and an educated mind. That link connected access to learning with greater opportunity and social equality. Both were seen as a natural consequence to the liberating call of God's kingdom. Yet, the school established in America was different from its British counterparts. The school chartered by American Methodists was to be a college of higher learning. Called Cokesbury College, the school sought to lift Methodist education to a new level while retaining that originating and ordinary impulse to join a deepening faith with advanced learning. In the Conference minutes of 1790, this assumption that faith and knowledge are common features to the church's life and mission are made explicit. Inserted by Bishop Asbury, the statement codified the Methodist instinct that all its educational efforts should "teach [students] learning and piety."[1] By founding a college as one of its first tasks, and by assuming that faith and learning were integral to its mission, the denomination expresses a durable commitment to higher education and a resolute conviction that faith should have a prominent role in its academic institutions.

While patient and persistent, this commitment and its related conviction are held in tension. However, this tension evolves. Importantly, what was assumed necessary to teach learning and piety in 1790 might not be the same in our contemporary contexts. In other words, while the impulse to hold together learning and piety may remain, its execution adapts. Despite these shifting needs to contextualize, the joint presence of learning and faith in these academic institutions generate the possibility that this tension will impact the culture, climate, and curricula at these schools, marking distinct the kind of education received at our church-related institutions.

Less theoretical than practical, this essay examines the possibility for positive impact that such a tension may offer when taken seriously and intentionally. This chapter tells the story of one campus's efforts to embrace religion and faith as a means to achieve and enhance its educational mission. More specifically, I will focus on one activity introduced to the campus meant to expand religious literacy and on a feasibly related outcome that resulted. However, before telling the story of one place, an overview of the current relationship of faith with knowledge on the college campus is useful. This overview provides the context that helps frame the work done on my specific campus. To tell this broader story, I turn to the assessment written by

Sam Wells when he was the dean of the Chapel at Duke University—a United Methodist–related school.

A Story: Told in Three Parts

> What I did not fully appreciate was that I would be responsible not just for Christian witness to the campus, but for the ministry of other faiths as well. . . . Leaving aside my philosophical puzzlement at the coherence of a notion called "religious life," I was amazed that non-Christians did not seem to feel humiliated that their spokesperson at the table of university authority and the gatekeeper of their interactions was the person that ran the Chapel.[2]

Reflecting on the current landscape of the American academy, Wells notes the relative advantage his perspective as an outsider affords him in seeing the myriad of unarticulated assumptions (about religion and religious-related institutions of higher education) that share the same intellectual space on our campuses. It took Wells nearly a year to begin to identify and articulate the unease those multiple and contrasting assumptions caused him to feel. Wells determined the underlying circumstances triggering his discomfort to be concurrent telling by members of the university community of three dissimilar chapters describing the relationship between religion and the academy. Discordantly, those who promoted each chapter assumed everyone was exclusively hearing their discrete tales. In response, Wells resolved to diagram these multiple stories to help give himself a better comprehension of what he was hearing and experiencing.

Wells believes that the story of church-related higher education in the United States involves, initially, a prologue. That prologue establishes the general institutional foundations for the church-related schools. The prologue is the story of "a time before 1900, when colleges and universities were founded, shaped and dominated by the major Christian traditions." The impact of that prologue remains. However, it is not the whole of the story. Wells claims that "history really begins in *chapter one*, which broadly covers the first half of the twentieth century—a time when faculties in many of the church-related colleges wrested control of those institutions away from the ecclesial hierarchies." In an effort to stay relevant and engaged in the intellectual enterprise of higher education, Wells surmises that denominations "traded their theological identity in order to retain their institutional influence." In other words, denominations made efforts to segregate the intellectual efforts of the university as a public good from the private ponderings of faith and the inner life. With a barrier in place and tacitly agreed to by the founding denominations, the relationship of faith to knowledge shifted from mutually informing each other to mutually tolerating each other while each occupied a different sphere on the same campuses. This is "chapter one."

While the story of chapter one was still being told, Wells began describing a second chapter. This chapter, chapter two, "refers to the period of significant social change in the third quarter of the last century. The way the story is remembered, excluded groups, notably African Americans and women, beat down the door of segregation and restricted access. White, Anglo-Saxon males stopped being seen as the source of all good and started being fingered as the cause of all evil." By adding new voices to the story of higher education, presumptions about the past and propriety are drawn into question, including presumptions about the place and role of faith and institutions of faith in the scholarly arts. In this chapter, the tension between faith and knowledge adjusts, again. This time, rather than occupying different spaces that tolerate each other, suspicion replaces tolerance and pluralism becomes a leveling mechanism. Pluralism, meant to supply an intellectual stalemate, assumes a central role in the academy. This is chapter two.

As chapters one and two sought place and priority in the narrative, Wells saw a third chapter emerging. This third chapter is one he represents and sees clearly given his position as someone from a post-Christian context—the United Kingdom—and the perception that his alien origin affords. He states:

American colleges and universities now find themselves in *chapter three*. . . . Chapter one was good for higher education in that it gave it purpose and coherence, but it impoverished higher education in that it excluded the majority of the population from any serious engagement with its endeavors and benefits. Chapter two was good for higher education in that it brought into the conversation many who should have been integral to it all along, but its legacy was an ambivalence about institutional development and an inarticulacy about final purposes."

In naming these positive contributions to the academic culture and climate written by the authors of chapters one and two, Wells identifies the negative impact those narratives had upon the church and the religious life exercised on its campuses: "Chapter one and chapter two meanwhile share a tendency to make the church invisible because they make it subservient to other causes such as the dominance of social elites, America, or the movement for social justice."

Wells and his coauthors of chapter three, most decisively, labor to protect his faith and all faiths from the marginalizing forces of chapter one that seek to sequester faith from conversations and thoughts that matter or from the diluting forces of chapter two that seek to relativize or equate everything. Wells asserts:

I did not believe my own faith, Christianity, was a manifestation of a broader genus known as "religion." My relationship with members of other faiths was not dependent on us all agreeing there was some kind of more fundamental subsoil from which we all derived, some kind of spiritual or philosophical nutrients. . . . I was not trying in an aggressive or imperialistic manner to say "I'm right—you're wrong." I was just pointing out that there was no philosophically coherent way in which we could both be right and that pretending otherwise only underwrote a culture in which it was widely assumed that neither of us were seriously interested in truth in the first place. Hence my fear that a definition of religion would render us all irrelevant—because it would expose us all as half-baked forms of self-help and therapy.

Wells sees a shift in the relationship of faith and knowledge as inevitable and necessary given the character of the third chapter he promotes. If the first chapter is characterized by marginalization and tolerance, and the second chapter is characterized by suspicion and pluralism, then the third chapter, in my estimation, is characterized by mutuality and hospitality. Mutuality is meant to be a recalibration of the system, rejecting the structural assumptions that faith is only relevant in intellectual discourse if it is privatized, or that faith is only acceptable in intellectual discourse if it is a subgenus of a larger claim that is general to all, irrespective of the particulars of a faith tradition. Rather, mutuality assumes the interlacing, informing, and sympathetic presence of discrete and (probably) disparate narratives. Hospitality is the methodology established to share that jointly occupied space while willfully naming a specific space as particular in character and disposition yet not intended to be hostile or dismissive of others.

What Wells articulates in his three-chapter formulation parallels the assertions couched in inclusivism, pluralism, and particularism, respectively. *Inclusivists* assert that truth claims—including religious truth claims—are really just one claim that represents absolute truth. Those other claims are merely derivations of this single claim more clearly spoken by one group or tradition. *Pluralists* avow that each claim is actually a different perspective on ultimately the same assertion with no one perspective holding any privilege over the others. *Particularists* contend that each claim should stand on its own and be presented to others and compared to others' claims without assuming the justifiability of any claims.

In Wells's estimation, we live in the mixing of these narratives, with all three chapters sharing space on our academic campuses. Those mixing narratives frame our campuses' assumptions about the relationship between faith and knowledge. Yet, these narratives are not necessarily communicating with each other or even aware of the others' presence. Each chapter and its advocates, he maintains, need to be aware that the other narratives continue to be told because the multiple simultaneous tellings are the source of the dissonance he experienced. That dissonance is the result of the three narratives using the same vocabulary but deploying it in different ways. As such, superficially, the narratives might seem to be telling the same story, describing the same space. But, in reality, they are saying substantively different things and speaking over each other. Hence, the dissonance. Wells seeks to make patent the obscured. By laying it bare, he works to fashion space for more honest and productive conversations about meaning, purpose, knowledge, and faith on our campuses.

Wells's observations are timely. According to some higher-education researchers, there is a growing interest among college and university students to engage in conversations about faith and meaning. For instance, Arthur Chickering and his coauthors in *Encouraging Authenticity and Spirituality in Higher Education* have identified this trend. Through their research, they detect that "in recent years, at colleges and universities around the country, an expanding and increasingly vigorous dialogue has begun, centered on examining personal values, meaning, purpose—including religious and spiritual values—as part of the educational experience."[3]

To Wells's point, if such dialogues are taking place, then it is incumbent to be clear as to what we are saying or think others are saying and what we mean by the words that we use and the assumptions that we bring to those conversations. Further underlining Wells's conclusion, Chickering's team determined that particularity and knowledge of the particular traditions informing our religious and spiritual assumptions is crucial to the kind of efficacious spiritual maturation and development institutions of higher learning should pursue.[4] In a potentially beneficial turn for institutions affiliated with the church, those same students who are interested in conversations around faith and meaning often assume that their institutions will be places that help them with those explorations.[5]

These intentional conversations about faith and knowledge do not happen in a vacuum. Historical and ecclesial expectations that shaped the church's higher-education institutions; aspirations of faculty, staff, and administration; assumptions by boards; and needs of students converge to create the environs in which these vital conversations are imagined and carried out. Broader cultural trends and perceptions affect the campus, particularly shaping the kind and substance of these conversations. Following the trajectory proposed by Wells and Chickering, the challenge for any conversation about faith, meaning, knowledge, and purpose that our institutions foster must be honest and self-aware by engaging its institutional community "where it is" while remaining dynamically connected to and informed by its tradition, authentically interpreting and adapting to the present environs. And those environs are shifting.

The larger culture is experiencing significant existential transition. Recent studies suggest that our society is moving from rigorous affirmations of absolutes toward more nuanced spiritual quests characterized by openness to unanswerable questions.[6] College and university campuses serve as the epicenter for this shift. Supporting this assertion, one study of college students indicates that interest in spirituality and religion increases nearly 20 percent during the first year of college.[7] Moreover, other research suggests that faculty, staff, and administration are experiencing similar increases in their personal interests in matters of faith and spirituality.[8] Such trends, while extending over many generations, find particular expression on today's campus. More than ever, students and nonstudents alike identify themselves as "spiritual."[9] For colleges and universities of the church, these trends offer both not-so-good news and great news. The not-so-good-news is that these institutions cannot remain solely fixed to past programs and institutional structuring. The great news is that being institutions of the church provides a natural and expected context for vigorous reality-making, meaning-finding language and practices—the very language and practices those on our campuses desire.

To this point, I have outlined a general superstructure to provide the theoretical rationale warranting my chapter. Below, I will give that chapter its substance and particular detail. This tracing of the story of higher education and its tension-filled and shifting dynamic between faith and knowledge is meant to press my project forward in two ways. First, this engagement with Wells's and others' observations names what is often unidentified, describing clearly the complex conversations shaping our institutions' environments. Those generated environments have the capacity to impact positively the culture, climate, and curricula of our institutions. Further, this naming and impacting may restore where lost and undergird where persisting that originating impulse informing all United Methodist–related schools, principally to bind learning to piety. This does not mean that learning should in any way require a faith test. Rather, what I am saying is that the kind of educational environments fostered within our institutions of higher learning must take seriously how a particular faith impacts knowledge formation and value claims. Stated even more pointedly, we must acknowledge that intellectual neutrality and purity is more illusory and, ultimately, diminished and unintelligible when divorced from grounded and specific assumptions. Second, with the context set, I am better positioned to tell the story of one campus's efforts to engage, head-on, faith and religiosity as a vital part of the education enterprise as a means to increase understanding and advance the mission of that academic institution of the church. That institution was Young Harris College, a small liberal arts college of The United Methodist Church, where I served for many years as the institution's chief religious officer as a dean and as an associate professor.

An Exercise: Beans-in-a-Cup

As Alexander Astin and his colleagues discovered in their seminal study on the spirituality of college and university students, most students' interest in spirituality and faith increases while in college. Concurrently, students' participation in religious and faith-based groups decreases. In addition, while in college, many students look to their institutions of higher education to help deepen their spirituality and in their exploration of meaning and purpose.[10] Detached from faith communities while concomitantly turning to their academic institutions for help, our institutions seem (1) often unaware of our students' increased interest in matters of spirituality and (2) generally unprepared to attend to those interests because of a lack of intentional, institutional strategizing and training of administration, faculty, staff, and students in how to address our students' increased spiritual curiosity or—sometimes—crisis. In an effort to address our students' spiritual questions and proactively prepare our institutions for the reality of our students' spiritual questing, I created a training module in spirituality and religious literacy.

Using data gathered from national and internal institutional surveys, I designed a short and customizable education module.[11] Called "Beans-in-a-Cup," the module presents this data in two formats— one based on percentages and another based on true/false statements. The procedure for the exercise is simple. Upon entering the room where the exercise is conducted, participants are asked to fill out a pre-participation survey. The completed surveys are collected. Participants, then, are each given a handful of beans. Thirteen cups— one set of eleven cups in graduated percentages in intervals of ten from 0 percent to 100 percent, and another set with the words "true" or "false" printed on them—are arranged in a central, convenient location. As statements and questions making claims about spirituality and religious practice are read, participants are asked to drop a bean into a cup best representing what they assume to be the most accurate response to the statement made or question asked. After each statement/question, participants are asked to support their assumption or reflect on their decisions. Following various responses from participants, the answer or specific datum is revealed. Additional conversations after revealing the answer or datum are encouraged. Participants are introduced to institutional resources in place to help students explore their spiritual and faith questions and advance their understanding of spiritual and religious practices. Before leaving, participants are asked to complete a post-participation survey. The post-survey is identical to the pre-survey. Over the course of several years, the module was utilized in different training sessions at the college; for example, as part of resident assistant training, as part of a professional staff in-service training, as part of orientation leader training, as part of human resources' new staff and faculty orientation, and as part of first-year seminar programs.

The module was designed to meet six goals. First, I intended the exercise to introduce participants to general levels of student spiritual exploration and interest while in college. Second, I wanted it to introduce participants to general religious data and to expectations specific to our institution's students. Third, I intended the exercise to introduce participants to resources at our institution that might aid them in addressing student questions and questing. Fourth, I designed it to empower participants to help feel better equipped to assist students who ask questions or who exhibit spiritual/faith-specific needs. Fifth, I meant the exercise to reaffirm the natural centrality and integrality of spirituality and spiritual questing as part of the higher education experience. Sixth, I designed the exercise to inform participants of the need for our institution to develop spirituality and faith-based resources for our students. For our purposes here, the data acquired from the pre- and post-participation surveys and the annual student surveys of the campus prove insightful and suggestive of how a program might take seriously religion's role in the academy as a source of faith formation and knowledge acquisition.

Results: In Two Parts

As mentioned in the previous section, each participant in the Beans-in-a-Cup survey is given a pre- and post-participation survey. The surveys are identical, allowing for comparative data. The surveys are short and use a common rating scale for responses, the numeral one representing a low degree of familiarity or knowledge and a numeral six representing a high degree of familiarity or knowledge. The results from comparing the two surveys taken from the more than two hundred participants suggest an overall positive benefit and increased knowledge from the module. Specifically, participants demonstrated a

- 37 percent increased knowledge regarding spirituality and religiosity in the United States;

- 31 percent increased knowledge regarding spirituality and religiosity among college students;

- 34 percent increased appreciation for the import of faith practices on the college experience;

- 13 percent increased understanding of the value of multi-faith interaction while in college;

- 33 percent increased appreciation for the role of spirituality and faith exploration as part of a student's higher education experience; and

- 10 percent increased knowledge of institutional resources and opportunities related to spirituality and faith.

The outcomes based on the data collected from the surveys were immediate but did not necessarily imply any long-term impact for the campus in increasing spirituality or religiosity or religious literacy among the student body. However, another survey taken on the campus many months removed from the individual Beans-in-a-Cup exercises might shift that assumption from a possible correlation toward a probable one.

Each year, students participated in other studies and surveys for the campus that were not exclusive to those administered by the religious life program. Some of those institutional surveys were internally generated and administered by the college to assess all aspects of the educational experience, while others were part of national surveys meant to gather data locally to be compared to data gathered at similar institutions around the country. The quantitative data generated by those institutional surveys suggest a parallel trend if not a correlation to what was calculated from the Beans-in-a-Cup survey data.

For instance, data from the College's 2013 Student Opinion Survey (SOS) identified a steady and increasing support for religious life programming by the student body, maintaining a high level of weekly, monthly, and semester participation. Statistically, over a four-year period, there was a demonstrated 50 percent rise in student participation in religious life programming. More specifically, according to the year-end data gathered through the college's 2013 SOS, student participation in religious life programming for that academic year exhibited board growth, with weekly participation increasing by 53 percent, monthly participation increasing by 76 percent, and semester participation increasing by 56 percent. Those results were all taken from internal data. Favorably, the external data described a similar narrative.

In a national survey, students indicated a stable maintenance or increase in their spirituality while at the college, confounding national trends. Over four years, Young Harris students report a 73 percent rate of maintenance or increase in their spirituality while at the college, according to the college's SOS. The National Survey of Student Engagement (NSSE) results for the campus found that the institution's students indicated a 34 percent greater sense of deepening spirituality compared to other college students in America. The NSSE survey data indicate that the school's students showed a 5 percent increase in their sense of deepening spirituality from their first year to their senior year. Finally, the NSSE found that other college students in America at similar institutions indicate an 8 percent decrease in their sense of deepening spirituality from their first year to their senior year, meaning that while attending the college, Young Harris students reported a 13 percent net increase in their sense of deepening spirituality compared to college students at similar institutions. The results from the exercise's survey, the college's internal data, and the national survey in which the college's students participated do not guarantee a link between that exercise and the positive results for increased faith/spirituality and religious literacy among the student body. However, the data certainly suggest a climate was created that positively shaped faith expression while advancing the academic mission of the institution, a mission that includes better understanding the broader world and the motivations for individual behaviors and commitments.

Conclusions

As my title for this essay implies, what I offer is meant to serve as an annotation on Wells's third chapter, the third chapter of American higher education he asserts is presently being written. By implication, my work with that chapter indicates that this third chapter is the more desirable narrative to tell in our contemporary academic context. The shift in the relationship of faith and knowledge that accompanies this chapter is not only inevitable and necessary given the character of the third chapter; but it is, ultimately, preferable, allowing for an authentic and honest means to engage difference and diversity on our campuses while respectfully acknowledging the unavoidable particularity that gives our contexts and claims intelligibility and grounding. Claims are never neutral and detached. They require context and content rooted in lived and narrated existence to convey anything meaningful or substantive. Such grounding brings particular assertions. Those particularities are not to be and cannot be circumvented or ignored but should be recognized, then engaged critically. This critical engagement is a hallmark of the higher educational enterprise. I contend that acknowledgment of and critical engagement with particular claims restores the possibility of a positive role for faith in relationship to knowledge as a vital partner in the academic mission.

As summarized earlier, if the first chapter is characterized by marginalization and tolerance, and the second chapter is characterized by suspicion and pluralism, then the third chapter, in my estimation, is characterized by mutuality and hospitality. Mutuality is meant to be a recalibration of the system, rejecting the intellectual structural assumptions (1) that faith is only relevant in intellectual discourse if it is privatized or (2) that faith is only acceptable in intellectual discourse if it is a subgenus of a larger claim that is general to all, irrespective of the particulars of that faith tradition.

Mutuality allows us to name the diversity among us; to begin to see more clearly the places of intersection and divergence; and to see how those particularities, intersections, and divergences impact the educational contexts of our institutions. Hospitality is the methodology established to share that jointly occupied space, while willfully naming a specific space as particular in character and disposition yet not hostile or diminishing to others. Much like recognizing that a particular celebration has a host and that the host infuses the celebration with certain assumptions and possibilities and characteristics, an institution grounded in a particular (faith) tradition and claims should not automatically mean a posture of hostility to others and their differences. Hosts create a space and give that space its character and establish—through intentional acts and recognized claims—the possibility for flourishing or not. In other words, particularity need not be an obstacle to creating a rich, diverse, and effective learning environment. To the contrary, particularity might be the indispensable context and the very cause of effectual learning.

> Higher education is not value free. Each policy and practice we adopt, each resource allocation judgment or staffing and personnel decision we make expresses a value priority.[12]

Notes

1 *Methodist Review* 93 (1911): 15.

2 Quotes and information from here to the next note number are taken from Samuel Wells, "The Possibilities of a Faith Council," *Journal of Scriptural Reasoning* 9, no. 2 (December 2010), http://jsr.shanti.virginia.edu/back-issues/vol-9-no-1-december-2010 -the-fruits-of-scriptural-reasoning/the-possibilities-of-a-faith-council/.

3 Arthur W. Chickering, Jon C. Dalton, and Liesa Stamm, *Encouraging Authenticity and Spirituality in Higher Education* (San Francisco: Jossey-Bass, 2005), 2.

4 Chickering, 7.

5 *Alexander W. Astin, Helen S. Astin, and Jennifer A. Lindholm*, "A National Study of Spirituality in Higher Education: Students' Search for Meaning and Purpose," *Spirituality in Higher Education* (2010), http://capabilities.templeton.org/2004/pdf/SPIRITUALITY _HIGHER_ED.pdf.

6 Chickering, *Encouraging Authenticity and Spirituality in Higher Education*, 72.

7 Chickering, 153–54. Cf. *Astin, Astin, and Lindholm*, "A National Study of Spirituality in Higher Education."

8 Chickering, 2. Cf., Cathy Lynn Grossman, "Young Adults 'Less Religious,' Not Necessarily 'More Secular,'" *USA Today*, February 17, 2010.

9 Cathy Lynn Grossman, "Survey: 72% of Millennials 'More Spiritual Than Religious,'" *USA Today*, April 27, 2010, https://usatoday30.usatoday.com/news/religion/2010-04 -27-1amillfaith27_st_n.htm.

10 *Astin, Astin, and Lindholm*, "A National Study of Spirituality in Higher Education."

11 The data acquired for the questions/answers varied over the years but typically came from relevant surveys. Some of those utilized include: (1) 2007 UCLA H.E.R.I. Survey, (2) 2008 American Religious Identification Survey, (3) 2009 Barna Group Survey of Young Adults, (4) Young Harris College Religious Life Surveys, (5) Young Harris College Student Enrollment Statistics, (6) Young Harris College Student Satisfaction Surveys, (7) Gallop Polls on Religion, and (8) Young Harris College First-Year Student Preference Surveys.

12 Elizabeth J. Tisdell, *Exploring Spirituality and Culture in Adult and Higher Education* (San Francisco: Jossey-Bass, 2003), 9.

3

The Grand Rallying Point

Methodists, Congregationalists, Baptists, Episcopalians, and Jews Forge a Lesson and Legacy in Interfaith Cooperation

Eva Semien Baham

Bishop Robert Elijah Jones stood between the proverbial rock and a hard place. He represented 350,000 African Americans at the 1908 General Conference of the Methodist Episcopal Church (North) as the only African American minister member of the Joint Commission on the Unification of the Methodist Episcopal Church and the Methodist Episcopal Church South.[1] Reunification aptly describes this early-twentieth-century effort by the Methodists to mend the seams of the schism of 1844. The Methodists, along with the Baptists and Presbyterians, split over the issue of the "evil" but not the "sin" of slavery. Surely semantics played slyly among the theologies of that differentiation, but not subtly enough to maintain one united church. The Mason-Dixon Line divided Methodists.

At the 1908 General Conference, the reverend's attendance and his appointments, although he served in Louisiana, came under the auspices of the northern church. He and Matthew Clair Sr. of Washington, DC, "were both elected bishops" by the northern Methodists at the 1920 General Conference, where—this time—they "were not members of the new commission to negotiate" reunification. Again in 1934, Bishop Jones, and this time, Rev. Willis J. King, were the lone African Americans among "sixty-five prominent Methodist leaders gathered in Chicago, Illinois, to begin discussion of the unification." Theirs was a delicate balancing act: "to represent faithfully African American Methodists without alienating their northern white allies." The conundrum for both regions of the white Methodist church involved segregating African American churches in the General Conference.[2] Bishop Jones and Reverend King were wedged between the regional white Methodist churches supporting a "Jim Crow Church," and African American Methodists who sought nothing short of an egalitarian religious institution. The outcome of the reunited church: "Six jurisdictional conferences—five based on geography and one, the Central Jurisdiction, based on race."[3] The affirmative "vote for the plan was for the greater good," its white adherents claimed. Bishop Jones and Reverend King faced criticism by some African Americans claiming that they acquiesced in this debate. The bishop said he was not an obstructionist; apparently believing that, after twenty years of debate, he could have no effect on the outcome. The *Crisis*, organ of the National Association for the Advancement of Colored People (NAACP), called it "Jim Crow for Jesus."[4]

Bishop Jones led the black Methodist Church in just about every facet of its existence from 1881 until his death in 1960. His role as presiding elder of African American Methodists for seventy-nine years and principal navigator for them through the networks of white Methodism illustrate the tethering of goodwill to racial diplomacy and social realism. This was the environment in which each of the religious organizations coming to the aid of freed African Americans post–Civil War had to function. Theirs was to carefully navigate the rocky terrain of a country that had wrapped itself in human bondage for almost 250 years. Among the several religious groups that—in the case of the American Missionary Association—followed freedom south on the heels of conquests by the Union Army, the *"greater good"* manifested itself in religious democracy more than in denominational sectarianism. Consideration of the racial climate of the era in which each religious group worked took precedence over the emphasis on the specific denomination espoused by each group. It would be inaccurate to conclude that these religious organizations cast aside their denominational doctrines and dogmas. Neither was that the case as the religious worked nor is it conveyed in this chapter. It is accurate to hold, however, that the greater good rested in the common cause for which the religious worked. The fire—although at times explosive—of this "good" ignited a faith common among all the groups.

The core question, simply put, was: How does my faith become active without, for the most part, being stifled by religious particularism? From the end of the Civil War in 1865 through the early 1950s, the period covered in this chapter, religious groups blurred denominational lines to work with and on behalf of African Americans. This work concerns New Orleans. Its religious and social diversity illustrates the intricately delicate dance of good intentions in a highly charged environment. Effective aid, therefore, required interfaith cooperation to forge progress for a maligned populace. This chapter examines that effort in the establishment of Dillard University, whose history begins in post–Civil War missionary work of black and white Baptists, Methodists, and Congregationalists, and whose hope for continued existence rested in the cooperation of a Christian and Jewish community.

Roots of a Missionary Spirit

The American Missionary Association (AMA) had no one denominational affiliation. Indeed, its founding grew out of the 1838 Amistad case,[5] which morphed into an abolitionist movement of black and white missionary groups in New England. Many of its founding members were either Congregationalists or Presbyterians. Congregationalists, Methodists (north), Baptists, Episcopalians, and later into the twentieth century, Jewish congregants, invoked a "missionary spirit" to educate anyone who hungered to learn, both academically and spiritually. Schools founded by the American Missionary Association were open to all, regardless of race, sex, religion, or class.

The AMA's mission "was a New Testament ethic: a gospel that adhered to religion's basic faith in the fatherhood of God and the brotherhood of all humankind."[6] The "strange warming" of their mission should not be confused, the AMA warned, with the conditions under which the workers must labor. This was hard work requiring unprecedented commitment to serve with unbridled resilience.

> No one need apply who is not prepared to endure hardness as a good soldier of Jesus Christ—to do hard work, go to hard places, and submit if need be, to hard fare. *Good health* [emphasis in quote]: This is not a hygienic association, to help invalids try a change of air, or travel at others' expense. *Culture and Common Sense*: (It is) a mistaken mischievous idea to think almost anybody can teach the freemen. Nowhere is character, in the school and out of it, more important. Only those persons least likely to make mistakes should be commissioned.[7]

In addition, Lewis Tappan, one of the founders of the AMA, warned applicants that they must "conquer their prejudices (lest they) evince indisputably that they are unfit for the high and responsible office of superintendent or teacher, and should be dismissed from the post they so unworthily fill."[8] Commitment, character, and an open mind and heart were uncompromising requirements to work with and for former slaves as free people. Nonetheless, workers faced dangerous assignments. Vigilantes shot to kill. Sometimes they missed; sometimes they hit their targets. That was the story of the brief life of one AMA teacher in New Orleans.

Edmonia Highgate believed herself qualified to "labor advantageously in the field for [her] newly freed brethren." She arrived in New Orleans, after having taught in Norfolk, Virginia, and having organized a school in Darlington, Maryland. Although Highgate traveled under the auspices of the AMA, her position was in government schools in New Orleans. She encountered the July 30, 1866 race riot in New Orleans, which she exclaimed was "horrible"; at least thirty-five were left dead (some sources claim in the hundreds), and more than one hundred wounded.[9] For respite, she traveled to an outpost in Lafayette Parish at Vermillionville, some two hundred miles southwest of New Orleans. Vigilantes shot at her school. She returned to New Orleans, where she threatened to "starve" or "resign and return to the country and once again risk rebel bullets" in protest of segregated schools. That had no impact. She did go back to the country, only to die young from a "cause unknown."[10] Yet, the need was still great. Booker T. Washington remarked, "It was a whole race trying to go to school. Few were too young, and none too old, to make the attempt to learn."[11] In that light, churches and teachers had all the incentive they needed to forge on in spite of the risks.

Invasion of the Protestants from the North

Methodists, Congregationalists, and Baptists from the North landed in New Orleans on the heels of the Civil War. They were on a fervent mission. The Methodist Church North began sending pastors and church representatives to the South a few months after the end of the Civil War. Church reconciliation, with the Methodist Church South, did not fit their immediate agenda. Rather, their purpose was to give aid to former slaves. Theirs was a mission to give people tools to live free. Freedom, therefore, began with schools.

The reverends (later bishops) John Phillip Newman, of New York, and Joseph Crane Hartzell, from Illinois, met in their "first session" December 24, 1865. First Newman, followed by Hartzell, pastored Ames Methodist Episcopal Church on St. Charles Avenue, the lone affiliate of the Methodist Church North in New Orleans.[12] They organized a trustee board, laid out plans for schools, selected faculty, and established the Thomson Biblical Institute. They were sponsored by the Methodist Freedmen's Aid Society, organized August 7, 1866. In three months, all were fully operational; at the end of the first full year, there were eight schools in Louisiana. The Union Normal School followed on July 8, 1869, with a Miss R. A. Coit as principal, and a staff of three women teachers. Students paid a "tax of $2 a term." The Thomson Biblical Institute and the Union Normal School merged and became New Orleans University, chartered March 22, 1873. Among the signers of the charter was "the unusually eloquent preacher" Emperor Williams. He was born a slave in 1826 and secured his freedom in 1858. His offer to buy his wife's freedom was denied. The fall of New Orleans to the Union early in the Civil War solved that problem and saved him two thousand dollars.

In keeping with the desirous diverse vision of its founders and a true sense of camaraderie in cause, New Orleans University, serving African American students, sat nestled "in the finest residence portion" on St. Charles Avenue "between a Jewish Orphanage and the Protestant Episcopal Asylum for boys." Its historical account revels at the picturesque scene of having the descendants of Jews, and African and European Christians, living harmoniously side by side. Each faith worked on causes common to the postbellum era. "Here," they noted, "is to be *the grand rallying point* of our church in the South."[13] The university admitted all who wanted to learn. Men and women like Newman, Hartzell, and Coit expected that men and women like Williams and Highgate would set progress in motion by continuing to prepare African Americans to live as free people and citizens. African Americans took the charge.

Graduates of New Orleans University traversed the state of Louisiana, teaching and establishing schools and churches. T. H. Harris, state superintendent of education, remarked that there was no place where there was not a New Orleans University graduate in service, and that included across the United States. "This is a contribution on the part of New Orleans University and other institutions of like character which shows over and over again that the heroic effort on the part of the early workers and the philanthropy poured out so generously and cheerfully by the Church were wisely invested."[14]

That characterization applied to Leland University, a Baptist affiliate, as well as to Straight University, founded by Rev. Joseph W. Healy, a Congregational pastor from Chicago, with the financial backing and social consciousness of Seymour Straight, a Baptist and an Ohio native doing business in New Orleans and Cincinnati. He committed himself to support the work of the American Missionary Association beginning in 1863. From 1864 to 1883, he was its vice president.[15] He corresponded with Rev. George Whipple, AMA corresponding secretary, questioning them for not sending missionaries to both New Orleans and Baton Rouge. Healy's pleas with the AMA went unanswered. As historian Shawn Comminey noted, the AMA was "overburdened" across the South.[16] Healy pushed the issue by telling AMA officials that the "American Baptist Home Mission, a northern missionary society approached him about ways to obtain Freedmen's Bureau aid for a theological school." Nonetheless, efforts to nudge the AMA by pointing to the work of other religious groups initially did not work. The Freedmen's Bureau was not impressed, as "interdenominational rivalry" in mission work "may have been a factor."[17] Straight questioned Healy as to the need for the Congregationalists to open another school. Duplicating efforts frustrated Straight, because of the drain on the same sources. Healy convinced him, however, that this school would have another purpose, higher education at the onset.[18] Straight guaranteed his financial backing as long as support from the AMA and other sources would be forthcoming, and the schools would be geographically strategic to avoid competition. Straight University came into fruition with financial support of the Freedmen's Bureau, the AMA, and private individuals like Straight. Finally, the school filed its charter in 1869.

Impact of New Orleans University and Straight University/College

While New Orleans University produced Bishop Alexander Camphor, Straight gave to the city the Reverend Dr. Alfred Lawless, founder of Beecher Memorial Congregational Church. In 1919, he became the general superintendent of the Southern Congregational church work. While on faculty at Straight, he developed the first temporary school for children in the neighborhood of North Miro and Allen Streets in New Orleans. He donated six lots of property to the public school board as well as property for Dillard, in what became Gentilly

Gardens. He served as superintendent of the Negro churches in the South on the Congregational National Church Board. The Lawless Memorial entrance to Dillard dedicated at the seventieth annual baccalaureate noted that Dr. Lawless's "influence in educational and civic affairs was as wide as that which he wielded in religion, for he worked to persuade public educations officials in the South to raise standards for Negro education, and to provide wider educational opportunities for Negro youth."[19] Dr. Alfred Lawless died in 1933. On October 23, 1955, the board of trustees of Dillard University dedicated its Lawless Memorial Chapel in his honor with a plaque to both him and his son, Dr. Theodore Lawless, noting, "inspiring father and devoted son."[20]

Through New Orleans University came a nursing school and a medical college. The Phillis Wheatley Club, composed of African American women, served the medical needs of their community with a sanitarium and training school for Negro nurses in 1896. New Orleans University came to the financial rescue of Phillis Wheatley, making it part of its medical school (founded in 1889). Generous gifts from Caroline Medge of Boston and John D. Flint of Fall River, Massachusetts endowed both the nursing and medical schools and hospital. In their honor, the names were changed to Sarah Goodridge Hospital in honor of Mrs. Medge's mother and Flint Medical College. The medical school and hospital became Flint-Goodridge Hospital of Dillard University.[21]

An ecumenical spirit pervaded New Orleans University's student body, which included "pastors irrespective of denominations"; the African Methodist Episcopal Church, the Colored Methodist Episcopal Church, and the Holiness Church. Its students represented a cross section of Christianity, both black and white. Further, two rabbis accepted invitations to speak at the university; they, in turn, welcomed faculty and students "in their own synagogues. The Jewish Children's Home, which parallels the University property . . . has had no misunderstanding with the University."[22]

Important contributions made by the women of Straight University demonstrate the impact that their faiths made among and for a progressive society through their professions. Straight graduates Valena C. MacArthur Jones, Fannie C. Williams, and Lucille Levy Hutton educated an entire generation of New Orleans's African American students. Two have roots in Mississippi, with Jones and Williams having been born on the Gulf Coast; Hutton in New Orleans. Jones's husband was Bishop Robert E. Jones. Williams and Hutton were Congregationalists. Among them there was no question about their roles in shaping the educational practices utilized in teaching New Orleans's children of color.

Two Shall Be One, Christians and Jews

Leo M. Coogan, representing the Edgar Stern Family Fund, submitted the last $20,500 of a $100,000 pledge to build a science building at Dillard University.[23] The Sterns' donation was the largest of any individual contribution. Hence, discussion among other board members and Dillard president Albert W. Dent began within a few months to name the building after Edgar Stern, at the time the first and only president of the university's board of trustees. Discussion gave way to minor debate as to the wording of the inscription for the cornerstone. The initial proposal by Dr. Will W. Alexander explicitly credited Stern with having "originated" the "idea" of Dillard. Monte M. Lemann, another trustee and a personal friend to Stern, went further for clarity, stating that Stern "first conceived the idea of Dillard."[24]

President Dent took issue with the intent of the proposed inscriptions.[25] He read them as making Stern the founder of Dillard, which he was not. The combination of both New Orleans and Straight universities formed Dillard in 1935, a merger more by necessity than by idea. Academic successes and spiritual accomplishments in educating students could not supplant financial needs. The Methodist Episcopal Church committed $15,000 per year through 1927. The Depression years dropped "this appropriation" to $1,500 a year for the eight years preceding 1935. The budget had to be reduced from $50,000 to $40,000, reflecting, as well, a drop from $6,000 to $1,000 in collections from the Louisiana Conference.[26]

Straight University fared the same. According to historian Joe Richardson, the Straight College president approached Edgar Stern either in 1927 or 1928 with a request for a $500 "emergency contribution." Stern reportedly refused the president, sending him to his "church board" and telling him to come back if he were "ever interested in bigger things." As the request suggests, financial problems mounted for some time. The AMA broached the subject as early as 1913, when its general secretary pointed to "Straight's weakness [and] emphasized the necessity of a plan of cooperation with other institutions in New Orleans."[27] Indeed, it is the difficulty that caused Seymour Straight to have misgivings about having multiple schools working on the same issue. To compound the problems of the two schools, they were losing their white New Orleans and national benefactors either to poor economic times, death (Seymour Straight died in 1816), or attrition at the schools. Seymour Straight's philanthropy largely exhausted his wealth during his lifetime because he eschewed having massive stockpiles of money, preferring instead to donate it. Another decisive factor involved new conversations between the two regional divisions of the Methodist Church North shortly after 1900 for reunification. This action redirected needed resources from former Northern benefactors to Southern Methodists, who were less inclined to see the need to educate African Americans. The boards of both New Orleans University and Straight faced critical decisions. Combine resources or fail. They chose the former. Leading this effort were Bishop Robert Elijah Jones and Rev. Merrill Holmes. As President Dent lamented, "there might be confusion over the statement that the idea of Dillard University originated with [Stern]. Bishop Jones and Merrill Holmes and others might think otherwise."[28]

Bishop Jones had a vested interest in a thriving legacy for New Orleans University. He was chair of its 1935 board of trustees and had been for fifteen years prior. Additionally, he received an honorary degree from the university in 1918, making him an alumnus. According to New Orleans University's historical account, "both the church and the school in Louisiana and in the nation has been greatly influenced by . . . Bishop Robert E. Jones," whose association goes back thirty-eight years.[29] Little occurred within the concerns of African American Methodists, especially in Louisiana, without the bishop's input. He worked in concert with Rev. Holmes, the secretary of the General Board of Education, whose charge it was to oversee Methodist schools serving African Americans. Additionally, the creation of public schools, such as the 1880 founding in New Orleans of Southern University, had a detrimental effect on the two private colleges. In light of those long-term issues, both New Orleans and Straight universities also realized that they needed to consolidate.

There was no hesitation from both New Orleans and Straight universities' trustees in their affirmative responses to the president of the Julius Rosenwald Fund, Edwin R. Embree's offer for support if the schools merged into one university. The merger included the Flint-Goodridge Hospital and Medical Schools. Embree received approval from trustees from each school and from their major financial supporting institutions: the General Education Board (GEB); Fred L. Brownlee, Congregationalist, of the AMA; and Rev. Merrill J. Holmes, secretary for the Department of Education for African Americans in the Methodist Episcopal Church. The terms required that the AMA, Methodist Board of Education, and the GEB each pledge $500,000; the "Rosenwald Fund committed . . . $250,000 from New Orleans; and $35,000 annual for at least ten years." The trustees had seventeen members: twelve whites, including Stern, his friend Monte M. Lehman, a noted New Orleans attorney, both Jews; Warren Kearny, an Episcopalian and owner of a building materials company; and five blacks. Three of the African American trustees were Bishop Jones and Congregationalists Fannie C. Williams and Dr. Alfred Lawless. Stern noted that the white community in New Orleans did not provide much support for causes affecting African Americans; therefore, he expected that soliciting monetary support would be an uphill battle. Nonetheless, Stern became the board's president, a position he maintained until his death in 1959.[30]

The new Dillard University Board of Trustees readily agreed on its name in tribute to the work of the president of the Jeanes and Slater funds and a former Tulane University professor. Under Dr. James Hardy Dillard's leadership, Frederick Brownlee wrote, the organizations found in him a "life [of] working not simply for but also truly with . . . principals, teachers, and preachers" in the African American community "who were doing grass roots work." He organized a Commission on Race Relations in the South, forerunner to the Commission on Interracial Cooperation (CIC), which was "inspired by [Methodist minister Dr.] Will W. Alexander," and the Southern Regional Council.[31] A 1940 tribute reminded readers that Dr. Dillard traveled rural areas and was able to engage "the cooperation of the southern whites, of northern philanthropists, and of the Negroes."[32] Naming the university proved to be an easier task than managing an unwieldy board of trustees and naming the university's first president.

An Unseemly Fire among the Religious

Tension lay waiting for its opportunity as the consolidated boards convened. Stern claimed that because there was not complete trust between the Methodists and Congregationalists, the board named "a Jew" as president. Bishop Jones reportedly and straightforwardly accused Dr. C. Jeff Miller, the head of the university's collection campaign, "with being racially prejudiced." This raised the ire of fellow board member Alvin Howard, close friend to Miller. Moreover, Bishop Jones charged two other board members with favoritism, as one nominated the other as architect for the university's building project. Although Stern did not like the charges, he was faced with another disruption.[33]

Stern did not want to rattle the segregationist's status quo in selecting a president. Neither Straight nor New Orleans universities had ever had an African American president. With Dillard came a faculty of different "races." Stern held that no African American president could supervise white faculty. Stern's preference was either a Southern white man or a Northern person with no "radical ideas on interracial relations." Brownlee continued to push but lost out, as Stern named Dr. Will W. Alexander, a white male, whom he believed would not upset any relationships that had been established with the white community. Alexander accepted the offer on a temporary basis. He spent little time at Dillard. Therefore, Dean Horace Mann Bond and Stern "practically ran the school."[34]

Stern immersed himself in Dillard. There was one problem after the other. White residents did not approve of the university in Gentilly, and they didn't want to ride the bus with black students. Stern worked with the city to get a separate bus. A new president was desperately needed, as Stern could not continue the pace. Dr. Alexander's regular commute between New Orleans and Atlanta forced the board to seek candidates for president.

Dr. Alexander met a young accountant at Morehouse. Although he had no business experience in running a hospital, Alexander hired him to run Flint-Goodridge. By all accounts, Albert W. Dent was a fast learner. When Alexander's temporary contract neared its end, Stern's support turned to Dent for president. His vote of confidence in the young hospital administrator was not shared by the majority of the board. Rather, they looked to another young man who was slightly older than Dent and had experience as president. William Stuart Nelson arrived from Shaw University and became Dillard's second president. Nelson did not meet expectations, and, Stern wrote, he strongly encouraged him to take a position at Howard University. Thus, the search began again in less than two years after the university opened its doors.

Early on, Trustee Brownlee did not support Dent, claiming he had not indicated any interest in the academic side of the university. He did not approve of several other candidates, holding that neither they nor Dent had the support of local African Americans.[35] He then set out to speak with one of the most noted figures among African Americans, Trustee Fannie C. Williams. He admitted that the board made a mistake in selecting William Stuart Nelson and had "been thinking and thinking, wondering about" where they erred. To keep from falling into the same trap, that is, hiring someone "spoiled with classical technique" as Nelson had been, Brownlee noted that he had been made aware that Dent's academic leanings were utilitarian. Brownlee could consider Dent, as he was Stern's choice, if that one last hurdle could be crossed. "No one has ever told me just why our Negro friends in New Orleans don't like him." He begged Williams to explain the mind of local African Americans to him. "I wish you would tell me," he implored, and "please do not hesitate to tell me frankly if my thinking is moving along a good or bad trace, and (once again) let me know how our Negro friends really feel about Mr. Dent and why."[36]

Although Brownlee kept up his writing campaign of inquiry about the African American community and its relationship with Dent, Miss Williams refused to take the bait. The Congregational minister and president of Lemoyne Owen College in Memphis at times appeared to stage an inquisition. To Stern, Brownlee said that the selection was between Charles Johnson, the sociologist, and Dent, but that he would choose Johnson over Dent. He named three others, none of whom "are what we need," he admitted. Some were too religious; others were not religious enough. As for Dent, he could not know where religion fit in his spiritual life.[37] Phillips Bradley, another board member, surmised that perhaps Dent did not suffer from criticism as an "aristocrat" by African Americans; rather, his "very warm welcome . . . from the white group in New Orleans would make him suspect among many classes of Negroes whose good will and active cooperation are indispensable to the future of Dillard." A reference to the *Washington Tribune*'s characterization of Dent contradicts Bradley's assumption: "He is not a white man's Negro. He wears no collar save his own."[38] In all of their conjectures about the nature of African Americans in New Orleans and their relationships one with the other, Bradley implored Brownlee to continue to pursue the inquiry with Miss Williams.[39]

Miss Fannie C. Williams, the dean of principals and noted educator of young children, finally addressed Brownlee. Her nuanced letter opened with four paragraphs of pleasantries but filled itself with diplomacy on the matter of Albert W. Dent's qualifications and his relationship with African Americans in New Orleans:

> For the President of an Institution like Dillard, I would like to have a man who was thoroughly trained and prepared in the administration of a College, who knew young people as well as elders, who had a way of life in human relations. I agree with you in the fact that Mr. Dent has done a corking good job at the hospital. He has been able to get the hearty support of the local Southern White man as well as men from all over the country. He has many friends among the people of his race. I admire him for his efficient method of conducting the hospital and for his courageous stand on problems in which specific principles are involved. Would he make a better President than a Superintendent of Flint-Goodridge Hospital? That is the question to be solved. My hope would be that a Dean of vision and education would be found to do the type of work which is so essential in a college where leaders and intelligent followers are being prepared.[40]

Her choice apparently was Dr. Felton G. Clark, "the youthful President of Southern University" in Scotlandville (Baton Rouge). She listed his credentials and stated that as "contemporaries" he and Dent "would make a good team if given the opportunity." She bid Brownlee well at LeMoyne but added, "I am also hoping that you will soon return to your field of larger service." That should have squashed Brownlee's fascination with the "Negroes" of New Orleans. However, as this matter dragged into the spring of 1941, Brownlee questioned each new candidate's ability to establish a relationship within the African American community. He begged the question with J. F. Drake, president of the Alabama State A&M College; and Edward Hope, son of the noted scholar John Hope, among others.[41]

Since the early 1930s and in the midst of the Great Depression, attention had been drawn to Dent with other opportunities. The assistant director of the National Association of Housing Officials contacted him because his "name has been suggested as a possible manager for one of the housing developments that the PWA (Public Works Administration) is at present constructing."[42] His interest was piqued at the request. He spoke by telephone with Florence Read, president at Spelman; then with Will W. Alexander, John Hope, and Edwin Embree. All were encouraging, although Alexander asked him to take a pause to consider where his strengths lay; to Alexander that was in public health and hospital administration and not as much with housing. Additionally, a fellow alumnus of Morehouse asked his permission to submit his name for president of the college. Dent "considered it a great privilege" but would not give his consent.[43] At one point, Embree advised him that Stern was "very anxious" for him to stay in New Orleans.

Dent and Stern

By May 1941, Stern called a trustee meeting and settled the presidency. He announced to all stakeholders, representatives of the General Education Board, Julius Rosenwald Fund, the Board of Education of the Methodist Church, and the American Missionary Association, that Mr. Albert W. Dent had been elected president of Dillard. He asked that they attend a conference to address the university's "financial problems" and said Dent would be present.[44] This began an eighteen-year collaboration between Dent and Stern. Neither Stern nor Dent made many decisions without consulting the other. They each seamlessly and interchangeably moved between Christian and Jewish patrons. Theirs became a close partnership and friendship. "Dent was a frequent guest in the Stern home at a time when blacks were rarely accepted in New Orleans society."[45]

The connections to the Methodist and Congregational churches, the AMA, and—through Stern—with the Jewish communities enabled Dillard to establish a permanent endowment. "At the Seventh Annual Commencement, June 3, President A. W. Dent announced the launch" of a $3 million endowment campaign, and the audience was astounded to learn that already $2.3 million had been assured by several foundations and boards "on condition that the remaining seven hundred thousand dollars be secured."[46] President Dent believed that present commitments gave them "a fair chance" to raise the remaining. To the thirty-four graduates, the guest speaker, Honorable William

H. Hastie, judge, and those in attendance, including the trustees, he reiterated the need for "sustaining funds" to continue the daily operations of the university. Collaborations with all of the religious groups continued to provide for a solid financial foundation for the school. It therefore increased opportunities—although Dent assured the trustees that Dillard did not have nearly enough to fulfill the requirements of its entire plant and to continue to hire outstanding faculty.

Through the Congregational Churches "Friendly Service" mission work, linen, homemaking kits for instruction, new clothing, and miscellaneous items flowed into Dillard each year near Christmas. Packages arrived from across the United States. The Congregationalists and the Methodists continued their institutional contributions to the university's endowment, as well as their yearly pledge toward the operating fund.[47] In addition, the General Conference of the Methodist Church urged annual conferences to raise extra money "through Race Relations offerings" toward strengthening "the financial structure" of the university.[48]

Correspondences abounded between Dent and Stern concerning financial support. Through the years and numerous times, Stern covered immediate shortfalls in addition to his annual pledges, which he paid in full by its promised date. In addition, Stern tapped the Jewish community in New Orleans, as well as Christians from various faiths to contribute to Dillard. He supported individual students by paying tuition for extra study at leading universities. He and Dent approached Tulane University doctors to supervise interns at Flint-Goodridge. As those African American doctors reached their levels of expertise, they assumed supervisory roles.

Perhaps Brownlee concerned himself with the local community because African Americans contributed to the university. Land donations such as Dr. Alfred Lawless's and the many small contributions from churches, schools, and families amounted to a fairly steady stream of cash for Dillard. Straight and New Orleans University alumni were now Dillard Alumni, and they supported the university. Nonetheless, their donations, though not enough to build a structure or finance an endowment, represented the investment of the people themselves; those for whom the "labor" originated in the mid-nineteenth century. The "Penny-a-Day" campaign for Flint-Goodridge care was manageable and needed. The African American community's support for Dillard served as its response to nineteenth-century religious groups' mission of providing tools for self-help.

Bishop Robert Elijah Jones made a decision to accept the direction of the plan of reunion to ensure that African Americans would have some semblance of self-determination. He understood that it meant recognizing the limitations of the consciousness of both religious people and society at large. His actions, then, fall in line with the various Christian and Jewish denominations who acted out their answer to "What was the greater good?" While there were grave limitations in the systemic change of the American social infrastructure, individuals claiming a religious belief, and religious institutions themselves, chose to address the immediate causes of transforming masses of people from the nineteenth century's dependence forced on them in bondage to living their lives as free people. Additionally, interfaith groups worked collectively not for, but with African Americans through the first half of the twentieth century in forging institutions such as Dillard University. This was progress, albeit segregated. The legacy and the lesson of those early interfaith workers are embedded in the crust of the common ideal of their faiths; there was a shared belief in humanity's responsibilities for one another. Those early organizations allowed the crust of their faith to direct their vision. Although they gave in to the illness of American society, perhaps their lesson also teaches us to seek ways to address immediacies while fashioning long-term progressive structures.

Notes

1   Robert Elijah Jones Papers, 1872–1975, Amistad Research Center, Tulane University, New Orleans, Louisiana.

2   Peter C. Murray, *Methodists and the Crucible of Race, 1930-1975* (Columbia, MO: University of Missouri Press, 2004), 35–37.

3   Murray, 38. Murray notes that "African American Methodists, in the Central Jurisdiction, would elect their own bishops, and have jurisdictional representatives on all (General) church boards and agencies, but they would remain otherwise segregated from their white brethren."

4   Paul A. Carter, "The Negro and Methodist Union," *Church History* 21, no. 1 (1952): 55–70, http://www.jstor.org/stable/3162070. For another treatment of the reunification of the Methodist Church, see Blake Barton Renfro, "The Reunification of American Methodism, 1916–1939," MA thesis, Louisiana State University, Baton Rouge, May 2010, http://digitalcommons.lsu.edu/gradschool_theses/400/.

5   The Amistad Case is documented in numerous sources. It involved Africans who mutinied in 1839 and whose ship landed off the coast of New York. The fifty-three African captives were taken into custody. Lewis Tappan led the fight to free them and obtained the services of John Quincy Adams to argue their case. In *United States v. The Amistad* (1841), the court ruled in favor of the Africans. They were freed and were able to return to their homeland.

6   Clara Merritt DeBoer, *Be Jubilant My Feet: African American Abolitionists in the American Missionary Association, 1839–1861*, Studies in African American History and Culture, ed. Graham Hodges (New York: Garland, 1994), xii, xiv.

7   Clara Merritt DeBoer, *His Truth Is Marching On: African Americans Who Taught the Freedmen for the American Missionary Association, 1861–1877*, Studies in African American History and Culture, ed. Graham Hodges (New York: Garland 1995), 9–11. Although DeBoer focuses on African American teachers, AMA cofounder Lewis Tappan's stern instructions and warnings applied to all who wanted to be commissioned to work in the South.

8   DeBoer, 11.

9   Historian Samuel C. Hyde Jr. notes in *Pistols and Politics: The Dilemma of Democracy in Louisiana's Florida Parishes, 1810–1899*, that the "riot . . . amounted to no less than a slaughter of blacks by armed whites." (Baton Rouge: Louisiana State University Press, 1996), 161.

10 Deboer, *His Truth Is Marching On*, 121.

11 Quoted in William H. Armstrong, *A Friend to God's Poor: Edward Parmelee Smith* (Athens, GA: University of Georgia Press, 1993), 195.

12 James B. Bennett, *Religion and the Rise of Jim Crow in New Orleans* (Princeton, NJ: Princeton University Press, 2005) provides a full discussion of interracialism in Ames Methodist Church, as well as in the city's religious culture. An earlier account of the church is Anne C. Loveland, "The 'Southern Work' of the Reverend Joseph C. Hartzell, Pastor of Ames Church in New Orleans, 1870–1873," in *Louisiana History: The Journal of the Louisiana Historical Association* 16, no. 4 (Autumn 1975): 391–407.

13 "Seventy Years of Service: New Orleans University (New Orleans: published by the Faculty, May 1935). The "Historical Sketch" also notes that eight schools including New Orleans resulted from the work of these first Methodists arriving after the Civil War and the Ames Methodist Church: Baton Rouge, Thibodaux, Franklin, Jefferson City, Natchitoches, Evergreen, and St. Martinville.

14 "Seventy Years of Service," 97.

15 Todd L. Savitt, "Straight University Medical Department: The Short Life of a Black Medical School in Reconstruction New Orleans," *Louisiana History, The Journal of the Louisiana Historical Association* 41, no. 2 (Spring 2000): 180.

16 Shawn C. Comminey, "The Origin, Organization, and Progression of Straight University, 1869–1880," *Louisiana History: The Journal of the Louisiana Historical Association* 51, no. 4 (Fall 2010): 407.

17 Savitt, "Straight University Medical Department," 181, 183.

18 Comminey, "The Origin, Organization, and Progression of Straight University," 410.

19 "Dedication of the Lawless Memorial Entrance to Dillard University," May 31, 1942, in *The Christian Advocate*, central ed., the Official Organ of the Central Jurisdiction of the Methodist Church (Chicago: Methodist Publishing House, June 11, 1942).

20 Noted in Robert Elijah Jones Papers, Amistad Research Center. See also Letter to A. W. Dent, president, Dillard University, from Edgar B. Stern, president of the Dillard Board of Trustees, June 21, 1951, acknowledging Dent's letter and article from the *Chicago Defender* noting Dr. Lawless's "investment" in Dillard's Gentilly Gardens Apartments. "I cannot but feel that many of our students, having lived their childhood in subnormal surroundings, must leave Dillard with a new taste for the beautiful in their own home lives," Stern wrote. He added that he would send congratulations to Dr. Lawless. Letter courtesy of Archives, Will W. Alexander Library, Dillard University, New Orleans, Louisiana.

21 "Medical History: The History of Flint-Goodridge Hospital of Dillard University," *Journal of the National Medical Association* 61, no. 6 (1969): 533–36, repr., courtesy of the Amistad Research Center. Also helpful in this history were Moise H. Goldstein and B. C. MacLean, "A Hospital That Serves as a Center of Negro Medical Education," *Modern Hospital* 39, no. 5 (November 1932); Raymond P. Sloan, "Five Years of Negro Health Activities," *Modern Hospital* 48, no. 4 (April 1937); and Darlene Clark Hine, "Flint-Goodridge Hospital of Dillard University: The Development of Black Collegiate Nursing, 1932–1950," unpublished.

22 "Seventy Years of Service," 48–49.

23 Letter to A. W. Dent, president, Dillard University, from Leo M. Coogan of the Edgar Stern Family Fund, April 14, 1952.

24 List of suggestive inscriptions, courtesy of the Archives, Will W. Alexander Library, Dillard University, n.d.

25 Letter to Dr. Will W. Alexander, Chapel Hill, North Carolina, from A. W. Dent, president, Dillard University, July 21, 1952. Courtesy of the Archives, Will W. Alexander Library, Dillard University.

26 "Seventy Years of Service," 37.

27 Joe M. Richardson, "Edgar B. Stern: A White New Orleans Philanthropist Helps Building a Black University," *Journal of Negro History* 82, no. 3 (Summer 1997): 329–30.

28 Letter to Dr. Will W. Alexander from President A. W. Dent, July 21, 1952.

29 "Seventy Years of Service," 47.

30 Richardson, "Edgar B. Stern," 330. Richardson incorrectly identifies Bishop Robert E. Jones as an affiliate of the AME (African Methodist Episcopal) Church. Bishop Jones was a Methodist Episcopal clergyman.

31 Fred L. Brownlee, "Educational Programs for the Improvement of Race Relations: Philanthropic Foundations," *Journal of Negro Education* 13, no. 3 (Summer 1944): 330–31.

32 "James Hardy Dillard," *Journal of Negro History* 25, no. 4 (October 1940): 585–86.

33 Richardson, "Edgar B. Stern," 331.

34 Richardson, 332.

35 Letter to Warren Kearny, New Orleans, from Fred L. Brownlee, September 20, 1940. Courtesy of the Amistad Research Center, Tulane University, New Orleans, Louisiana.

36 Letter to Miss Fannie C. Williams, New Orleans, from Fred L. Brownlee, September 23, 1940. Courtesy of the Amistad Research Center.

37 Letter to Edgar B. Stern, New Orleans, from Fred L. Brownlee, September 26, 1940. Courtesy of the Amistad Research Center.

38 Quoted in Richardson, "Edgar B. Stern," 337.

39 Letter to Fred L. Brownlee, the Board of Home Missions, New York, from Phillips Bradley, Queens College, Flushing, New York, September 27, 1940; and to Brownlee from Bradley, October 4, 1940. Courtesy of the Amistad Research Center.

40 Letter to Fred L. Brownlee, New York, from Fannie C. Williams, Valena C. Jones School, October 29, 1940. In his letter of May 26, 1941, Brownlee thanked Williams for her response and asked for a meeting with her in New Orleans. Courtesy of the Amistad Research Center.

41 Letter to Edgar B. Stern, New Orleans from Fred L. Brownlee, May 5, 1941. Courtesy of the Amistad Research Center.

42 Letter from Elizabeth Longon, Chicago, to Albert Dent, October 23, 1935. Courtesy of the Amistad Research Center.

43 Correspondence among those individuals and Dent cover several offers in Atlanta and Washington, DC, as well, and span a four-year period, 1935 through 1939. Courtesy of the Amistad Research Center.

44 Letter to Raymond B. Fosdick, president, General Education Board, New York, from Edgar B. Stern, president, Board of Trustees, Dillard University, New Orleans, June 12, 1941. One member, Leon Favrot, declined election to the Board of Trustees but noted that Dent "possesses vision and executive capacity" and that he would continue to support "his effort" at Dillard (June 12, 1941). Courtesy of Amistad Research Center.

45 Richardson, "Edgar B. Stern," 337

46 "News of Methodism," in *Christian Advocate*, June 18, 1942. Courtesy of the Archives, Will W. Alexander Library, Dillard University.

47 For one example among many, see letter to Edgar B. Stern, from A. W. Dent, informing him that Stern's $100,000 pledge had been paid in full, as had the Methodists'. He

waited, however, on the remaining $66,000 from the Congregationalists, in order to collect the match from the General Board of Education, which would not be fulfilled until all the pledges were made (June 30, 1952).

48 Letter to Edgar B. Stern from John O. Gross, General Board of Education, The Methodist Church, Nashville, Tennessee, April 2, 1954.

TRANSFORMATIVE INTERSECTIONS

4

Change in Heart and Mind

Reflections on the Intersection between a Nonbeliever
and a United Methodist–Affiliated Institution

Kent Andersen

Working and teaching at a United Methodist–affiliated residential liberal arts college changed me. More specifically, participating in service-learning projects at Glide Memorial United Methodist Church through Birmingham-Southern College's January interim term prompted me to reexamine my attitudes toward religious communities and how best to work with students who hold religious commitments. Glide, based in San Francisco, describes itself as "a radically inclusive, just and loving community mobilized to alleviate suffering and break the cycles of poverty and marginalization."[1] During the January term project, students and staff from my institution in Birmingham, Alabama travel to San Francisco to participate in Glide's programs and meet with directors, staff, and clients to explore how Glide enacts its mission. This project was developed as a result of my college's affiliation with The United Methodist Church. I've participated in this project five times, the first time in 2002. My experiences provide insight into the conditions under which a change in thinking and feeling occurs and, specifically, how such change might occur in the intersection between an educator's professional identity and religiously affiliated higher education institutions.

Two Incidents: Side by Side with Students

Two incidents illustrate the difference between my former self and my present self. The first incident took place before my employment at Birmingham-Southern. I was working as an adjunct instructor at a community college, teaching introductory writing. As part of the course, I used an essay by Bertrand Russell titled "Why I Am Not a Christian."[2] Ostensibly, my point in teaching the essay was to provide an example of forecasting: the ways a writer guides the reader through his or her writing. I had chosen the essay because I liked it; I also thought at the time that it was an effective argument. In retrospect, Russell's essay does provide an effective model of forecasting—the thesis is clearly stated, the transitions explicit, and the headings appropriate—but the argument is less effective, I would now say, because it works best for those readers already sympathetic to his view, as I was at the time. In the essay, Russell lays out his position against Christianity, which he defines as having some belief in God and immortality as well as "some kind of belief about Christ."[3] His argument refutes common propositions in support of a deity (e.g., the first-cause argument, the argument for remedying injustice), and then goes on to impugn the character of Christ. I was first introduced to Russell's argument in an undergraduate course on the philosophy of religion, and I remember thinking it was quite right. In conjunction with other materials I encountered at the time, I came to identify as a nonbeliever and to hold an adversarial stance toward religious belief.

Although my focus for class that day was on Russell's approach as a writer, following class I was drawn into conversation with a student about the content of the essay. The weather must have been pleasant because I remember we spent a long time sitting side by side on the bench outside our classroom, looking out over a wooded area near the campus. I don't recall the student's name, but I do remember that he was from Romania, that he was an Orthodox Christian, that he wasn't much younger than I was at the time, and that most of our conversation concerned the logic and evidence one might marshal to justify a belief in God or acceptance of Christ. The conversation was never heated, and my memory of the student was that he was primarily interested in why I found Russell's argument so compelling. Likely, I rehearsed for him arguments against blind faith and why I did not view religious belief as necessary for moral and ethical actions. I did not ask why or how the student had come to be at the community college, I did not ask about his family or his background or even what he was planning to study in the long-term, I did not learn anything about his home in Romania and what that was like, and I did not find out how he responded to Russell. I am curious now how a student from Romania came to be there, at that moment—but I missed the opportunity to make these discoveries, though our conversation lasted for some time.

The second incident occurred in January 2017 at a San Francisco Starbucks. I was again sitting side by side with a student. It was raining outside, and we were talking about the required reflection essay she was going to write; we sat at a table facing a window that looks out on the street. The reflection essay required students to identify and then examine a "starting point," defined as a moment or experience when things don't seem right, when things seem off, or when things don't go as one expects or desires.[4] The task for students is to first describe this incident and then go on to make new sense of it through critical reflection, eventually identifying a new or changed understanding about the incident or the assumptions that guide their thoughts and actions. Writing these essays is often very difficult because it requires surfacing one's underlying, deeply held assumptions, examining those assumptions, and then making a conscious choice about whether or not to hold on to them.

In this case, the student wanted to write about her experience at Glide's "Speak Out" session a few days earlier. In a Speak Out session, individuals share—they speak out—with an audience. What people share is wide-open, although the use of language that demeans or is derogatory toward individuals or groups is forbidden. Our entire Birmingham-Southern team was present, as were other volunteers. There also appeared to be regulars, because the facilitator called individuals to the front of the room to share. The session concluded with a raffle, in which audience members—some of whom were staying in shelters, in single-occupancy hotels in the area, or living on the street—received care packages with groceries and other supplies. The facilitator also shared about her experience as a trans woman, about her previous drug use, about the abuse she experienced as a child, and ultimately about how she came to Glide and was drawn into Glide's recovery programs. The facilitator felt that God had led her to be there with us at that moment.

The student's starting point concerned her surprise at how comfortable she felt in the facilitator's presence, and, more important, the impression she had that the facilitator was talking directly to her and was perhaps channeling God in doing so. At this point during the project, I had learned a lot about this particular student, including details about her family background, which was not typical, and her varied life experiences. I had also come to respect this student in a very deep way. I admired her ability to enter openly into a situation, to accept others without any apparent reservations. She had admitted to me that she had not completed the readings about Glide until she was on the plane, at which point she became apprehensive about what she had gotten into. Yet, I saw no evidence of this apprehension in her actions. With regard to the Speak Out session, she wanted to explore what it meant that she felt God was speaking to her through the facilitator—not what she expected—at the same time that the facilitator was talking explicitly about illicit and sometimes illegal behaviors.

This moment in our conversation stands out to me because it places in vivid relief how I've changed in my approach to students and in my attitudes about religious commitments. In an earlier time, I would have balked at the idea that God can "work through" someone or that deities are somehow trying to clue us in to something. A previous version of me would have sought to shape the conversation in such a way that we could debunk the idea. It's not so much that I would have sought to coerce the student into accepting a particular view—I'm not like that—but I would have introduced a counterview that interpreted such comments skeptically, essentially from Russell's perspective.

But in that moment at Starbucks, I followed the student's lead and explored with her what it would mean to have Jesus speak through a trans woman in an old church in a poor neighborhood in San Francisco, and how that differs from other ways the student has come to understand the role of Jesus in her life, the accepted manner that Jesus can speak to us, and even what Jesus can say. In doing so, I saw that I was less interested in exercising the attitude of skepticism and more interested in collaborating with the student to make new sense of her experience on her own terms. In doing so, we had not stopped thinking critically, as my former self might have assumed, but in fact, just the opposite. We were able to unearth the student's assumptions about gender, about propriety, about the "masks" people wear to hide their true selves, and ultimately about what it means to love unconditionally, one of Glide's and Jesus's main messages.

Intersection with Glide: Unconditional Love

Unconditional love is a central tenet of Glide's mission and services. As an organization they've identified five values that ground achievement of their mission. One of these values is "loving and hopeful" and includes the assertion that "we love unconditionally." The other four values draw from a similar emphasis, asserting that Glide is "radically inclusive" and "truth telling," as well as committed to breaking barriers between groups and celebrating together as a community.[5] They refer to Sunday services as celebrations. During these services, speakers identify as Glide members and share their personal stories— stories that typically involve rejection or shame in other communities, followed by acceptance and inclusion at Glide. The prompting to love unconditionally appears regularly on banners, flyers, and other Glide materials, including the T-shirts and sweatshirts that bear the logo of a heart with the words "love unconditionally." In our meetings with Glide staff in January 2017, they talked specifically about how loving unconditionally is an aspiration, something one must continually strive toward, not something one merely accomplishes.

Unconditional love also figures centrally in *Beyond the Possible,* the memoir written by Glide founder Cecil Williams and longtime executive director of the Glide Foundation Janice Mirikitani. In a chapter titled "Love," they tell the story of Glide's relationship with the gay community in 1960s San Francisco and the negative reaction from other churches about Glide's work with homosexuals and support of a gay advocacy group.[6] "Today," the authors wrote, "about 40 percent of Glide's congregation are proud lesbian, gay, bisexual, and transgender (LGBT) folks."[7] Further, the first openly lesbian bishop of The United Methodist Church served as senior pastor at Glide. According to Williams and Mirikitani, "the way gay people have changed over the years offers a useful lesson about unconditional love."[8] They observe that in the past, the gay community "wagged their finger in the face of rejection," insisting that they be acknowledged. Now, in the wake of increasing acceptance, Williams and Mirikitani reflect that the LGBT community appears to say, "We embrace you, whatever society you belong to."[9] This message of radical inclusion, acceptance, and unconditional love informs much of what the students and I experience while at Glide.

For many of the students, Glide's radical inclusion comes as a surprise: they are surprised to see openly gay people attending a church service, to learn about Glide's outreach to drug users through harm reduction and recovery programs; and, if they are Christian, to hear of Cecil's decision, early in his tenure, to remove the cross from the sanctuary. As relayed in the memoir, Cecil came to understand that the cross often conveyed a message of exclusion and oppression, particularly for individuals who had been marginalized or ignored in traditional church contexts.[10] Because he envisioned Glide as an "all-inclusive church that practiced unconditional acceptance," he realized the removal of the cross was necessary if they were to convey that message.[11] This message of radical inclusion frequently serves as a starting point for reflection.

Two More Incidents: Suspension of Doubt and Methodological Belief

My approach toward students with religious commitments and my attitudes toward the church changed as a result of my time at Glide. Central to this shift, as indicated in the incidents with students relayed earlier, is how I work side by side with students to help them think more creatively and critically. While I've always aspired for collaboration, I think I am more successful in the second incident with the student at Glide than in the first with the student at the community college. In the first, I spent too much time arguing about nothing and learning little. In the second, I successfully suspended my perspective long enough to learn with the student and to help her make new sense of her experience without limiting ourselves to her or my initial understandings and reactions alone. How did this happen? Two additional experiences provide insight. The first has to do with people, and the second with ideas. From these, we can discern the conditions for a change in mind and heart. I will eventually place these conditions in the broader context of an aspirational pedagogy.

In my first year at Glide, I did not serve as the project leader. Instead, a professor of psychology, in collaboration with a student leader, facilitated the learning part of our service. Despite my title, I was more of a student than an instructor. Being a student was important, because it meant I could negotiate my own experience before having to help others manage their own. I remember vividly one of this group's reflective discussions. We were in one of the sleeping rooms at the youth hostel where we stay each year. Four or five bunk beds were arrayed in a tight rectangle, and students sat in pairs on each bunk. The psychology professor stood at one corner of our group, facilitating our conversation, gesturing and inviting people to talk. I was cross-legged on the floor, with my notebook and a pen. The specific substance of our conversation escapes me, but I remember clearly the professor's words toward the end of our discussion: "I don't know what it's like in your faith tradition, but in mine, we think it's important to . . ."

I have held on to that phrase. It was simple, respectful, inclusive, and honest. It also exposed a flaw in my thinking that I would have found difficult to identify in any other context: on some level I appeared to assume that all reasonable people reach the same conclusions, adopt the same perspective, and practice the same routines and rituals. Divergence from these conclusions and actions indicated flawed thinking. Thus, I appeared to assume that if one held a conviction—a faith—one was obligated to sway others into holding it as well. Had someone told me I believed this, I would have denied it. Yet, when the psychology professor extended herself in this way, making herself vulnerable by sharing an aspect of herself with the group, I was able to metaphorically "try on" her position and perspective without immediately giving up my own. This kind of metaphorical "trying on" of different life stories has been a common feature of our times at Glide. Recall that one of Glide's core values is "truth telling," which requires that "we each tell our story; we each speak our truth; we listen."[12]

A second incident involved ideas. At the same time that I was first experiencing Glide, I was also working to sharpen my craft as a teacher for introductory writing and literature courses. Pivotal in my thinking about how to teach such courses was the work of Peter Elbow, who introduced me to the idea of methodological belief. Elbow identifies methodological belief as a tool for prompting students to generate more and better ideas as well as better interpretations of literary texts.[13] He realized that people rarely change their minds or develop new ideas by "arguing" about things—that is, by laying out reasons and logic alone. More important to changing minds, he discovered, was experience and the ability to enter into other perspectives. In his own classrooms, Elbow observed how discussions about textual interpretations often turned into unproductive quarrels.

These unproductive discussions presumed that getting to the best interpretation required that every interpretation be subjected to rigorous skeptical tests, with no idea left unexamined. Yet, the result of these discussions rarely yielded changed minds, let alone new insights. As an alternative, Elbow started practicing methodological belief.

Methodological belief differs from methodological doubt. As Elbow says, "When we doubt, we spit out or fend off." In contrast, "when we believe we swallow or incorporate."[14] Both processes are valuable, and both need to be learned. "To doubt well," he says, "we learn to extricate or detach ourselves."[15] Doing so makes possible the identification of propositions and exposes contradictions. Doubting relies on distance. Methodological doubt looks a lot like Russell's exercise in "Why I Am Not a Christian" of first defining Christianity, debunking arguments, and identifying flaws in the character of Christ. What Russell missed is the experience of the believer, the phenomenology of being a Christian, and the value such belief might provide. As Elbow emphasizes, belief involves experience and proximity. Unlike doubt, which requires distance, effective believing requires that "we learn to invest or insert ourselves."[16] When I was younger, I sought out fallacy and poor logic. Once I started teaching and thinking more about the craft of teaching, Elbow's methodological belief provided a different orientation. Methodological belief is "the rhetoric of experience," and Elbow goes on to say that "trying to *experience* our understandings helps us see as someone else sees."[17] I needed this capacity in order to teach more effectively.

Elbow does not advocate for blind or naïve belief. Recall that his aim is to get past the impasse of quarreling. To do that, we need to use our imaginations to metaphorically "try on" other perspectives and to get into the experiences of others. Methodological belief requires that we try to see what's "interesting or helpful about the view," asking, "What would you notice if you believed this view? If it were true?"[18] To methodologically believe, we ask, "In what sense or under what conditions might this idea be true?"[19] That suspension of disbelief is what occurred in response to the psychology professor's turn of phrase in the reflection discussion during my first trip to Glide. It is also what I made a deliberate choice to do when working with the student on her reflection essay about the Speak Out session.

I don't mean to imply that my change in mind and heart happened suddenly. It did not. It happened over time, and my consciousness of it probably has yet to be fully realized even at the time of this writing. Biases and blind spots likely remain, and I know I fall into old habits of quarreling when suspension and methodological belief would lead to more productive results. But, in sum, my experiences at the intersection between my work as a professional educator and my religiously affiliated institution suggest four conditions necessary for change. (1) For one, my change was grounded in my own goals and aspirations. I had a predisposition to seeing myself as a collaborator but increasingly saw a gap between aspirations and actions. (2) Second, working at a religiously affiliated institution afforded me the opportunity to experience Glide. While the experience alone would not have been enough, witnessing a diverse religious community opened me to change. It helped, of course, that Glide's values accorded with my own. Rejecting or "spitting out" Glide ran the risk of rejecting at least some parts of myself. (3) Third, I encountered individuals—the psychology professor who led my first project, as well as many others I have not discussed here—who welcomed me, often on my own terms and without expectation. I was loved unconditionally. (4) Finally, I had developed a language—methodological belief and methodological doubt—for naming and identifying what I was thinking and feeling. Elbow had already convinced me that doubt was insufficient for prompting critical and productive thinking. Glide provided the experience that solidified that approach.

Implications for Educators and Institutions: *Sentipensante*

The implications here, I think, are clear. (1) If educators hope to affect people's hearts and minds, they need to identify learners' goals and interests—the things people care about most. (2) If educators wish to prompt learning and growth, they also need to ensure learners encounter a wide array of life experiences and views. For many of my students, this means encountering trans people. For me, it meant encountering individuals—such as the Speak Out facilitator—who identified as believers but held similar convictions and values as my own. Maintaining misunderstandings or false assumptions becomes more difficult as evidence accumulates. (3) My experiences also imply that educators interested in changing hearts and minds need to provide contexts that are inclusive and welcoming. It's important for people to learn to identify and challenge their assumptions, but this is most likely to happen when they feel welcomed and valued as they are, not as others expect them to be. (4) Finally, to prompt learning, educators need to assist learners in developing a language that increases the capacity to name the challenges and difficulties they face.

Glide sets these conditions, and I've been fortunate to have powerful learning experiences while there. The challenge is to consider how to extend these contexts into our classrooms and other learning sites. Laura Rendón's pedagogy of *sentipensante* offers a model for doing this. The pedagogical approach also provides additional context for reflecting on the three-way intersection between religiously affiliated institutions, religiously committed students, and skeptical, nonbelieving educators like me. According to Rendón, *sentipensante* "represents a teaching and learning approach based on wholeness, harmony, social justice, and liberation."[20] The term *sentipensante* combines two Spanish words: *sentir*, which means "to sense or feel," and *pensar*, "to think."[21] The point is to balance and ultimately integrate intellectualism with intuition. Intellectual work is outer work in that it is objective and concerned with objects and ideas in the world. Intuition is inner work in that it involves connecting these outside objects and concerns with one's own life and inner, subjective experience. The goals of this pedagogical approach are threefold: first, it "disrupts" the teaching and learning assumptions in academic culture that hinder wholeness; second, it cultivates "*personas educadas*," or well-rounded learners capable of integrating knowledge and experience and acting wisely; and third, the approach prompts social change and commitment to social justice.[22] Adopting this orientation provides a way forward by extending Elbow's notion of methodological belief as well as the insights gained from my experiences.

Adopting *sensipensante* as a pedagogical approach requires revising commonly held assumptions in academic culture about teaching and learning. For example, Rendón asserts that educators replace the agreement to privilege intellectual or rational knowing with an agreement "to work with diverse ways of knowing in the classroom."[23] By "diverse ways of knowing," Rendón means several different approaches, including emotional intelligence, spiritual intelligence, and heart intelligence, as well as non-Western and indigenous knowledge.[24] Similarly, she asserts that educators replace the agreement of separation with an agreement to "embrace connectedness, collaboration and transdisciplinarity."[25] In this case, Rendón imagines faculty collaborating across disciplinary boundaries, rather than working in disciplinary silos, and connecting with students in a manner that supports validation and care for students' subjective realities, not merely intellectual development.[26] Likewise, she challenges educators to revise the emphasis on outer knowing, and instead embrace the need for examining how to balance personal and professional work, with a particular emphasis on meaning and replenishment, as well as self-reflexivity on the status and role of the educator.[27]

Putting the pedagogy of *sentipensante* into practice requires employing a range of pedagogical techniques, as well as developing curricular content that "affirms diverse ways of knowing and the dignity and worth of all people."[28] The approach has obvious similarities to the unconditional love expressed at Glide, as well as the necessity of meeting people on their own terms and in their own language. Rendón anticipates that many traditional pedagogical activities would remain, including critical reading and analysis of texts, research, lab work, and classroom discussions. However, to emphasize inner work, these activities would also include contemplative activities, such as meditation, deliberate silence, and storytelling. Also necessary, she argues, will be opportunities for out-of-class learning that involve students with social change initiatives that foster "critical consciousness."[29] Such activities work best, she insists, when coupled with introspection where faculty and students identify their underlying assumptions and how those assumptions may enable or hinder the enactment of social justice and the accomplishment of wholeness. Self-reflection and self-examination, Rendón imagines, "can serve as a means for faculty and students to probe more deeply into what they are learning and how the learning is transforming them."[30]

Birmingham-Southern College, as espoused in its mission, prepares students to "live lives of significance."[31] While one might debate what constitutes a life of significance, the mission statement provides parameters, grounding significance in the idea of a well-rounded education as well as the college's relationship with The United Methodist Church. The mission asserts, for example, that the college "honors its Methodist heritage of informed inquiry and meaningful service," and that it fosters students' "intellectual and personal development . . . by challenging [them] to engage their community and the greater world, to examine diverse perspectives, and to live with integrity."[32] In other words, the college seeks to develop *personas educadas*, although not precisely in those terms.

One way the college has honored its tradition of informed inquiry and meaningful service is by offering service-learning projects. These projects were initiated by the chaplain's office and have been ongoing since the 1980s, many of them developed through the college's relationships with The United Methodist Church. When I initially arrived at the college, I was skeptical of these connections and saw these relationships as a potential weakness. But I've changed. My participation in these projects changed me by prompting me to reassess my orientation toward students, toward religious communities, and ultimately toward my own pedagogical practice. I do not yet identify as a person of faith, but I do now see a strength in the relationships such collaborations between institutional partners afford, specifically the way partnerships can draw on traditions and provide support, validation, and unconditional love for the individuals engaged in learning at these institutions. I don't want to overstate the case, but I feel now that religiously affiliated institutions are well positioned to support the educational objectives of wholeness, harmony, social justice, and liberation. As for me, and as for the staff we talked with at Glide, such institutions may not always live up to their aspirations, although I believe they are most valuable and meaningful to their members when they attempt to. In the end, my experiences provide insight into the necessity of drawing individuals and groups of varied faith traditions and belief systems together to share their stories, reflect on their experiences, and aspire to develop well-rounded individuals committed to the radical practice of unconditional love.

Notes

1   Glide, "I Am Glide," accessed November 7, 2017, https://www.glide.org/.

2   Bertand Russell, "Why I Am Not a Christian," in *Why I Am Not a Christian and Other Essays on Religion and Related Subjects* (New York: Simon & Schuster, 1957), 3–23.

3   Russell, 4.

4   Barry C. Jentz and Joan W. Wofford, *Leadership and Learning: Personal Change in a Professional Setting* (New York: McGraw-Hill, 1979), 7.

5   Glide, "Mission and Values," accessed November 7, 2017, https://www.glide.org/mission.

6   Cecil Williams and Janice Mirikitani, *Beyond the Possible* (New York: HarperCollins, 2013), 103.

7   Williams and Mirikitani, 109.

8   Williams and Mirikitani, 111.

9   Williams and Mirikitani, 111.

10   Williams and Mirikitani, 132.

11   Williams and Mirikitani, 60.

12   Glide, "Mission and Values."

13   Peter Elbow, "Methodological Doubting and Believing: Contraries in Inquiry," in *Embracing Contraries: Explorations in Learning and Teaching* (Oxford: Oxford University Press, 1986), 254–300.

14   Elbow, 264.

15 Elbow, 264.

16 Elbow, 264.

17 Elbow, 264.

18 Elbow, 275.

19 Elbow, 275.

20 Laura Rendón, *Sentipensante (Sensing/Thinking) Pedagogy: Educating for Wholeness, Social Justice, and Liberation* (Sterling, VA: Stylus, 2009), 132.

21 Rendón, 131.

22 Rendón, 136.

23 Rendón, 32.

24 Rendón, 28–32, 42.

25 Rendón, 36.

26 Rendón, 35.

27 Rendón, 45–49.

28 Rendón, 142.

29 Rendón, 137.

30 Rendón, 137.

31 Birmingham-Southern College, "About BSC," accessed November 7, 2017, https://www.bsc.edu/about/index.html.

32 Birmingham-Southern College.

Sources

Birmingham-Southern College. "About BSC." https://www.bsc.edu/about/index.html.

Elbow, Peter. "Methodological Doubting and Believing: Contraries in Inquiry." In *Embracing Contraries: Explorations in Learning and Teaching*, 254–300. Oxford: Oxford University Press, 1986.

Glide. "I Am Glide." https://www.glide.org/.

Glide. "Mission and Values." https://www.glide.org/mission.

Jentz, Barry C., and Joan W. Wofford. *Leadership and Learning: Personal Change in a Professional Setting.* New York: McGraw-Hill, 1979.

Rendón, Laura I. *Sentipensante (Sensing/Thinking) Pedagogy: Educating for Wholeness, Social Justice, and Liberation.* Sterling, VA: Stylus, 2009.

Russell, Bertrand. "Why I Am Not a Christian." In *Why I Am Not a Christian and Other Essays on Religion and Related Subjects.* New York: Simon & Schuster, 1957.

Williams, Cecil, and Janice Mirikitani. *Beyond the Possible.* New York: HarperCollins, 2013.

5

How the Story of Job May Help Us All Get Along

Chad J. Pevateaux

Each of them set out from his home. . . . They met together to go and console and comfort him. When they saw him from a distance, they did not recognize him, and they raised their voices and wept aloud; they tore their robes and threw dust in the air upon their heads. They sat with him on the ground seven days and seven nights, and no one spoke a word to him, for they saw that his suffering was very great.

—Job 2:11–13

Acts of horror seemingly happen faster and faster today. When we hear of all these troubles, we struggle to respond in ways that would aid interfaith relations rather than exacerbate the strife. How can we counter hate and lessen violence arising from and directed at religious communities? Especially when we see that the suffering of one faith group is very great, what are we to do?

I worked as a youth minister in an Episcopal church for many years, but after seeing the suffering of September 11, 2001, I decided to go to graduate school to develop resources to help us avoid religious violence and oppose hate of religious others. I feared a cycle of violence that could plunge the world again into the horrors of the twentieth century that saw global war revolving in part around a "final solution" of purging the religious other from our midst. In the shadow of the Shoah and 9/11, I spent my master's and PhD studying comparative religions to try to help us all get along. Whether because of hate violence or catastrophe, when suffering befalls any one faith community, it affects all people of faith. From the Abrahamic traditions, the story of Job shows us a possible process for an interfaith response to such suffering. That is: to (1) know, (2) go, (3) gather, (4) recognize, (5) cry, (6) and share silence.

Know: "Now when Job's three friends heard of all these troubles . . ."

Somehow, the friends had come to know that Job suddenly had everything violently taken from him—his loved ones, his possessions, his health. From this, we see that we must first be friends. Without waiting for further calamity, we should already cultivate a climate of friendship among different religious traditions. As friends, we should have a system of communication capable of quickly informing all when some violence or hardship befalls one.

Some fear, however, that friendship with a religious other means watering down their own faith. The fearful think that those people over there who believe differently, worship differently, and act from different convictions cannot be our friends because they believe wrongly, worship wrongly, and act from the wrong convictions. To befriend them would mean to condone their wrongness and discount our rightness. If full agreement were a precondition of friendship, though, then we all would be friendless. How, then, can we forge friendships across religious differences?

People working on interfaith issues often use the key term *pluralism* to discuss religious differences, though that same word oftentimes has different meanings. When I teach the meaning(s) of pluralism in my classes, I begin with a distinction between descriptive and pre-scriptive. On the one hand, descriptive pluralism simply refers to the fact that there are in human cultures certain diverse systems that we deem religious, such as Judaism, Christianity, Islam, Hinduism, and Buddhism. We might debate the word "religion" as an overly West-ern, socially constructed concept with a colonialist history (as indeed we should and it is), but we also all should agree that, however we de-fine what we now call "religions," there are more than one of them, or plural. Pluralism, then, simply describes an undeniable reality of reli-gious diversity. On the other hand, prescriptive pluralism recommends an orientation in regard to that religious diversity. People who use the term in this sense, then, proclaim pluralism a virtue and offer it as a prescription for how we might all get along.

I further explain to my students, though, that there are at least two types of prescriptive pluralism, and that's where things get con-fusing, because in interfaith discussions it's not always clear which is which. Failing to clarify the differences of the term can cause confu-sion for many and create fear for some. For instance, I had a student in an upper-level comparative religions seminar who was deeply suspi-cious of pluralism. We read and discussed Eboo Patel's *Sacred Ground: Pluralism, Prejudice, and the Promise of America*, and from the first she seemed skeptical.[1] Knowing that Patel was coming soon to our campus to speak, I thought that after hearing him herself her hesi-tancy would, if not disappear, then at least soften. When she heard of all these ideas, though, her resistance hardened further.

Patel defines pluralism according to the contributions of diverse peoples. He makes a helpful distinction between diversity and plural-ism, the former being descriptive and a problem, with the latter being prescriptive and an opportunity. He tells a bold and convincing story of America's strength arising in great measure from our shared collective effort to embrace different opinions and peoples while persistently striving to form a more perfect union. Hearing diverse perspectives and having vibrant contributions from various communities helps us forge a brighter path ahead because the new ideas and additions might always be better. Any person or community willing to contribute to creating a better future, Patel argues, should be embraced not in spite of their differences but because of them. We do not have to agree on all matters to work together side by side volunteering at a food pantry, cleaning up a stream, or cooperating on ending sex trafficking.

When my student first heard Patel advocate for pluralism, however, she heard him asking her to water down her faith in Jesus Christ as the only way to salvation. Now the mother of grown children, she had seen her way through many struggles in life with her strong faith sustaining her. Along the way, when she was first exposed to the idea of pluralism, she had encountered the type that prescribes believing in a more ascendant truth than any of the particular traditions claimed. Pluralism in this mode means embracing an unknowable universal sacred of which the individual traditions preach only partial approximations. Advocates of this type of pluralism hope we can all get along by accepting all religious worldviews as reflections of the more ascendant truth, albeit refracted through each one's particular limited perspectives. My student feared pluralism in that guise because it made Jesus not *the* way, as she heard in the Bible (John 14:6), but merely *a* way, which threatened the faith that had seen her through so much. Though Muslim, Patel clearly was not proclaiming such a message either in his writing or in his talk at Texas Wesleyan. Nevertheless, that's what she heard when she heard the word *pluralism*.

Thankfully, she was a good student who had committed to my class. Thus, we were able to spend an entire semester in dialogue on interfaith issues, reading great religious thinkers from many traditions and beyond, with Patel's book and his talk as parts of the continuing discussion. In other words, she had committed to work through a process of hearing diverse perspectives and listening for what they might contribute to her life, our community, and the world. In still other words, she had committed to Patel's vision of pluralism, but not under that term as she at first understood it.

For her final presentation, she revisited Patel's contributive pluralism (after a little urging from the professor), paying special attention to how his differed from the other ascendant pluralism. After undergoing a semester's worth of communal process of intentional interfaith engagement, she had developed the ears to hear the differences in the term *pluralism* and became committed to the type that values the contributions of diverse persons and communities. For her final project, she designed a blueprint for a mostly silent contemplative retreat that took the spiritual wisdom of Alcoholics Anonymous's 12-step process and adapted it to interfaith cooperation, with fear of the other as the addiction to overcome. Needless to say, it was amazing.

Before we can hear the troubles of our friends of other faiths, we must first cultivate those friendships, but we must also develop the ears to hear. Oftentimes developing the ears for interfaith work and dialogue means perhaps undergoing a long process of education and transformation.

Go: "Each of them set out from his home . . ."

Job's friends left the comfort of their homes to go and join Job. Praying in our own communities for the afflicted is good; going to their side is better. We cannot stay inside our places of worship—our churches, our mosques, our synagogues—and simply wish our neighbors well. We must leave our comfort zones to join in solidarity with those who suffer.

The metaphor of a journey frames my introductory courses on "world religions."[2] At the beginning of the semester, we take stock of where we are now and what we have to take with us on our trip exploring diverse dynamics deemed religious. We tell our own personal travel stories from our pasts that involve wild and wonderful sights as well as unexpected trials and travails. So too, I say, will and should our journey together thinking critically about religious dynamics involve not only amazing and uplifting insights but also challenging and difficult experiences. Journeys always involve risk, and going on a journey of exposure to different traditions might mean seeing our own formative traditions differently.

Having each been born at a particular place, at a particular time, to a particular set of parents, in a particular society, we all have stories from home that will affect how we hear and see whatever we encounter on our travels. In that sense, we all have been formed by the traditions of our upbringing, even if not by explicitly identified religious ones. Asking questions about these traditions will make us more aware of the lenses through which we see the world, and therefore better able to faithfully render the object of study. Responsibly accounting for our own subjectivity, then, makes us more objective, not less. Before embarking, we think critically about the terms we use and the methods of our study. Then, for the bulk of the semester, we journey far and wide across time and clime exploring peoples and processes deemed religious. I even offer extra credit for students to literally go to visit the sites, worship services, or gatherings of an unfamiliar tradition.

When students walk out of my classroom at the end of the semester, I hope to have equipped them with tools for thinking critically, reading against the grain, asking and responding to difficult questions, and responsibly dealing with difference, while at the same time seeking commonality. Ultimately, the goal of the class is for students to "return home" enriched and perhaps transformed by their exposure to different religious worldviews, even having risked the journey of viewing their own tradition, whatever it may be, from the outside. To know one is to know none, as the scholar Max Müller famously quipped. Setting out from our homes on a journey of exposure to diverse religious dynamics hopefully will give us not only an empathic understanding of others' traditions but also an enhanced understanding of our own.

Gather: "They met together to go and console and comfort him."

The friends do not separately offer aid but rather gather together in collective consolation. We should gather our various faith communities to stand together against hate and violence. We must have well-laid plans to organize such gatherings quickly in response to unforeseen and unforeseeable acts and events.

Interfaith gatherings must be not only periodic events occurring after calamities but also regular events in the ordinary life of our campus and civic communities. To facilitate such meeting together, campuses must foster places for students to assemble and interact. From comfortable benches and hammocks in the shade of trees to outdoor amphitheaters capable of accommodating groups of various sizes, and from small dedicated interfaith rooms to large auditoriums, our colleges should provide places for people to congregate.

Many religious congregations, however, see fewer and fewer people gathering together each week. Rejecting organized religions, more and more people, especially young adults, embrace the affirmation of being "spiritual but not religious" or simply "none of the above." Such "nones" may find little use in interfaith endeavors or may feel unwelcome at interfaith gatherings. While some seek sacred ground inside traditional places of worship, others see the sacred underneath their feet wherever they walk. Still others think religions are part of the problem and should go away, instead planting their feet firmly in faith in science and rationality. For these reasons, I prefer to define faith quite broadly and to seek common ground elsewhere than disputed sacred ground.

"Faith," argues the philosopher William James in *The Will to Believe*, "means belief in something concerning which doubt is still theoretically possible; and as the test of belief is willingness to act, one may say that faith is the readiness to act in a cause the prosperous issue of which is not certified to us in advance." Since it is always theoretically possible that even our most assured confidences can be revised by something other to come, then faith is the very air all of our actions, concepts, and experiences breathe. "The necessity of faith as an ingredient in our mental attitude," James notes, "is strongly insisted on by the scientific philosophers of the present day; but by a singularly arbitrary caprice they say that it is only legitimate when used in the interests of one particular proposition—the proposition, namely, that the course of nature is uniform."[3] James proposes that we all walk by faith—whether rationalists or fideists. Reason and religion, then, are "over-beliefs" built upon the ground of faith, which is really the hope in future possibilities to come. New data, insights, and experiences may always arrive to challenge and transform any and all of our prior certainties. Thus, realizing that ignorance and error are as common to all humans as our fundamental dignity, I believe we can deal with complex questions from the common ground of admitting, "I don't know."

We all suffer human finitude. Even the most ardent atheists and fervent fideists should quiet down enough to agree that they do not know everything. From this shared place of silent humility, fruitful dialogue across beliefs and backgrounds may blossom. When we meet together in our shared human fallibility, we may better go forth with empathy for others. Like the friends in the Book of Job, our meeting together should be with the goal of going out in consolation and comfort for those who suffer.

Such gatherings to go compassionately forth for others might take the form of marching against hate, violence, and injustice. Protesting racial and economic injustice, Rabbi Abraham Joshua Heschel walked arm in arm with the Reverend Martin Luther King Jr. in Selma. Sensing the holy in such prophetic protesting, Heschel famously said, "I felt my legs were praying."[4] When we gather together to go compassionately forth, all of our actions may become prayer.

Recognize: "When they saw him from a distance, they did not recognize him."

Job's afflictions left him unrecognizable to his friends. The sight of him did not align with the righteous and blessed person they were used to seeing because for them righteousness and blessings were aligned. Good people get good things, and bad people bad. Righteousness, so they thought, is something you can see in someone's health and wealth and happiness. The sight of poor Job challenged all of that.

The story of Job asks the age-old question: "Why do bad things happen to good people?"

Job himself did not recognize any of the traditional theological answers as satisfying. He rejected all attempts to explain his suffering, waiting instead for God to explain. When God finally showed up in the story, the answer God provided was a barrage of questions meant to humble Job in the face of Ultimate Mystery. Properly recognized, we can hear God's words to Job from out of the whirlwind as ultimately comforting, in essence proclaiming: "You're not God! You cannot know! Get over yourself and live!"

Given life amidst a constitutive opacity, humans are marked by both capacity and incapacity. As finite and fallible human beings who nevertheless exercise substantial creative and destructive power, we find ourselves possessed of or by agency as well as dispossessed by the unavoidable passivity of affectivity. The interplay of agency and passivity perhaps unavoidably generates indeterminate realms that we construct as more or less human—a more of whatever or whoever exceeds our grasp and control, like death or God, and a less of that which falls under our ability to manipulate, like nonhuman animals and the environment. This "more" we call sovereign, supernatural, or mystical, and the "less" we call beastly, natural, or material. We wage wars about the more of gods and sovereign states, and we turn the natural into technology and visit unspeakable violence on nonhuman animals, ecosystems, and on other humans we deem as less-than-human. All too often we fail to recognize those who differ from us along whatever categories—religion, race, class, gender, or species—as deserving of the dignity accorded to humanity. In such misrecognition, we demean not only others but ourselves.

Whatever or whoever we recognize as ourselves and our others, perhaps we should ever remain vigilant in striving to recognize the unrecognizable who may come (back). "The unrecognizable," wrote the French Jewish philosopher Jacques Derrida, "is the beginning of ethics."[5] What he might mean by that can be explained partly with the story of the old monastery that had fallen into disrepair.[6] Not only were the walls and buildings crumbling, but also the worship and brothers were faltering. When they sang the hymns, their hearts weren't in it. When they did their chores, they did them grudgingly. When they passed each other in the halls, they grumbled and groaned. At his wit's end, the abbot who oversaw the miserable monastery journeyed into the forest to seek out the wisdom of the secluded rabbi. While sharing a small pot of soup, the rabbi listened to the abbot's woes. When the abbot finally fell into an exasperated silence, the rabbi slowly leaned forward, squinted an eye, and said that he had a secret to share. Then he whispered, *"The Messiah is among you"* and spoke no more.

As the abbot walked back to the monastery, he pondered this new insight. Was it Brother Timothy, who was terrible at carpentry but sang so beautifully? Or Brother John, who was so clumsy but always tried so hard? Or perhaps Brother Peter, who grumbled loudly in groups but always whistled quietly while sweeping the floors alone? The others received the news in shocked silence. From then on, however, the monastery was transformed. Now when they passed each other in the halls, they wondered whether the other brother might be the Messiah, and smiled affably. When they did their chores, they worked joyously wondering whether the Messiah would walk on the floor they scrubbed. The walls were rebuilt, the buildings restored, and once again from the old monastery the hymns rang out happily with resounding love.

Perhaps we must dare to unknow ourselves and our others through participation in unrecognizable mystery beyond recognized divisions—natural and supernatural, secular and sacred, self and other.

Cry: "They raised their voices and wept aloud."

Just as wailing loudly, tearing their clothes, and covering themselves in dirt are unmistakable signs of the friends' deep identification with Job's affliction, so too should our cries of common cause in response to an attack against a faith community be unambiguous and apparent to all. Publicly and in concert we must unequivocally express our shared grief, sorrow, and outrage.

Society tends to devalue displays of emotion, especially by men. In fact, all things associated with emotion and vulnerability largely have been disparaged historically and cross-culturally, though, of course, notable exceptions can always be found. All too often, however, women, embodiment, and the earth are deemed lower in the hierarchy of values. To engage students in thinking critically about such denigrated dynamics, I like to use a video clip of a comedian explaining why he doesn't let his daughters use cell phones. The comedian explains that technology removes us from interconnection and empathy, which are facts and skills we need to cultivate just as part of what it means to be human.

The comedian also tells a story of texting in traffic to avoid the realization that life involves deep suffering just by being in it (I also use the clip to explain some of the basics of Buddhism, like the Four Noble Truths. The comedian does a great job, unintentionally I think, of explaining basic Buddhist *dharma*, or teaching). One time, when a particularly nostalgic song comes on the radio, though, he puts aside the phone and decides to just sit there and let the feelings wash over him. He pulls over and cries. And at that moment, when he's trying to explain the intensity of the feeling and the tears, he blurts out the term for a female dog. Why?

Perhaps because those societal associations with femininity and animality arise whenever we (especially, maybe, white men) experience the unavoidable exposure to vulnerability that comes with deep feeling. The comedian tells the story to teach us that we need to set aside distractions and practice the ability to just sit there while watching good and bad feelings ebb and flow. That's what it means to be human, he says, and that's why he won't let his daughters have smartphones. If we could better cultivate such skills, especially embracing the unavoidable associations with vulnerability, we could better build empathy for one another across our differences. Moreover, I would argue, if we transform our relations with emotion and the body, we may transform society as well.

Better learning to cry without shame may help upend some of the oppressive hierarchies that limit our efforts to cultivate the skills of interconnection, like interfaith work. Whether we see, understand, or acknowledge it, we are all connected by our shared exposure to suffering and vulnerability. When I was six years old, I went to ride bikes with my big brother. Just like everyone else back then, we wore no helmets. Riding hard to keep up with him, I jumped off a root wrong and hit my head on a rock. The blow caused my brain to swell in such a way that I could not see, or remember who I was. Someone told me afterwards that I spent the entire time asking for my mother. For hours and hours, I kicked and cried and tried to get away and get home to mom. What I know now is that my mother was the one holding me the whole time. She was there when it happened. She rushed me immediately to the hospital. And she hugged me while I was kicking and crying for her. In the dark and not knowing where or who I was, I called out for the very love that was embracing me all the while.

Share Silence: "They sat with him on the ground seven days and seven nights, and no one spoke a word."

The best solace one can give another during a time of crisis may simply be one's comforting presence. Platitudes and explanations can hurt more than help. And Job's friends give him seven days and seven nights of nothing but their presence. So too should we lend more of simply our comforting presence than our words of interpretation to an affected faith community. Indeed, the friends err when later they open their mouths and start to tell Job what's what, presuming to speak for God. Thinking we know best will surely be the death of interfaith endeavors. Silence that is not silencing may actually offer our greatest hope for nurturing the mutual understanding among religious people that will form friendships in the first place.

For monologue to yield to dialogue, one must be silent and listen to the other. Beginning, ending, and punctuating gatherings with long periods of silence could cool heated arguments and help us all learn to listen more. Cultivating a discipline of sitting in silence with people who believe differently may grow to become a core practice of creative nonviolent action. When violence takes the form of hate speech, our active nonviolent resistance might take the form not of counter-rhetoric but of silence. How might the hurlers of hate speech be affected by the faithful of all religions sitting together in silent prayer?

When the time came, the friends would have better served Job by adding action rather than words to their silence. They did not need to discuss theology in order to care for his wounds, rebuild his house, and work to restore his livelihood. Practices of silence paired with practical action can counter violence and foster peace.

Embracing Mystery: Christian Interfaith Resources

The moral of the story of Job is that we need to faithfully accept the limitations of human finitude in the face of Ultimate Mystery. Toward that end, I would like to offer by way of conclusion a few underappreciated, specifically Christian resources for interfaith work. Contrary to much Christian (self-)righteousness today, the historical depth of the tradition offers resources for humbly embracing mystery, and doing so not simply from a lack in human capacity but moreover from the fullness of God's inherent incomprehensibility. For many, Christ reveals God as unrevealable. Thus, I would also like to suggest that Christians might not have so much to fear from even the ascendant version of pluralism as it at first may seem.

If ascendant pluralism affirms meeting amidst an unknowable mystery above and beyond all traditional approximations, then what have we to fear? After all, at the heart of our faith, is not mystery inscribed? The Trinity: three persons, one substance; Jesus: both God and human—to claim final resolution of these paradoxes is the height of heresy. Mystery remains as participation in the life of faith involves us in a paradox of wills: it takes a supreme act of will to submit one's will to God. I must will the giving of my will to God. How can such an impossible kenosis be possible? Perhaps only by grace, but by this do we not mean that God's will must (not) overwhelm human will?

Mystery and unknowing may also be found at the heart of our ethical teachings. Is not hospitality to the unknown and unrecognizable other inscribed in Christian scriptures in Matthew 25:37-39?

> Lord, when was it that we saw you hungry and gave you food, or thirsty and gave you something to drink? And when was it that we saw you a stranger and welcomed you, or naked and gave you clothing? And when was it that we saw you sick or in prison and visited you?

In other words, the righteous did not know. Such unknowing would entail not idolatrously living in confidence of one's own interpretive powers in regard to people, texts, or events. Instead, it would involve always wondering when, where, and how we are attending or failing to attend to the least. That future wonder should spur us to present questioning, always asking of any context, "Who is least?"

Ultimately, however, the least may be the one we do not even yet recognize as deserving of our attention, respect, or care. At some mysterious level, then, the other whom we miss or marginalize becomes indistinguishable from our God. Ethics and faith conflate in the effort to see the invisible. Gregory of Nyssa (335–395), one of the people most responsible for solidifying Nicene orthodoxy, taught that though the trinitarian God may be represented through various images, all images are inadequate finally to reflect the incomprehensible God. Arguing that any one image must be destabilized by others, he offered an array of analogies: three men (from "On Not Three Gods"), gold and coins ("On Not Three Gods"), breath (*The Great Catechism*), grape and wine (*Against Eunomius*), and archer-arrow-ointment (*Commentary on the Song of Songs*). Preeminently, Gregory prescribed a complex process of spiritual purgation that involves alternation between seeker and sought, active and passive, masculine and feminine in a perpetual ascent into intimacy with the divine.[7] In his allegorical interpretation of the Old Testament, *The Life of Moses*, Gregory says, "This truly is the vision of God: never to be satisfied in the desire to see him. But one must always, by looking at what he can see, rekindle his desire to see more."[8]

"We, however, following the suggestions of Holy Scripture, have learned that His nature cannot be named and is ineffable," Gregory of Nyssa wrote in "On Not Three Gods" of Christian orthodox belief.[9] Thus, the Nicene formulation of the Trinity affirming God as Three-in-One and the Christology (study of the two natures of Christ) of Chalcedon that affirms Jesus himself as both human and divine seem composed in part to direct Christians toward ever-deepening mystery. The Christian creedal response to the human condition, then, deems three mysteries—beyond, without, and within—to all be one and the same mystery. Indeed, the sacraments or "mysteries" of the faith may have been in part designed to deepen participation in such paradoxes.

"What is the significance of the unnameable name of which the Father speaks when he says 'Baptize them in my name,' without adding the signification uttered by this name?" Gregory of Nyssa asks of the baptismal blessing in the name of Father, Son, and Holy Spirit. Eunomius, a later follower of Arius, asserted that the word *agennetos,* "unbegotten," literally signified the nature of the divine. Against such an assertion of literal understanding of the divine communicable through any formulation of words, however fundamental, Christian orthodoxy according to Gregory affirmed:

> Only the uncreated nature, which we believe to be the Father, the Son, and the Holy Spirit, surpasses all signification that a name can convey. This is why the Word, in saying this name, did not add to the tradition of faith what it is (how could he have found a name which indicates the supereminent nature and which is equally fitting to the Father, the Son and the Holy Spirit. . . . And this, it seems to me, is what the Word decreed by this formula—in order to convince us that the name of the divine essence is unsayable and incomprehensible. (*Against Eunomius Book II.3*)[10]

Humans created in the image of such an incomprehensible God must also be at heart incomprehensible. Christian praxis may well be designed, then, to empower the believer to relinquish unhealthy attachment to grasping knowledge of God and self, in favor of participation in ever-deepening and ascending mystery, fueled by ever-increasing love.

"Let us change," argues Gregory of Nyssa in his treatise, "On Perfection,"

> in such a way that we may constantly evolve towards what is better, being *transformed from glory to glory*, and thus always improving and ever becoming more perfect by daily growth, and never arriving at any limit of perfection. For that perfection consists in our never stopping in our growth in good, never circumscribing our perfection by any limitation.[11]

For the Christian, then, perfection means perpetually striving to be more perfect. Thus, we should welcome as neighbors and friends any who also walk along with us on the path of persistently working to form a more perfect union.

Notes

1 Eboo Patel, *Sacred Ground: Pluralism, Prejudice, and the Promise of America* (Boston: Beacon, 2012).

2 For more on this metaphor in introductory classes, see the textbook *Comparing Religions: Coming to Terms*, by Jeffrey J. Kripal (Malden, MA: Wiley-Blackwell, 2014).

3 William James, *Writings, 1878–1899* (New York: Library Classics of the United States, 1992), 524.

4 As quoted by his daughter, Susannah Heschel, in her introduction to his *Moral Grandeur and Spiritual Audacity: Essays* (New York: Farrar, Straus, and Giroux, 1996), vii.

5 Jacques Derrida, *The Beast and the Sovereign* (Chicago: University of Chicago Press, 2009), 1:108. For a similar analysis of the more or less human, see Judith Butler's *Bodies That Matter: On the Discursive Limits of "Sex"* (New York: Routledge, 1993), esp. p. 8.

6 Though anonymous and old, this story first came to my attention through a version found in the Jesuit priest Anthony De Mello's *Taking Flight: A Book of Story Meditations* (New York: Doubleday, 1988), 51–52.

7   For more, see Sarah Coakley's *Powers and Submissions: Spirituality, Philosophy and Gender* (Malden, MA: Blackwell, 2002), esp. chap. 9, "The Eschatalogical Body: Gender, Transformation and God."

8   Gregory of Nyssa, *The Life of Moses* (Mahwah, NJ: Paulist Press, 1978), 116.

9   Gregory of Nyssa, "On Not Three Gods," in *Christology of the Later Fathers*, ed. Edward R. Hardy (Philadelphia: Westminster, 1954), 259.

10 Gregory of Nyssa, as quoted by Jean-Luc Marion in *In Excess: Studies of Saturated Phenomena* (New York: Fordham, 2002), 156.

11 Gregory of Nyssa, as quoted by Jean Daniélou in *From Glory to Glory: Texts from Gregory of Nyssa's Mystical Writings* (Crestwood, NY: St. Vladimir's Seminary Press, 1997), 51–52.

Prioritizing Questions for Religious Literacy at United Methodist–Affiliated Colleges

Nathan Eric Dickman

I n this paper, I will examine tensions some colleges face between religious affiliation and welcoming religious diversity to show how exploring questions of meaning and purpose can affect colleges' identities, in order to help my readers understand that prioritizing open-ended questioning is a productive way to engage religious and secular pluralism.

On many religiously affiliated college campuses that try to welcome students, staff, and faculty of diverse ways of life, a disconcerting issue is what we can call "pervasive structures of religious privilege."[1] The structures of privilege are especially problematic when they go unrecognized by the majority who identify with a college's affiliated religion. In concrete terms, many students, staff, and faculty who identify as Christian at United Methodist–affiliated colleges are unaware that others who identify as humanist (or Muslim, or "none," etc.) feel the campus climate as unwelcoming or even hostile. The unrecognized privilege is pervasive because it extends from extracurricular student affairs to curriculum and course learning interventions to institutional traditions and policies. One unconscionable problem is the effect this prejudice has on the academic vitality of a college, raising suspicions about its capability to provide genuinely liberal arts education. How can you claim to provide liberal arts learning if religious limits on imagination, empathy, and understanding are not recognized and thoroughly addressed?

I approach the topic with the following method. First, together we will traverse tensions between religious affiliation and recognition of many religions and narrow in on The United Methodist Church's (UMC) unique support for exploration of questions of meaning and purpose. Second, I develop a theory of questioning to explain how questions of meaning and purpose should work, especially with regard to interreligious literacy. Third, I propose ways to move us from apathy about religious diversity to productive engagement with each other consistent with liberal arts values. I conclude by identifying key risks we face in radical openness to inquiry—especially as this transcends typical philosophical responses to religious diversity. My underlying thesis is that pervasive structures of religious privilege at religiously affiliated colleges undermine engaged inquiry—especially deep existential inquiry—not due to direct adversarial argument or explicit persecution but through indirectly placating us in a contented religious exclusivism.

Before proceeding, I want to lay out a couple parameters for our inquiry. My first parameter is a theory of the "liberal arts." Some UMC leaders no longer use "liberal arts," due to political polarization between liberals and conservatives, and instead say their institutions prepare students to respond to "complexity, diversity, and change."[2] This is a missed opportunity to educate. I anchor my theory in the ancient Greek origins of the academy. The Greeks defined the purpose of human beings as realizing *eudaimonia* or flourishing through the maximal exercise of our definitive powers.[3] Intellectual virtues such as rational consistency and ethical virtues such as courage facilitate realizing this purpose; vices inhibit it. What differentiates us from other animals is that we are peculiarly discursive or "rational." In light of our yearning for fulfillment, Aristotle believed the highest kind of *eudaimonia* is the maximal exercise of our mind, the life of study. My students always find "study" anticlimactic as an answer for how to be happy, given our contemporary assumptions about what studying is and what happiness should feel like. Studying is not cramming for exams. As a shared activity of inquiry, we expand horizons of our understanding through it. Through dialogue, we integrate experiences, enrich them by emphasizing some features rather than others, remember them from different perspectives, create community with each other about them, and resolve conflicting interpretations of them. This is what "studying" something means on a rudimentary level.

We can study, ideally, without external inhibitions in "schools," derived from the Greek *skole*, which means "leisure." Leisure is a privileged condition free of environmental threats, biological needs, and economic demands, where you can "take time" to ask questions and think through possible responses without distraction. It is in academic institutions that we can, as Bourdieu elaborates, "deal seriously with questions that 'serious' people, occupied and preoccupied by the practical business of everyday life, ignore."[4] The liberal arts are literally the crafts of free people. They are what we do once we no longer need shelter, food, genetic progeny, and so forth. To stave off boredom, perhaps one smashes grapes, stains a wall, and thereby paints. Perhaps one explores an animal's biology without eating it, performing anatomization. These imaginative experiments clarify ways that standard liberal arts and sciences—from history to biology—involve the exercise of the freedom to ask questions dislodged from practical needs.

My second parameter I want us to keep in mind is classifying religious prejudice among social injustices—such as racism, sexism, homophobia, and others—that higher education tasks itself with addressing. For nearly twenty years the Association of American

Colleges and Universities (AACU) has emphasized, as Rice states, "the critical link between diversity in our institutions of higher education and civic learning in a diverse democracy."[5] The primary diversity initiatives include race and ethnicity, gender and sexuality, economic class and politics, and more. Despite many accomplishments achieved by civil rights movements in the 1960s, the brutalization of Rodney King in the 1990s led many higher education institutions to, as Patel highlights, "take race seriously at every level."[6] From prioritizing welcoming environments in student affairs to equal opportunity efforts in human resources to the development of African American Studies programs in academics, campuses sought to respond by providing educational opportunities for students to enhance their freedom in and responsibility to our ethnically diverse society.

Many of us have placed religious diversity among these other diversity initiatives over the last ten years. As Patel wrote, "Religious prejudice is a serious problem, and it ought to be considered just as un-American as racism or sexism."[7] A crucial freedom in liberal arts education is the freedom from unjust prejudice. And one crucial prejudice inhibiting our freedom of mind is religious prejudice. This is apparent in all sorts of contexts. Pew Polls indicate Americans perceive atheists as least trustworthy among their coreligionists. Politicians garner support for their agendas through populist rhetoric urging the banning of Muslims from entering the country.[8] The list could go on.

In light of these parameters—that liberal arts concern mental and spiritual freedom, and that religious prejudice fits among the social injustices inhibiting freedom—let us turn to tensions between religious affiliation and recognition of religious diversity.

I. Tensions between Affiliation with a Religion and Responsibility to Religious Diversity

In this section, I note America's shifting religious landscape as religious diversity and consumerism affect it. Then we will examine some key features of the mission of and guidelines for UMC-affiliated colleges published by the National Association of Schools and Colleges of The United Methodist Church (NASCUMC), particularly the push for colleges to provide opportunities to *"delve into questions of meaning and purpose."*[9] What are these, especially in a diverse religious landscape?

We receive many benefits from engaging diverse communities. Students show higher motivation for learning and greater gains in academic achievement.[10] With regard to research, there are greater leaps in innovation, and researchers are more thorough in their considerations. According to Bryant, students also become more culturally aware and tolerant through exposure to "heterogeneous peer groups and diversity-related activities (workshops, classes, and the like)."[11] Bryant elaborates:

> To promote the development of cultural awareness, it is critical that student communities strive for diversity so as to avoid homogeneity and insularity from otherness . . . Because students need to encounter diversity to enhance personal development and cultural awareness, homogeneous peer groups may not provide the triggers necessary to prompt critical reflection and understanding of otherness.[12]

The "triggers" should include both extracurricular social experiences as well as course assignments (what I prefer to call "achievement-endangering risks"), which would enhance students' maximal exercise of freedom of thought.

We can capture the diverse American religious landscape by analogy to a shopping mall. Wuthnow, for example, describes Americans as "spiritual shoppers," a mind-set toward religion shaped by capitalist consumerism. Religions have become commodities, shaped by supply and demand. Think of mass production of dream catchers, miniature Zen rock gardens, yoga classes, crucifix necklaces, and more. Or reflect on what a family might do to find a new church or place of practice when they move to a new city—they attend one place and then another, "shopping" for one that they feel fits them best. We should see in this a paradigm permeating all attitudes toward religious diversity that religion is voluntary and based on personal preferences.[13] Whereas in the past, people were of a religion by virtue of their birth in a particular region, today it is assumed we choose to identify with a religion (or none).[14]

What complicates this picture of discrete religions available for individual consumption is a general illiteracy about religions.[15] In 2010, a Pew Research survey studying religious knowledge gathered results measuring how well Americans know religions, including their own.[16] One crucial result correlated general knowledge about religions with general academic success. That is, those who know about religion also know more. But the general average seemed disturbingly low relative to a populace that purports on the whole to be religious in some way or another. This pervasive lack of literacy goes beyond merely exposing that, say, many self-identifying Christians are unfamiliar with things such as the Apostles' Creed. There are numerous popular surveys indicating that self-identifying Christians increasingly believe in a form of "reincarnation," an apparently Hindu notion.[17] Some people explicitly identify with one religion yet incorporate conflicting religious notions of the afterlife into their worldview. The general lack of literacy affects pervasive religious privilege on campuses because the people on the ground who embody that prejudice do not really even know their own religion, let alone the religion of others.

Student demographics reflect and intensify these American trends. While most still identify with a particular religion, many refer to themselves as "spiritual but not religious," or identify as "none."[18] Since 2003, the Higher Education Research Institute (HERI) at UCLA has examined the place of religion in American higher education.[19] They have found that the majority of students have an interest in spirituality, seek meaning and purpose for their lives, and discuss this with their friends.[20] Students, on the whole, are "seekers," desiring existential fulfillment, but they also tend to distinguish these spiritual values from traditional religious institutions.[21] Yet, despite students showing a strong interest in and involvement with spirituality and religion, faculty and colleges, according to Rice, "do little to foster student . . . *questions of meaning and purpose.*"[22]

This is an explicit goal of UMC-affiliated colleges. As Overton explains in the NASCUMC handbook:

> Rather than either isolating faith as something outside the curriculum or mandating a particular set of beliefs, United Methodist–related colleges and universities provide courses and cocurricular programs *that enable students to delve into questions of meaning and purpose.*[23]

Moreover, the UMC's University Senate recognizes, based on *The Book of Discipline*, that declaration of affiliation differs from college to college, and so each college can individually tailor and design affiliation for themselves.[24] Nevertheless, the University Senate has adopted a number of "principles" or guidelines institutions can use to ensure they help students explore questions of meaning and purpose. These include such things as respecting and providing "the teaching of religion," respecting the practices of students and faculty who "choose to participate in the Christian tradition," and encouraging "the exploration of the place of religious belief and practice in the larger society."[25] A particularly significant guideline is that the ideal UMC-affiliated college "*allows* faculty and students to explore the *place* of religious belief and practice, and specifically, the intellectual dimensions of Christian faith, in *all* academic disciplines and co-curricular activities."[26]

Let us pin down this wording more exactly. First, it emphasizes faculty and students are "allowed" to explore, as in, they may choose to but do not have to. This indicates awareness of others who may prefer not to explore religious commitments in general or Methodism in particular. Second, the emphasis on "place" reorients exploratory inquiry away from personal religious feelings. Exploration of the place of religion consists foremost of humanistic, existential, historical, and natural scientific questions—such as asking about the ways religions influence art and architecture, or about the ways religions have been tied to politics, or about the ways religious practices might impact brain chemistry. Through such questions, students and faculty can explore the places of religion in human culture, whether they are themselves religious or not. Third, it indicates this is not the sole responsibility of one department. Students may explore places of religious commitment in a history course, a chemistry course, the anime club, or any other extracurricular organization. Students might not take any religious studies courses for some reason or another, however much we might want it to be a requirement for all students. Faculty assigned to other programs might never teach or take religious studies courses. What is a physics professor to do if she wishes to explore the place of religion in general or the place of intellectual dimensions of the Christian faith on campus? By the guidelines, she is allowed to explore the place of it, perhaps in advising an extracurricular religious student group, or in her research, or even where it is relevant within her discipline-specific courses.[27]

Making all this explicit helps to determine with some precision those "questions of meaning and purpose" definitive for a uniquely UMC-supported liberal arts education. Let us turn to examine the nature of questioning more closely.

II. The Priority of Questioning in Interreligious Literacy

In this section, I formulate a theory of genuine questioning that is radically open-ended. I then contrast this with one example of a UMC-affiliated institution's narrow construal of the "big" questions. I point out how this narrow construal falls short of liberal arts ideals for inquiry and raises concerns about credible accreditation. I cover all this to emphasize the need for a robust account of questions of meaning and purpose when navigating tensions between religious affiliation and religious diversity.

Although this may seem odd, we should ask, "What even is a question?" Questioning is a complex phenomenon put to many uses, from classroom management to police interrogations to clinical therapy and more.[28] Within educational settings alone, we have inherited numerous taxonomies of questions, often rooted in Bloom's taxonomy of learning goals. Yet an interesting feature of most pedagogical questions is that they are not genuine questions. Consider what would happen if an exam consisted solely of multiple-choice questions to which the instructor did not already know the answers. How would she measure a student's learning? Genuine questioning gets subordinated to measuring student comprehension. These sorts of questions aim at getting "the" (or at least an) answer. Genuinely open-ended questions, alternatively, aim primarily at getting the conversation partner to share the question. Consider this question: "In what ways might religious commitment enhance or undermine liberal arts learning?" Rather than narrowing considerations to get "the" answer, this sort of question opens up consideration of multiple responses. But this is only if the conversation partners share the question so both can consider responses as possible answers. Sharing questions and considering possible responses are what ground questioning's priority in liberal arts learning.

As Gadamer wrote, "To understand a question is to ask it. But to understand meaning is to understand it as an answer to a question."[29] Gadamer's axiom about questioning can help us clarify two things about the priority of questioning. First, questioning is a unique discursive phenomenon that binds conversation partners together. It is not that we consider and weigh a question to decide whether or not to ask it before we ask it. In our very considering of a question, we are already asking it. Like understanding a request involves doing what was requested (e.g., "Please pass the salt."), this is what we do when we understand a question—we ask it. Thus, another person's question becomes both of our question when we understand the question. We both ask it and come under the influence of the topic at issue. Whereas our answers—especially our religious answers—often seem to divide us, it is this feature of *having* to ask questions that allows us to relate with others in a way beyond assimilative empathy.[30] We do not experience another's question as an authoritarian imposition when we find ourselves so captivated. Instead, the question—if we genuinely ask it with one another—motivates us to understand options for response.

The second feature of questioning's priority is that it helps us specify a useful concept of "meaning." In addition to asking what questions are, we should ask, "What is 'meaning'?" Meanings are responses to questions that we actually ask. As Gadamer wrote, "one speaks with motivation, and does not just make a statement but answers a question."[31] The lack of motivation helps explain why, for instance, students sometimes struggle to understand assigned texts for classes. The students do not understand—that is, they do not actually ask—the question(s) the text tries to address. If the students do not ask the question, then the text will be merely a stream of statements arbitrarily bound together in a book. By asking the text's question, students find motivation to consider the text as a possible response. Indeed, one cannot receive answers to questions one is not actually asking. Raising this to an interreligious level, consider Tillich's reflection on effective evangelism:

> The difficulty with the highly developed religions of Asia, for example, is not so much that they reject the Christian answer as answer, as that their [conception of] human nature is formed in such a way that they do not ask the question to which the Gospel gives the answer. To them the Christian answer is no answer because they have not asked the question to which Christianity is supposed to answer.[32]

We need not endorse here the potential implication that effective tactics for Christian missionaries involve positioning others to ask the question(s) to which Christianity responds. Our point is merely that without actually asking the questions oneself, whatever statements made are lost on one.

We should note that this approach to meaning focuses on sentential meaning or semantics. Semantics is distinct from, though relevant to, existential "meaning" or one's feeling of purpose in life. A question is a kind of sentence. Sentences always consist of at least a subject and a predicate, even if one is merely implied. Sentential subjects identify the topic or subject matter through proper names, pronouns, definite descriptions and more. In declarative sentences, predicates place the subject in a context. That is, they put the subject in its proper predicament.[33] Questions, though, are statements in the interrogative mood. Rather than placing a subject in a predicament, they suspend either subjects or predicates (or both) in abeyance. Consider someone asking, "Where are my car keys?" The subject matter identified by the sentential subject "car keys" is lifted up, and we consider a number of predicaments in which those keys might be—such as on the counter in the kitchen, locked inside the car, in a pocket, and more. But let us not get too distracted by this brief detour into the grammar of questions. How does this apply with regard to religious diversity?

We need to keep rigorous about the difference between subject terms and predicate terms in religious languages. Even though some contemporary Buddhist evangelists refer to the historical Buddha by simply calling him "Buddha," we know that is not his proper name.[34] His family name was Gautama of the Shakya clan, and later disciples ascribed the legendary first name "Siddhartha" to him. The early Buddhist community inherited a language with the predicate "Buddha" and asked the question, "Who will be my Buddha?" When Gautama started teaching, they found an answer to their question: "Gautama is the Buddha." In comparison, even though many contemporary Christians call Jesus of Nazareth "Christ," we know that is not his proper name. First-century Palestinians inherited a language with the predicate "Messiah," and asked the question, "Who will be my Messiah?" Some of them found an answer to their question: "Jesus is the Messiah." This analysis applies across religions, where the terms are primarily predicates—however much they may be taken as sentential subjects. This is most prevalent with regard to the word *god*. I have developed this in detail elsewhere, but in brief, like "Buddha," "Christ," "Prophet," "Sage," "Guru," and "Hero," the word *God*, too, is a predicate or title and not a proper name.[35] A community inherits a language in which "god" is a live predicate, and members might ask, "Where is my god?"[36] For early Hebrews, the personal name of their god is represented by the tetragrammaton, and they understand the meaning of "YHWH is my god" as a response to the question. This is especially crucial in the context of religious diversity. A prevalent assumption among many contemporary American Christians is that Muslims worship an inherently different god, named "Allah."[37] But the word "Allah" is the Arabic word for "god" and so is not a proper personal name.[38] Without keeping subjects and predicates straight, we get seduced into potentially explosive misunderstandings, such as with Wheaton College's suspension of and move to fire tenured professor Larycia Hawkins for stating that Muslims and Christians worship the same "God."[39]

I highlight this close analysis of religious predicates (or "symbols") because the study of religions is analogous, but not equivalent, to the study of foreign languages. How can one acquire the appropriate use of predicates without fluency in the language? How can one understand the meaning of sentences expressed by religious others without being motivated actually to ask their questions? Perhaps one might worry here. If students get motivated to ask the questions of religious others, will they convert? Will we lose them from our own religion to another (or none)? Is their faith at risk? These worries show why it is crucial, at least at first, to distinguish semantic meaning from existential meaning. My answers to questions, that is, the meanings I understand based on asking questions, may—but need not—inform my existential meaning. Just as I can understand what a Republican says without necessarily becoming one, I can understand what a Lutheran says without necessarily becoming one. We can—as the NAMBUMC guideline encourages—study the intermediary "place" of religion. A further benefit of a semantic theory of meaning is a therapeutic effect on the anxiety people often experience over the existential meaning of their lives. When someone feels crushed by the weight of the question, "What is the meaning of my life?" we might respond with the simple rejection of presuppositions within the question by saying, "'Life' is not a complete sentence" or "'Life' is not an answer to a question." Regardless, engagement in religious diversity includes genuine asking of many questions, which requires learning multiple language-like fields of discourse.

Yet some leaders of UMC-affiliated colleges do not seem to approach questions of meaning and purpose with this level of appropriate expansiveness. This is not surprising, and is a widely common phenomenon, illustrative of religious privilege. For example, J. Cameron West (Huntingdon College President) claims that the biggest of the "big" questions paradigmatic for UMC-affiliated colleges are:

> What am I called to do with the life God has given me? What are my gifts? What does it mean to be great? Who is my neighbor? What does the command to love require me to do? What about the command to do justice? How often must I forgive someone who wrongs me? Can I love money and also love God? What is life like when I make the accumulation of money my sole reason for being? Is it permissible to kill, even in order to defend myself? What does it mean to be faithful to my wife, my husband? What must I do to receive eternal life?[40]

Like many others, West believes questions like these shape the unique mission for UMC colleges. According to West, the mission should make relevant the perspective of what he calls "the Judeo-Christian" narrative. And this seems as it should be for colleges that claim to be grounded in the UMC. But note how these questions seem to be mere prompts for the answers lying in wait within that narrative.

West situates these questions as key for engaging deeply in what he further describes as "the Mind of Christ and . . . the minds of those who through the centuries have engaged questions put to us by the Judeo-Christian narrative."[41] This is because West formulates the purpose of UMC-affiliated colleges foremost to make disciples of Jesus Christ and to nurture Christian leaders for the Church and the world.[42] Do such colleges only allow faculty, staff, and students who already confess Christianity, or if they have "open enrollment" are the non-Christians targets for conversion into disciples of Christ? West roots this approach in Paul's encouragement to "let the same mind be in you that was in Christ Jesus" (Phil. 2:5). The mind of Christ is juxta-posed with the life of the mind caught up in modern materialism and consumerism, and even in purportedly disinterested theoretical spec-ulation. Rather, according to West, living the mind of Christ involves living "as servants who love our neighbors and God, in the same way Jesus loved his neighbors and God."[43] (Note that we already have the answer to one of the "big" questions here before anyone has even asked it. Yet, was Jesus really a good neighbor? Does textual scrutiny bear this out?) He continues:

> Consequently, it is *our responsibility as church* to offer a unique higher education experience, differentiated from the experience that can be offered at any public institution, so that our young women and men will have the *opportunity to explore intellectually* what it means to have the mind of Christ and live with that mind.[44]

I do not want to be misread here. I intend this as constructive criti-cism of a case study of a general pattern. I want to point to the phrase "our responsibility as church" as the clue—that The UMC supersedes liberal arts. The Church seems to take priority over the college, and this is precisely the prevalent religious prejudice experienced by those not in the religious majority on many open campuses affiliated with Christianity.

West also adds, "Any liberal arts education worth its salt will give students the tools to understand the major world faiths."[45] This primarily takes place at Huntingdon College, where West serves as president, in a college-wide required general education "Compara-tive Religions" course, offered by the religion department that sup-ports both a "religion" major and a Christian ministries major.[46] In the course, students engage major religious traditions of the world—such as Judaism, Hinduism, Confucianism, and atheism—*in dialogue with* the Christian faith.[47] If this is so, then students are not engaging these religions on their own terms; they do not learn to understand the predicates and questions that these religions seek to address. Instead, these religions seem to be *translated* into Christian terms. The course description explains that it "assumes that people all over the world ask similar questions" about the origin of human life and shared responsibility on the planet—apparently universal and neutral questions.[48] It further assumes that people have written texts, developed rituals, and created art and institutions in attempting to address these questions.[49] Are these questions and responses subordinated to Christian predicates (in the way West's "big" questions are above)? Can the course be taught without dialogue with the Christian faith? How can students be genuinely motivated to ask questions and consider responses from alternative religious forms of life if the biggest of the big questions always are posed in Christian terms?

What I want you to see is that the exclusive use of Christian predicates as the fundamental discourse of intelligibility atrophies our understanding and imaginative possibilities. Consider, for example, the use of the phrase "the Judeo-Christian tradition." While this is a very common phrase, there are two problems with it. One is that from a generally Jewish perspective, this phrase is supersessionistic, subordinating Judaism to its purported fulfillment in Christianity in the same way referring to the Hebrew Bible as the "Old Testament" does (especially problematic if this label is used for a course in the academic curriculum).[50] How many Jewish leaders and thinkers actually use this phrase? Why not show respect, since Jews do not see Christianity as fulfilling Judaism? Another problem involves the use of the definite article "the" and the ahistorical use of "tradition," implying that there is an uncontested essence definitive for both Judaism and Christianity, let alone across all the diverse forms of life all claiming to be Christian—including, say, the Church of Jesus Christ of Latter-day Saints. Do Catholics and Southern Baptists and nondenominational Christians all subscribe to the "same" tradition? With lucidity about religious diversity, even intra-religious diversity, we need to recognize that when someone asks, "What do Muslims believe?"—our first response should be, "Which Muslims?" Just so with affiliation of a college with a particular religious tradition. If a college like Naropa University identifies with "the Buddhist tradition," then we should ask, "Which form of Buddhism?"

If the biggest of the big questions are restricted at a religiously affiliated college, then we might be suspicious about the credibility of its accreditation. In 2014, the *Chronicle of Higher Education* published a number of reflections proposing that national accreditation of some religiously affiliated colleges should be discontinued.[51] Peter Conn criticizes the accreditation industry at large by arguing that although conferring accreditation on an institution ought to prove its legitimacy as an institution of higher learning to the general public, accrediting religious colleges undermines that ideal. He contends, "By awarding accreditation to religious colleges, the process confers legitimacy on institutions that systematically undermine the most fundamental purposes of higher education." Some Christian colleges, such as Bryan College, Shorter College, and Wheaton College demand that faculty members sign a statement of faith, requiring them to consent to "scientifically preposterous propositions." Such religious boundaries intellectually compromise faculty teaching and research, where they have to abandon what Conn calls "the primacy of reason." The issue is not, Conn emphasizes, that there are religious colleges. It is, he notes, that accreditation symbolizes legitimacy beyond their denominational or religious insularity. For example, it provides public financial benefits to a religious college, such as making students eligible for *federal* financial aid. The federal benefits symbolize general public recognition of such colleges' academic legitimacy.

Of course, we could note areas of narrowness in Conn's argument—he assumes a notion of "religion" normatively defined by a contemporary Christian fundamentalism and neglects unquestioned presuppositions in his advocacy for "skeptical and unfettered inquiry" or an objective account of "reason" itself.[52] Moreover, accreditation merely shows an institution is meeting its mission—even if that mission adheres exclusively to a single religious worldview that forgoes genuine liberal arts values of free inquiry.[53] Accreditation does not actually confer public legitimacy to a college as successfully promoting free intellectual inquiry. Conn is best interpreted as urging it should. But much like West, Conn neglects comparative analyses between institutions like Shorter College and, say, Naropa University in Colorado or Maharishi University of Management in Iowa. These institutions are never mentioned. This is an oversight on Conn's part, but this is consistent with the atrophied imagination due to pervasive religious privilege granted to Christianity on American campuses—even on the part of critics!

I want these two extremes represented by West and Conn situated with regard to our account of the liberal arts and our account of the priority of questioning. If the predicates of questions, and thereby the answers, are already prescribed at religiously affiliated colleges, then are the questions actually free? Or, perhaps worse, *are the questions actually being asked*? Are the questions mere prompts for the chorus of answers? Such pervasive religious privilege illustrated above undermines actively engaged free inquiry through placating a contented religious exclusivism. It atrophies imaginative possibilities for both questioning and for responding to that questioning, and living ethically in a diverse community.

Let us turn to look at ways engaging in genuine questioning with regard to religious diversity may help with this.

III. Moving from Apathy to Responsibility

In this section, I conclude by explaining how this approach to questions can help transition colleges suffering pervasive apathetic attitudes about religious diversity toward responsible attitudes about it, and how this approach transcends the usual philosophical responses to religious diversity.

Stewart, Kocet, and Lobdell urge that transformative engagement in religious and secular pluralism requires

> faculty, staff, and students to invest in the long-term work
> of examining and revising institutional structures to dismantle
> privilege, while contemplating what it means to live life to-
> gether as a campus community, mobilizing our beliefs about
> meaning and purpose to enhance the educational journey.[54]

They believe religiously affiliated colleges with open admissions and employment should resist religious hegemony but without inherently undermining the institution's guiding religious tradition(s). They lay out general institutional attitudes toward religious diversity on a spectrum from mere apathy, to awareness, to acceptance, to active engagement. I want to detail briefly these four options to isolate the unique character of active engagement. An apathetic institution mutes dialogue about religious diversity and leaves unexamined its "mono-religious heritage." Religious privilege goes unrecognized and unchallenged. Apathy creates what religious minorities perceive as a hostile or at least unwelcoming campus climate, and religious minorities often form alliances "rooted in the need to oppose religious hegemony on campus." Aware institutions, alternatively, use an "additive approach" to tolerate religious and secular diversity.[55] Needs are accommodated given specific requests, but general privilege goes unquestioned. Religious minority students, faculty, and staff might request and receive accommodations for holiday absences, for example, but unlike their Christian colleagues they will have to announce that they will be absent. People are outed even if they believe religion or spirituality should be radically private.

Accepting institutions recognize "the epistemic value of religious diversity" by promoting dialogue across differences.[56] These campuses strive to move beyond tolerance to achieve a socially pluralistic education that incorporates multiple perspectives in the pursuit of liberal arts learning. At actively engaged colleges, though, there is an even deeper respect and empathy for differences, *where those differences are sought out in order to raise questions about privilege and identity construction.* Engaged institutions actively confront systems of privilege and collectively reenvision their campus's traditions and symbols.

In this way, "members of religious minority groups can function as partners with equal voice in shaping the campus climate, beyond merely combating oppression." How can we ensure recognition of religious others as having an equal voice? *Are we actively looking for places we might put privilege in check?*

What might questions of meaning and purpose look like at engaged institutions? Stewart, Kocet, and Lobdell do not address this but instead suggest that faculty could represent varying religious holidays in their syllabi calendars and that student affairs can infuse discussions of spirituality and pluralism into staff meetings and programming.[57] They encourage establishing ally training for facilitating open dialogue about religion, secularism, and spirituality where students' diverse voices are heard and encouraged. Stewart, Kocet, and Lobdell note that many professionals might not "choose to integrate questions of meaning and purpose from a religious and secularist pluralist perspective into curriculum or staff training because they may not feel adequately prepared." They answer this by proposing that campuses need to have "key leaders actively serving as advocates who recognize that religious and secular pluralism falls under the model of multicultural competence."[58] These dedicated and contracted advocates would be tasked with promoting the existential well-being of all campus members and with addressing inequities of treatment or access through policy proposals, as well as with examining how religious diversity affects learning.

While colleges should integrate questions of meaning and purpose into their model of liberal arts learning, this integration needs to include diverse ways of meaning-making. Whose questions of meaning and purpose will be asked? Which predicates form the fundamental language(s) of inquiry? Stewart, Kocet, and Lobdell do not specify content for the questions of meaning and purpose they say need addressing in multifaith contexts. I think an informed philosophical approach will help us take a closer look. The practical act of including various religious holidays on a syllabus schedule may seem different from philosophical theories about religious diversity. We will see, however, that even a small act of respect involves philosophical presuppositions. All questions of meaning and purpose are existential philosophical questions. Religious symbols and narratives can helpfully be conceived of as possible ways of addressing these philosophical questions. The "big" questions have always been, and should remain, the domain of philosophy.

Western philosophy, influenced by Christian theology, has developed three to five broad options for response to religious diversity.[59] Exclusivism, for example, presupposes only one religion is true and one must subscribe to it in order to gain ultimate fulfillment. Pluralism, as another example, presupposes that human concepts and symbols are too limited to capture ultimate reality completely, and so all religions are partial perspectives on but not direct descriptions of ultimate reality. Some people even presuppose relativism, where all religions are true, or skepticism, where no religions are true. These dominant Western presuppositions, though, all start with single religious belonging as normative. Single religious belonging is a recent development, primarily in Abrahamic monotheisms. Many throughout history and across cultures have not perceived participation in multiple religions as problematic. This implicit privilege of exclusive commitment is reflected in descriptions of Japanese participation in both Buddhist and Shinto rituals as "ambiguity tolerance."[60] Why not instead refer to presuppositions of exclusive monotheists as "extreme dichotomy tolerance"? Moreover, no exclusivist argues that a religion besides her own is the truth. Imagine an exclusivist saying that she believes only Islam is true, but she happens to be Daoist. All these philosophical strategies betray an aversion to genuine open-ended and responsible inquiry into religious diversity. These evasive tactics placate resting contentedly in religious exclusivism.

People who make these presuppositions probably do not realize there is an alternative approach to the issue of religious diversity. This alternative belongs, in part, to the rise of the humanities field of religious studies as an autonomous academic discipline from Christian theology.[61] With the *School District of Abington Township*

(PA) v. Schempp family Supreme Court decision in the 1960s, this field opened up for study about religions without necessarily being religious. That is, it shifted the terms of exploration from conflicting truth claims to questions of meaning and purpose. Whether or not a religion is "true" (in the sense of an accurate representation of reality), it is meaningful to its adherents. Through phenomenological and hermeneutical methods, with postcolonial and historical criticism, religious studies scholars seek to comprehend the meanings of religions throughout history and in contemporary society. The unique role of religious studies is that it maintains academic and political focus on structures of pervasive religious privilege as well as how other social injustices affect religions (e.g., patriarchy in religions). The campus advocates whom Stewart, Kocet, and Lobdell call for need rigorous training in religious studies.

Our development of genuine questions transcends inherited philosophical and practical tactics for response to religious diversity in two particular ways. First, we need to realize that religions are not about the description of reality. All the usual responses to religious diversity presuppose that the purpose of religious language is to describe reality accurately. If that is so, then what year is it? Is it "AD" 2017 or 2017 "CE"? Even secularizing the era-naming system, we know that year zero really concerns Christianity. But, for many Buddhists, it is 2560. For Jews, 5778. For some Hindus, 5119. For Muslims, 1439. Is only one of these correct? Rather than running parallel to the world, our temporal predicates raise up a moment in the flux of our experience into a field of intelligibility structured by our inherited religious traditions. The predicative function runs perpendicular, not parallel, to the world. Our inherited religious and secular predicates help us organize or make sense of our experiences of time. They are not primarily about accurate representation of reality.

Second, engagement will change who we are. Questioning and considering possibilities for response affect our self-understanding to the point where we cannot demand to retain some stable identity on the other side. What is the purpose of dialogue concerning religious

NATHAN ERIC DICKMAN

diversity? That is, what is it that we gain from dialogue that we cannot get another way? If it were just to get information about other
perspectives, then we could look up information about humanism or
Hinduism in an encyclopedia or a textbook summary. We would not
need shared questioning for that. Instead, to question and share questions is to listen well. Active listening displays respect for the other's
autonomy over what she has to say. Active listeners suspend their perspective's claim to sole superiority by regarding their conceptions and
constructions as revisable. As Fiumara wrote, "Listening involves the
renunciation of a predominantly moulding activity and ordering activity, a giving up sustained by the [anticipation] of a new and different
quality of relationship."[62] Listening to and understanding what someone says breaks down rigid distinctions between "inner" and "outer,"
between mine and yours, because the sounds and understandings
they deliver reverberate throughout our entire system. Moreover, genuine questions put our inherited predicates, our prejudices, and our
pretensions to understand at risk. To ask such a question is to suspend
the tyranny of hidden prejudices that make us Deaf to others. Inas-
much as we are constituted by our inheritances and biases, to suspend
them is to suspend ourselves, and thereby open ourselves to possibilities that will transform us. Such dialogue is, as Gadamer wrote,
"not merely a matter of putting oneself forward and successfully asserting one's point of view, but [involves] being transformed into a
communion in which we do not remain what we were."[63] Prioritizing
questioning in this way is to be rigorously undogmatic. Changes in
self-understanding through learning religiously diverse discourses pro-
ceeds aoristically, a lateral movement, little by little, perhaps to such
an extent that our previous commitments no longer hold the same influence. In sharing questions we yield our horizons to the importance
of what the other asks and answers. At engaged institutions this is
done even at an institutional level—hopefully even before religious
others have to ask for it.

In these ways, religious studies can serve as a model for what
is possible on college campuses and can help us see a distinction

only implicit above concerning West and Conn. On the one hand, colleges "grounded" in the UMC restrict the big questions to distinctively Christian forms of asking and answering them. On the other, colleges historically "affiliated" with the UMC benefit from support in their radical openness to engaging truly philosophical questions—where they facilitate asking and answering questions wherever the subject matters might lead the inquirers. An institution that respects religious diversity and genuinely promotes engagement in philosophical questions should be open to many forms of meaning-making and thereby open to its own revision to such an extent that it is no longer recognizably "Christian" as it currently (or popularly, really) is defined. It takes courage to understand and ask the others' questions in their terms in order to consider their answers. Yet, there ought to be nothing to fear in the genuine pursuit of truth, knowledge, and freedom. For institutions of higher liberal arts learning to address pervasive religious privilege satisfactorily, we have to put that privilege in check, and that means putting institutional identity at risk. This might involve, for example, reenvisioning what "Christian" can mean. For example, could a "Christian service" award be given to someone who keeps her religion radically private? Could it be given to a self-avowed Shin Buddhist? This would also involve lucidity about word choices for events and organizations. A "Spiritual Life" event dominated by Christian participation ether should rename the event to clarify its commitments or it should recruit religious others and plan inclusive activities. If such a call is met with resistance, or merely dismissed for more urgent priorities, then the institution is missing an opportunity to actively engage religious diversity. An engaged college might affirm and respect its history, but it does not allow that history to dictate the terms of or nature of the questions or the answers to those questions. Pervasive and contented religious privilege prevents genuinely free inquiry.

Some colleges have tried to work through their identity and vision by becoming more inclusive (such as Wagner College) or by reaffirming their religious roots in the midst of their affirmation of cultural pluralism (such as Elmhurst College).[64] In my own experience, some faculty who decided to join Young Harris College felt reassured about the college by seeing diverse campus organizations—such as the Gay-Straight Alliance, the Student Inquiry Group for Humanist Thought, and the Buddhist Meditation and Mindfulness Gathering. This growth in diversity of faculty and staff leads to a growing interest and commitment to increasing the inclusiveness of the campus through policy revision and revision of the mission. Students also gain from their increased literacy in being able to detect the difference between academic and intellectual approaches to the study of religion and confessional approaches to religion. And this skill transfers into other realms, such as studying politics, where students can detect the difference between teaching about politics and propaganda promoting a particular political perspective. While the method of engagement I propose helps students gain fluency in engaging with people across multiple religious commitments, I think we still fall short of ideal efforts and effects. The main problem is contented apathy, which involves not seeing the value in engaging religious diversity and not recognizing religious diversity as among the crucial injustices at issue in multicultural education, such as race, gender, sex, class, and so forth. My hope is that by actually focusing on questions of meaning and purpose, we will find ourselves captivated by the adventure of liberal arts learning in spiritually vital settings and fearlessly engaging religious and secular pluralism.

I have proposed what it is to genuinely question in liberal arts settings, and I have urged that this account clarifies what it is for the UMC to support colleges that promote exploration of questions of meaning and purpose in the context of religious diversity. Other advocates for religious diversity encourage avoiding polarizing debate and encourage instead engaging different others through activist and service projects. Patel emphasizes that overcoming religious prejudice is most effective through developing a friendship with a real person of another religion. I do not want my project to be seen as disagreeing with their efforts but merely supplementing them. How else is friendship realized except through shared experiences, service, and dialogue together? By investigating questions, we have seen that religions fittingly are conceived of as languages, and that learning about religious diversity is similar to becoming multilingual. We have seen this reveals a "perspectival" character of religions. But how might this play out institutionally at colleges that affiliate with a religion yet maintain openness to all religious and secular perspectives?

Notes

1 I draw this phrase from Dafina Lazarus Stewart, Michael M. Kocet, and Sharon Lobdell, "The Multifaith Campus: Transforming Colleges and Universities for Spiritual Engagement" in *About Campus* (March–April 2011).

2 Sandra S. Harper, "Drawing Out," in *Conversations: Leading United Methodist–Related Schools, Colleges, and Universities*, ed. M. Kathryn Armistead and Melanie B. Overton (Nashville: GBHEM, 2015), 31.

3 See Aristotle, *Nicomachean Ethics*, 2nd ed., trans. Terence Irwin (Indianapolis: Hackett, 1999), 3–8.

4 See Pierre Bourdieu, *Pascalian Meditations* (Stanford: Stanford University Press, 2000), 13–18.

5 R. Eugene Rice, "Religious Diversity and the Making of Meaning: Implications for the Classroom" in *Diversity & Democracy: Civic Learning for Shared Futures* 11, no. 1 (Winter 2008): 1.

6 Eboo Patel, *Sacred Ground: Pluralism, Prejudice, and the Promise of America* (Boston: Beacon, 2013), 110.

7 Patel, 68.

8 Negative prejudice is not the only sort atrophying freedom of thought. Lopez and others show how the modern West's reception of various forms of Buddhism indicate an orientalist prejudice, exoticizing the foreign other. See Donald S. Lopez Jr., ed., *Curators of the Buddha: The Study of Buddhism Under Colonialism* (Chicago: University of Chicago Press, 1995).

9 Melanie B. Overton, *Handbook for Leaders at United Methodist–Related Schools, Colleges, and Universities: Understanding, Energizing, and Communicating the Relationship* (Nashville: GBHEM, 2016), 3, emphasis added.

10 Eve Fine and Jo Handelsman, "Benefits and Challenges of Diversity in Academic Settings," Women in Science and Engineering Leadership Institute, University of Wisconsin–Madison, 2010.

11 Alyssa N. Bryant, "The Effects of Involvement in Campus Religious Communities on College Student Adjustment and Development," *Journal of College and Character* 8, no. 3 (2007): 14.

12 Bryant, 14.

13 Taylor describes this as the "immanent frame," the default neutral framework from which we select our (ir)religious preferences, and he claims this is definitive for our contemporary "secular" age. Charles Taylor, *A Secular Age* (Cambridge, MA: Harvard University Press, 2007).

14 See Robert Wuthnow, *America and the Challenges of Religious Diversity* (Princeton, NJ: Princeton University Press, 2007). As Wuthnow shows, not only do so-called "immigrant" religions, such as Hinduism and Islam, increase in visibility each year; so also do mainstream participants continually redefine their comportment to religion. Wuthnow discovers three tendencies for navigating religious diversity. There are "resistors," those who restrict their social networks to their religious sect. Wuthnow labels another group "acceptors." These people identify with a particular religion but tolerate living alongside alternative religious forms of life. The third tendency Wuthnow labels "embracers." These people select aspects from this or that religion to invent an individualized spirituality. They sometimes refer to themselves as "spiritual but not religious."

15 See Stephen Prothero, *Religious Literacy: What Every American Needs to Know—and Doesn't* (New York: HarperOne, 2007). A further complication is the question in religious studies challenging the "world religion paradigm," a question of whether "religions" even exist or if the notion of religion is just a function of imperialist rhetoric. See Tomoko Masuzawa, *The Invention of World Religions: Or, How European Universalism was Preserved in the Language of Pluralism* (Chicago: University of Chicago Press, 2005).

16 Pew Research Center's Forum on Religion & Public Life, "U.S. Religious Knowledge Survey: Executive Summary," Pew Research Center, 2010, http://www.pewforum.org/2010/09/28/u-s-religious-knowledge-survey/.

17 See, for example, Lisa Miller, "We Are All Hindus Now," *Newsweek*, August 15, 2009.

18 See Michael Lipka, "A Closer Look at America's Rapidly Growing Religious 'Nones,'" Pew Research Center, May 13, 2015, http://www.pewresearch.org/fact-tank/2015/05/13/a-closer-look-at-americas-rapidly-growing-religious-nones/.

19 See A. W. Astin et al., *The Spiritual Life of College Students: A National Study of College Students' Search for Meaning and Purpose* (Los Angeles: Higher Education Research Institute, 2005).

20 "The Study of Religion in the United States," *Diversity & Democracy* 11, no. 1 (2008): 21.

21 See Conrad Cherry, Betty A. DeBerg, and Amanda Porterfield, *Religion on Campus: What Religion Really Means to Today's Undergraduates* (n.p.: University of North Carolina Press, 2001).

22 Rice, "Religious Diversity and the Making of Meaning," 1, emphasis added.

23 Overton, *Handbook for Leaders at United Methodist-Related Schools, Colleges, and Universities*, 3, emphasis added. The UMC's General Board of Higher Education and Ministry (GBHEM) primarily focuses on "preparing global leaders for a global church." The NASCUMC focuses specifically on advancing "the work of education and scholarship" while cooperatively addressing "issues of mutual concern to the church and the

academy." I highlight this to underscore the UMC's explicit recognition of a difference between seminary-modeled education and liberal arts–modeled education.

24 Overton, 8.

25 Overton, 9.

26 Overton, 9, emphasis added.

27 I want to make a strong caveat here, though, that any reasonable academic will respectfully defer to disciplinary experts for guidance. Just as an institution should discourage an English professor from performing and directing chemistry experiments as if she is an expert for students, so should an institution discourage professors in fields other than religious studies from leading and running inquiries into the place of religion in culture (let alone leading and running religious services on campus!)—at least not without proper guidance.

28 See Nathan Eric Dickman, "The Challenge of Asking Engaging Questions," *Currents in Teaching and Learning* 2, no. 1 (2009): 3–16.

29 Hans-Georg Gadamer, *Truth and Method*, 2nd rev. ed., trans. Joel Weinsheimer and Donald G. Marshall (New York: Continuum, 2004), 368.

30 Gadamer, 304. See also Emmanuel Levinas, "Philosophy and Awakening," in M. Smith and B. Harshav, trans., *Entre Nous: On Thinking-of-the-Other* (New York: Columbia University Press, 1998), 86.

31 Hans-Georg Gadamer, "Language and Understanding," in R. Palmer, ed., *The Gadamer Reader: A Bouquet of the Later Writings.* (Evanston, IL: Northwestern University Press, 2007), 104.

32 P. Tillich, "Communicating the Christian Message: A Question to Christian Ministers and Teachers," in *Theology of Culture* (Oxford University Press, 1964), 204–5.

33 See N. E. Dickman, "Transcendence Un-Extra-Ordinaire: Bringing the Atheistic I Down to Earth," *Religions* 8, no. 4 (2017).

34 Thich Nhat Hanh, *Living Buddha, Living Christ* (New York: Penguin, 2007).

35 See Dickman, "Transcendence Un-Extra-Ordinaire."

36 See John D. Caputo, *On Religion* (London: Routledge, 2007), 27.

37 Scholarly publications sometimes reinforce this. See, for example, Kevin Schilbrack, *Philosophy and the Study of Religions: A Manifesto* (West Sussex: Wiley-Blackwell, 2014), 169.

38 Al Rahmin, the Arabic superlative for "the Most Merciful [One]" is one among the ninety-nine names for the god in Islam—yet "Allah" (merely the Arabic word for "god") is often used in English as if it were a proper name. See Sumbul Ali-Karamali, *The Muslim Next Door: The Qur'an, the Media, and that Veil Thing* (Ashland, OR: White Cloud, 2008), 35–36.

39 Manya Brachear Pashman, "Wheaton College Reverses Efforts to Fire Professor, but She Won't Return to Teach," *Chicago Tribune*, February 6, 2016.

40 J. Cameron West, "Jesus, the Big Questions, and United Methodist–Related Higher Education," in *Conversations: Leading United Methodist–Related Schools, Colleges,*

and Universities, ed. M. Kathryn Armistead and Melanie B. Overton (Nashville: GBHEM, 2015), 60.

41 West, 60.

42 West, 7.

43 West, 59.

44 West, 59, emphasis added.

45 West, 61.

46 See Huntingdon's General Education core curriculum, http://www.huntingdon.edu/academics/general-education-core-curriculum/.

47 West, "Jesus, the Big Questions, and United Methodist–Related Higher Education," 61.

48 See Huntingdon's catalog, 2016–2017 draft, http://hawk.huntingdon.edu/2016-17_Draft_Catalog.pdf.

49 Upon a cursory look at Huntingdon's official website, there seem to be no extracurricular representations of religious traditions other than Christianity.

50 Oversight of diversity occurs in other UMC documents. The Book of Discipline states, "The practice of homosexuality is incompatible with Christian teaching" (220, paragraph 304). The statement continues: "self-avowed practicing homosexuals are not to be certified as candidates, ordained as ministers, or appointed to serve" in the UMC. What about other forms of sexual orientation, such as bisexual, asexual, questioning, queer, and so on? What if someone self-avowedly identifies as bisexual but is currently in a heterosexual marriage? The point here is that, as with religious diversity, are the terms imposed onto others, or are others allowed to define themselves from themselves on their terms? This betrays an atrophied imagination. I hope this exclusive prejudice will be removed altogether, rather than be reworded to exclude even more LGBTQIA individuals.

51 See Peter Conn, "The Great Accreditation Farce," Chronicle of Higher Education, June 30, 2014.

52 See Adam B. Westbook, "Religious College, Peter Conn, and the 'Bill Mahr Dichotomy,'" Chronicle of Higher Education, July 10, 2014; and Thomas K. Wolber, "Orthodoxy Does Not Trump Reason as Every Church-Affiliated College," Chronicle of Higher Education, July 3, 2014.

53 Rosemary Royston (vice president of planning and research, chief of staff, and lecturer of English at Young Harris College), email message to author, April 23, 2017. See also The Principles of Accreditation: Foundations for Quality Enhancement, 5th ed. (Southern Association of Colleges and Schools Commission on Colleges, 2011), 23–25.

54 Stewart, Kocet, and Lobdell, "The Multifaith Campus," 12.

55 Stewart, Kocet, and Lobdell, 13.

56 Stewart, Kocet, and Lobdell, 14.

57 Stewart, Kocet, and Lobdell, 15.

58 Stewart, Kocet, and Lobdell, 17.

59 See Dickman, "Ethical Understanding"; Dickman, "Why do so many people think that only one religion can be right?" in *Religion in 5 Minutes*, ed. Aaron W. Hughes and Russell T. McCutcheon (Sheffield, South Yorkshire; Bristol, UK: Equinox, 2017); and Michelle Lelwica, "Religious Diversity: Challenges and Opportunities in the College Classroom," *Diversity & Democracy: Civic Learning for Shared Futures* 11, no. 1 (Winter 2008).

60 Michael D. Coogan, *The Illustrated Guide to World Religions* (Oxford: Oxford University Press, 2003).

61 See Schilbrack, *Philosophy and the Study of Religions*; Russell T. McCutcheon, *Critics Not Caretakers: Redescribing the Public Study of Religion* (New York: SUNY, 2001); and Bruce Lincoln, "Theses on Method," *Method & Theory in the Study of Religion* 8 (1996).

62 Gemma Corradi Fiumara, *The Other Side of Language: A Philosophy of Listening*, trans. Charles Lambert (New York: Routledge, 1990), 123.

63 Gadamer, *Truth and Method*, 371; see also Gadamer, "Language and Understanding," 96.

64 Allie Grasgreen, "Faith Reconsidered," *Inside Higher Ed*, April 1, 2011.

Sources

Ali-Karamali, Sumbul. *The Muslim Next Door: The Qur'an, the Media, and that Veil Thing.* Ashland, OR: White Cloud, 2008.

Aristotle. *Nicomachean Ethics.* 2nd ed. Translated by Terence Irwin. Indianapolis: Hackett, 1999.

Astin, A. W., H. S. Astin, J. A. Lindholm, A. N. Bryant, S. Calderon, and K. Szelenyi. *The Spiritual Life of College Students: A National Study of College Students' Search for Meaning and Purpose.* Los Angeles: Higher Education Research Institute, 2005.

Bryant, Alyssa N. "The Effects of Involvement in Campus Religious Communities on College Student Adjustment and Development." *Journal of College and Character* 8, no. 3 (2007).

Caputo, John D. *On Religion.* London: Routledge, 2007.

Cherry, Conrad, Betty A. DeBerg, and Amanda Porterfield. *Religion on Campus: What Religion Really Means to Today's Undergraduates.* University of North Carolina Press, 2001.

Conn, Peter. "The Great Accreditation Farce." *Chronicle of Higher Education.* June 30, 2014.

Coogan, Michael D. *The Illustrated Guide to World Religions.* Oxford: Oxford University Press, 2003.

Dickman, Nathan Eric. "Ethical Understanding: The Priority of Questioning in Interreligious Dialogue." *Listening: Journal of Communication Ethics, Religion, and Culture* 50 (2015).

Dickman, Nathan Eric. "The Challenge of Asking Engaging Questions." *Currents in Teaching and Learning* 2, no. 1 (2009).

Dickman, Nathan Eric. "Transcendence Un-Extra-Ordinaire: Bringing the Atheistic I Down to Earth." *Religions* 8, no. 4 (2017).

Dickman, "Why Do So Many People Think That Only One Religion Can Be Right?" In *Religion in 5 Minutes*, edited by Aaron Hughes and Russell McCutcheon. Bristol: Equinox Press, 2017.

Fine, Eve, and Jo Handelsman. "Benefits and Challenges of Diversity in Academic Settings." Women in Science and Engineering Leadership Institute. Board of Regents of the University of Wisconsin, 2010.

Fiumara, Gemma Corradi. *The Other Side of Language: A Philosophy of Listening*. Translated by Charles Lambert. New York: Routledge, 1990.

Gadamer, Hans-Georg. "Language and Understanding." In *The Gadamer Reader: A Bouquet of the Later Writings*, edited by R. Palmer. Evanston, IL: Northwestern University Press, 2007.

———. *Truth and Method*. 2nd rev. ed. Translated by Joel Weinsheimer and Donald G. Marshall. New York: Continuum, 2004.

Goodman, Kathleen, and Daniel Hiroyuki Teraguchi. "Beyond Spirituality: A New Framework for Educators." In *Diversity & Democracy: Civic Learning for Shared Futures* 11, no. 1 (Winter 2008).

Grasgreen, Allie. "Beyond Tolerance." *Inside Higher Ed*, January 31, 2012.

———. "Faith Reconsidered." *Inside Higher Ed*, April 1, 2011.

Harper, Sandra S. "Drawing Out." In *Conversations: Leading United Methodist–Related Schools, Colleges, and Universities*. Edited by M. Kathryn Armistead and Melanie B. Overton. Nashville: GBHEM, 2015.

Lelwica, Michelle. "Religious Diversity: Challenges and Opportunities in the College Classroom." *Diversity & Democracy: Civic Learning for Shared Futures* 11, no. 1 (Winter 2008).

Levinas, Emmanuel. "Philosophy and Awakening." In *Entre Nous: On Thinking-of-the-Other*, 77–90. Translated by M. Smith and B. Harshav. New York: Columbia University Press, 1998.

Lincoln, Bruce. "Theses on Method." *Method & Theory in the Study of Religion* 8 (1996).

Lopez Jr., Donald S., ed. *Curators of the Buddha: The Study of Buddhism under Colonialism*. Chicago: University of Chicago Press, 1995.

Masuzawa, Tomoko. *The Invention of World Religions: Or, How European Universalism Was Preserved in the Language of Pluralism*. Chicago: University of Chicago Press, 2005.

McCutcheon, Russell T. *Critics Not Caretakers: Redescribing the Public Study of Religion*. New York: SUNY Press, 2001.

Miller, Lisa. "We Are All Hindus Now." *Newsweek*. August 15, 2009.

Overton, Melanie B. Introduction to *Conversations: Leading United Methodist-related Schools, Colleges, and Universities*. Edited by M. Kathryn Armistead and Melanie B. Overton. Nashville: GBHEM, 2015.

———. *Handbook for Leaders at United Methodist–related Schools, Colleges, and Universities: Understanding, Energizing, and Communicating the Relationship*. Nashville: GBHEM, 2016.

Pashman, Manya Brachear. "Wheaton College Reverses Efforts to Fire Professor, but She Won't Return to Teach." *Chicago Tribune.* February 6, 2016.

Patel, Eboo. "In Promoting Campus Diversity, Don't Dismiss Religion." *Chronicle for Higher Education.* March 11, 2015.

———. *Sacred Ground: Pluralism, Prejudice, and the Promise of America.* Boston: Beacon Press, 2013.

The Principles of Accreditation: Foundations for Quality Enhancement. 5th ed. Southern Association of Colleges and Schools Commission on Colleges, 2011.

Prothero, Stephen. *Religious Literacy: What Every American Needs to Know—and Doesn't.* New York: HarperOne, 2007.

Rice, R. Eugene. "Religious Diversity and the Making of Meaning: Implications for the Classroom" *Diversity & Democracy: Civic Learning for Shared Futures* 11, no. 1 (Winter 2008).

Schilbrack, Kevin. *Philosophy and the Study of Religions: A Manifesto.* West Sussex: Wiley-Blackwell, 2014.

Stewart, Dafina Lazarus, Michael M. Kocet, and Sharon Lobdell. "The Multifaith Campus: Transforming Colleges and Universities for Spiritual Engagement." *About Campus,* March–April 2011.

Supiano, Beckie. "A Group for Secular Students Finds Its Way on a Christian Campus." *Chronicle for Higher Education,* February 27, 2011.

Taylor, Charles. *A Secular Age.* Cambridge, MA: Harvard University Press, 2007.

Thich Nhat Hanh. *Living Buddha, Living Christ.* New York: Penguin, 2007.

Tillich, Paul. "Communicating the Christian Message: A Question to Christian Ministers and Teachers." In *Theology of Culture.* Oxford: Oxford University Press, 1964.

———. *Dynamics of Faith.* New York: HarperCollins, 2001.

United Methodist Church (US). *The Book of Discipline of The United Methodist Church.* Nashville: United Methodist Publishing House, 2012.

West, J. Cameron. "Jesus, the Big Questions, and United Methodist-Related Higher Education" in *Conversations: Leading United Methodist-related Schools, Colleges, and Universities.* Edited by M. Kathryn Armistead and Melanie B. Overton. Nashville: GBHEM, 2015.

Westbook, Adam B. "Religious College, Peter Conn, and the 'Bill Mahr Dichotomy.'" *Chronicle of Higher Education,* July 10, 2014.

Wolber, Thomas K. "Orthodoxy Does Not Trump Reason as Every Church-Affiliated College." *Chronicle of Higher Education,* July 3, 2014.

Wuthnow, Robert. *America and the Challenges of Religious Diversity.* Princeton, NJ: Princeton University Press, 2007.

CAMPUS
INTERSECTIONS

Interreligious Community Engagement and Service-Learning in Higher Education

Pedagogical Considerations

Hans Gustafson

erving as a primary starting point for faculty thinking about adding interreligious community engagement (service-learning) to one's pedagogy, this chapter lays out the essentials for course design and implementation, especially at the undergraduate level. It shares key readings, student learning outcomes, types of community partners, and strategies for student assessment (e.g., critical reflection on course content and community engagement). Further, it provides background context to the theory and practice behind college-level course-based community engagement insofar as it relates to and enhances intentional "interreligious" course-based community engagement. Essentials for course design include the necessity of clear and well-defined student learning outcomes, the fostering of adequate community partners that facilitate interreligious encounter between and among students and nonstudents with various religious identities, and the implementation of critical reflection exercises on the interreligious encounter that also draw on classroom content and readings. In addition to offering examples that link student learning outcomes to readings, engagement experience, and critical reflection on the readings and experience, this chapter sketches some "best practices" for course-based interreligious community engagement and comment on the promises and challenges that may arise.

Melanie B. Overton, formerly the assistant general secretary for schools, colleges, and universities in the General Board of Higher Education and Ministry's Division of Higher Education for The United Methodist Church, draws our attention to The United Methodist Church's promotion of interreligious dialogue "as a tool for deepening and extending faith, gaining insight into the wisdom of other traditions, and overcoming fears and misapprehensions."[1] This chapter endorses, as a primary way to overcome fears and misapprehensions and to cultivate constructive relationships across lines of religious difference, the implementation of course-based interreligious community engagement and service-learning into undergraduate curriculum. In so doing, it sketches the essentials for course design and implementation by sharing theoretical and practical insights. These include student learning outcomes, community partners, key texts, assessments, and best practices.

Theoretical Considerations

Community Engagement and Service-Learning

Do you want to incorporate community engagement or service-learning into your course curriculum? The answer to this may very well end up being based on your student learning objectives. What is it that you want your students to do and achieve? Why are you incorporating an element of course-based community engagement in the first place? To get at these questions, it may be helpful to first consider the nature of community engagement and service-learning.

Service-learning, perhaps the older (and perhaps outdated and somewhat controversial) model, emphasizes the giver-receiver relationship in which students, or student groups, often engage the community outside the classroom in a manner that provides a needed (hopefully) service. This might entail volunteering at the local soup kitchen or food shelf or tutoring or mentoring in after-school programs. Indeed, the service performed under the rubric of service-learning ought to be related to the content and curriculum of the course and its classroom learning experiences. The University of Southern California emphasizes this point by describing service-learning in the following way: "At the core of service-learning is the principle that community service can be connected to classroom learning in such a way that service is more informed by the theoretical and conceptual understanding and learning is more informed by the realities of the world."[2]

Community or civic engagement de-emphasizes the service, or giver-receiver, aspect and instead emphasizes, perhaps to a larger degree, engagement over service. However, many modes of community engagement implicitly include an element of contribution to the community. For instance, the University of St. Thomas in Minnesota defines it as follows: "Civic engagement, formerly known as service-learning, incorporates meaningful community partnership into coursework, allowing the students to contribute to the community while gaining knowledge relevant to their academic and professional lives. It is a link between the classroom and community through required, academic experiences."[3]

There may be rationale for why an instructor might go with either or both service learning and/or community engagement. As discussed below, it may depend in large part on the learning objectives of the course. Keep in mind, however, that both have in common the connection of community with curricular content. For instance, in the courses I teach that incorporate community engagement, I tell my students, orally and in writing, that the essential nature of a community engagement reflection paper (whether short low-stakes or longer final, reflection papers) "is the exploration of the connections between course material and a person's individual life or psyche" and is assigned "to elicit students' responses to complex, difficult, or troubling readings and invite the writer to 'speak back' to the reading in a musing, questioning, and probing way."[4] Simply put, I ask the students to "speak back" to the content of the course, in light of their engagement experience.

Interreligious Community Engagement

What makes community engagement interreligious? This is a question each instructor ought to spend some time considering prior to reaching out to potential community partners. Before I offer the criterion I employ to determine whether or not a community engagement experience is interreligious, it will be helpful to review a few modes of community engagement.

One mode of engagement is to have each student individually serve a particular community partner. The advantage of this mode is that its great flexibility allows each student to tailor his or her engagement hours to their own schedule in collaboration with their chosen community partner. Another mode is to commission the class to serve as a group with a community partner. This is the mode described by Eboo Patel in his talk at Interfaith Youth Core's 2003 Spring Sacred Stories Performance.[5] Patel advocates for giving the students, ideally a "religiously diverse group"[6] of students, "a common service experience."[7] These modes of engagement are not mutually exclusive. In my classes, I often have some students doing their own individual engagement placements with a particular community partner while others work in groups to do a project with another partner.

The criterion I employ in my courses that qualifies particular engagement experiences as interreligious requires that students serve or engage, or serve or engage alongside, those from a religious tradition other than their own or the one they were raised in. By interreligious, I have in mind the interaction between and among those with various religious identities (agnostic, atheist, and secular humanist included). I do not have in mind intra-religious or ecumenical encounter. Although valuable, and necessary for fostering interreligious understanding, I exclude this option from my courses. Therefore, if a United Methodist student requests to engage the local Roman Catholic, Lutheran, or Evangelical church, I decline her request. Given this sole criterion, in addition to my student learning objectives proposed below, I am able to offer a wide variety of community engagement experiences to my students (some examples of which are given below under the heading "Community Partners"). I find that this criterion ensures interreligious engagement; that is, it fosters encounter between and among those with different religious identities.

The Value of Interreligious Community Engagement

Lived Religion. Perhaps the most obvious reason for adding this element to a course is to expose students to the reality of lived religion. It is one thing for a student to read about Hinduism in her textbook, but it is another thing for her to encounter a living, breathing Hindu in her local community. Last year, a few of my students served at a local Hindu mandir (temple) outside the Minneapolis–St. Paul area. After a day of service at the mandir, one of my students struck up a conversation with the director of the mandir. He asked her about how Hinduism helps its practitioners deal with negativity in their lives. The director gave him a warm smile and explained how she understood the role of the inner spirit in relation to feelings and emotions. Their conversation became more intimate, bouncing around topics such as gratitude, karma, giving freely, sincere compassion, the power of positive thinking, and the role of desire. From this student's reflection paper, it was evident that this Hindu woman in Minnesota made a significant impression on him, certainly in a way a textbook could not. The student concluded his reflection with a statement about how "awesome" it was to have much of what he had read about Hinduism presented to him by a Hindu woman living in a small town in Minnesota.

My Aunt Susan and Friend Al. In their article "America's Grace: How a Tolerant Nation Bridges Its Religious Divides,"[8] political scientists

David Campbell and Robert Putnam demonstrate what they refer to as the Aunt Susan Principle (ASP) and the My Friend Al Principle (MFAP). ASP speculates that we all have an Aunt Susan in our lives, someone "who epitomizes what it means to be a saint, but whose religious background is different from our own. . . . But whatever her religious background (or lack thereof), you know that Aunt Susan is destined for heaven. And if she is going to heaven, what does that say about other people who share her religion or lack of religion? Maybe they can go to heaven too."[9] Putnam and Campbell suggest "that having a religiously diverse social network leads to a more positive assessment of specific religious groups."[10] MFAP speculates that "upon realizing that you can become friends with Al, a member of a religious group you once viewed with suspicion, you come to reevaluate your perception of other religious groups too."[11] If ASP and MFAP are accurate, then interreligious community engagement that fosters simply building relationships between and among people with different religious identities works toward addressing, and hopefully achieving, any student learning outcomes that call for students to reevaluate their perceptions of religious groups other than their own, and in the process, hopefully, leading to a more positive assessment of those groups.

Student Learning Objectives

One of the very first questions an instructor interested in incorporating interreligious community engagement into the classroom ought to ask is what learning objectives she intends to satisfy through the engagement experience. Not only is this simply good practice for clear pedagogical thinking, but ultimately it will most certainly determine what community engagement experiences and community partners will meet the needs of the class and students. Further, these learning objectives will grow directly out of the content of your course. Therefore, a course in world religions is likely to have different objectives than a course in politics and religion. Likewise, a course in religion and peacemaking is likely to have different objectives than a course in interreligious dialogue. Having one or two clear objectives for the learning experience of community engagement will also help the instructor respond to student requests to custom design their own interreligious community engagement experience (which I do not discourage). When such occasions arise, the student learning objectives are helpful in determining whether or not the students' ideas adequately meet them. Further, as most instructors know, students simply want to know "why are we doing this?" And they justifiably deserve a well-articulated answer that can be directly linked to the content of the course.

When I teach courses in interreligious encounter, interreligious dialogue, world religions, and the like, I prefer to keep it rather simple when it comes to articulating clear learning objectives. The students will be able to easily find them on their syllabus and assignment sheet (as well as hear them from my mouth). They will read that the overarching learning goal of the community engagement experience is to "provide students the opportunity to develop interreligious relationships in the context of service and examine their experience in light of course material" and to "apply factual and conceptual course content to their own experience." Clearly stating these goals early and often impresses upon students the logic and value behind the learning experiences. In addition, as stated above, the primary criterion I use to determine whether or not a particular community partner or community engagement experience can be considered is whether it facilitates students serving or engaging, or serving or engaging alongside, those from a religious tradition or with a religious identity other than their own or the one they were raised in. Using this criterion in conjunction with the two learning objectives above allows the instructor to determine whether a community engagement project proposed by a student will qualify. Below I discuss some of the wonderfully creative projects and placements my students have proposed and implemented, in addition to some of the standard options I usually offer.

Preparing the Students

Preparing students and instructors for community engagement and service-learning is a vital part of the process and one that should not be taken lightly. Questions for the instructor to consider at the outset include: Will the community engagement experience be required or optional? If not required, what will the alternative options be? Will the alternative options address the same learning objectives as the interreligious community engagement option? If community engagement is required of all students, will the students be notified upon registering for the course that it will be a required part of the course? How many hours of engagement will be required?

Many institutions already have robust offices for service-learning and community engagement in place, with dedicated staff to assist in the design and implementation. This should be the instructor's very first contact before going any further. Some institutions already have in place rigorous requirements and protocols for implementing community learning into courses. Some have special engagement course designations to alert students upon registering for the course, and some require that all students complete a community engagement course upon graduating. Many institutions have a minimum number of hours of community service for all students (whether it be completed through curricular or cocurricular activity) to complete in order to graduate. Instructors ought to consider whether the engagement experiences in their courses will count toward these requirements and thus perhaps be more attractive to students who might not otherwise consider registering for such a course.

Another reason the office of community/civic engagement or service-learning (if your institution is fortunate to have one) should be an instructor's first stop is to draw on their wisdom and services, especially for preparing your students. Invite their staff to visit your class the first week to give a basic introduction to service-learning and community engagement. If they do not provide this service, then suggest it! If no office or support exists, a great place to start is Jacoby and Howard's *Service-Learning Essentials*.[12]

To prepare students for *interreligious* community engagement, instructors might consider devoting a class period or two during the first weeks to specific readings on interreligious encounter, dialogue, engagement, and service-learning. Consider readings such as Eboo Patel's "Interfaith Service-Learning,"[13] Catherine Cornille's "Conditions for Inter-Religious Dialogue,"[14] Tanden Brekke's "Why Interfaith Engagement? A Civic Imperative,"[15] and Kate McCarthy's "When the Other Is Neighbor: Community-Based Interfaith Work."[16] Consider pairing one of these readings with a brief presentation on the concept of dialogue and how it can take shape in a variety of ways. Often my students come into a course with a preconceived idea of interreligious dialogue as sitting down at a table with people of various religious identities to rigorously hash out religious doctrines, beliefs, and practices. To them, at first, dialogue is literally dialogue. However, to broaden the concept of dialogue, I introduce them to the very well-known four types or models of dialogue made famous by the 1991 Vatican document "Dialogue and Proclamation."[17] The models are the dialogue of life (sharing in joys and sufferings of our neighbors regardless of religious identity), dialogue of social action (collaborating across lines of religious difference in a mutual effort to serve poor, marginalized, and suffering peoples), dialogue of theological exchange (deepening our understanding of religious heritages, including histories, beliefs, and practices), and the dialogue of religious experience (sharing the spiritual riches of our traditions, such as prayer, contemplation, and the like). The dialogue of life and the dialogue of action, in particular, help students to frame interreligious dialogue beyond literal theological conversation and begin to think of encounter and engagement around civic action and neighborly service as dialogue as well, and perhaps a more urgent and immediate form of dialogue. It also removes any anxiety they might harbor over not being well equipped to carry out informed theological exchange. Rather, it instills confidence that they too, perhaps more than many others, have a skill set that can immediately contribute to constructive interreligious dialogue and engagement.

Community Partners

Perhaps the single most important factor determining successful student learning experiences comes down to the community partners chosen for the course. To begin with, the instructor ought to consider whether all of the students will partner with the same community partner, or whether they will have a few options to choose from. As noted earlier, there are reasons why an instructor might choose one partner over several, or vice versa.

Preliminary Considerations

Identifying and Cultivating Community Partners. Begin the process by identifying a few partners that may fit the student learning objectives of the course. You may already have some connections in your social and professional network you can call upon. Survey the directory of local nonprofits that might offer volunteer opportunities that cultivate interaction between and among people of various religious identities. Be creative and think broadly. Are there organizations devoted to particular aspects of your course (e.g., the local Interfaith Power and Light chapter)?[18] Some partners might, at first, not seem to offer explicit interreligious encounters; however, you'll never know until you reach out to them to discuss further (e.g., perhaps the local nonprofit devoted to immigrant assistance has an after-school tutoring and recreation program with which your students can volunteer). Once you have identified a few promising partners, contact them and request to meet at their site. Some partners will be a natural fit, and you'll sense this almost immediately once you meet with them. For others, it might take longer to find a project that meets both their needs and your course's. Do not give up too easily. If a partner doesn't work for one semester, keep them in mind for later on down the road. Many community partners go through cycles of needs, initiatives, staffing, and funding. If something does not work out one semester, it might for another semester later. Some of the partners I work with took a couple years to cultivate a relationship with and find projects that meet both the needs of my class and the needs of their organization.

Communicating Goals and Establishing Clear Expectations. When entering into a potential relationship with a community partner, it is of the utmost importance to be very transparent and up front about the learning objectives you have for your students. Further, it is crucial to stress to them your desire for the students to meet a particular need the organization might have or, at the very least, provide some valuable service. The last thing I want to do is create unneeded work for a community partner. Your students will be representing not only you, but their university, in the community. You want it to be a positive and productive experience on both ends, not only for the sake of the organization and your students, but for yourself as well! Hopefully, if everything goes well the first time, they will invite your classes back in future semesters.

There are several ways to establish this in your first meeting with potential community partners. You could provide a short single paragraph articulating your expectations for the students in their community engagement experience, and inquire of the partner what needs energetic college students might be able to fill at their organization while simultaneously satisfying the student learning objectives. It is essential to be frank and respectful in this initial conversation in order to avoid any misunderstandings once the semester is under way. You might ask a potential community partner to provide a list of needs they envision your students could meet. Follow this with a conversation with the partner by going through the needs one by one, either accepting or rejecting it based on your course goals. I did this once with a local Hindu community mandir that gave me a long list of needs. Most of the items on the list were outstanding. They included helping prepare food and art with the community for an upcoming festival, attending community gatherings, helping design an interfaith peace garden, and others. However, some of the needs, though great needs of the community, did not match my learning goals. These included tasks such as mowing the lawn and doing masonry work.

Sometimes community partners become so excited about the possibilities of having college students work with them that they create new initiatives designed to meet both their needs and those of the course. For instance, a community partner once created a project designed especially for the communication and journalism student in mind. It tasked a student or two with attending their events, interviewing the participants, and then writing short articles to be published in the local newspapers or online in blogs. The community partner would gain much-needed publicity while the students would put into practice their journalism skills by actually publishing articles, not to mention having material to add to their résumés. Of course, to properly do this the students would be required to interact with people with various religious identities. Above all, it is important to establish clear lines of communication between both the instructor and community partner, but also for the time during the semester when you may expect your students to be communicating directly with the community partner.

Introducing Community Partners to Your Students. There are several effective ways to do this. I encourage all instructors, however, to help facilitate a personal introduction instead of leaving it to your students to reach out to the partners. I have found greater success with getting my students in the same room as the community partners for a formal introduction to their organization. I often devote one class period during the first week to do this. I invite all of my community partners (often between three to five partners) to class to give a ten-minute presentation to "sell" my students on why they should work with their organization. As one might expect, it can be rather challenging to schedule three to five people for a set class time, so start the scheduling process early. If it is simply not possible, which is not unlikely, consider using time from multiple classes.

Another option is to find out whether your institution holds a volunteer or service fair at the beginning of each semester. If they do, ask the organizers to invite your chosen community partners, and then require your students to attend this fair and make contact with their chosen partner. If you choose this option, be sure to introduce the community partner options in class and by way of handout before the fair. The advantage of this option, if you are fortunate to have it, is that it does not require you to give up a class period. Also, it may be more enticing to the community partners, as they will, hopefully, by being present at the college-wide service fair, be able to make connections with other students outside your classes. Regardless of the path you choose, make the introductions as early as possible. Many community partners will require your students to complete background checks before working with them. These can sometimes take from seven to ten days, which means, realistically, that most students will not be able to begin their community engagement until two weeks of the semester have expired.

Examples of Community Partners

The following is a list of community partners I have either collaborated with in creating robust course-based interreligious community engagement programs or have started the conversation with as potential partners for future classes. The aim of this section is to give instructors a sense of what is possible. Ultimately, the instructor knows best the local region, town, or metro area. The uniqueness of each region will determine what is possible for community partnerships. It is then only a matter of getting out there and making contacts.

- Sholom is a "non-profit organization providing a broad continuum of residential, social service and health care services primarily for older adults and within a Jewish environment."[19] This service site routinely serves as a favorite among my students. At Sholom home, at which both Jewish and non-Jewish residents live, students first and foremost are afforded the opportunity to develop relationships with those with religious identities other than their own. The students socialize with the residents, play games, help them with tasks such as painting fingernails, listen to their stories (and sometimes record them in writing or via audio for the residents' family members), serve as bartenders at the daily nonalcoholic happy hour, prepare meals, and help the staff rabbis set up for weekly Shabbat services, among other activities. Students who serve with Sholom learn quickly that interreligious dialogue need not be only about sharing religious beliefs, but rather simply entering into relationship and sharing in life (i.e., the dialogue of life). Further, Sholom offers the advantage of engaging seniors with a rich wealth of life experiences. Not all residents at Sholom are Jewish; thus, the students witness interreligious living at a senior level. They witness conversations between and among people who come from different countries, have different native languages, and maintain different cultural and religious identities.

● The Minnesota Hindu Milan Mandir is a growing Hindu community outside St. Paul, Minnesota. They started in family room of a house, then moved to a larger two-car garage, and eventually were able to purchase a Lutheran church building in downtown Farmington, Minnesota (about thirty minutes south of St. Paul). The community responded swiftly and warmly to my inquiry regarding partnering with my course. I asked them to envision how students could contribute to their needs while satisfying my course's learning goals. A representative from the community visited my class with a substantial list of projects. I had students eventually help paint artwork on the walls of their space (assisted by projecting sketches and outlines onto the walls), prepare dishes for the Diwali celebration (and then attend), assist in the design of a meditation garden, and assist in thinking through the initial design of an inaugural website for the mandir. The work my students did was fruitful, but the genuine learning took place in their encounter and collaboration with the Hindu community members. To accomplish all of these tasks, the students had to develop relationships with the community, ask questions about what they want and why, and in the process learn about lived Hinduism in small-town Minnesota (as the story in the previous section "The Value of Interreligious Community Engagement" narrates).

● Interfaith Youth Connection "is a group of high school students who work together to increase cultural awareness and religious tolerance, reduce prejudice and misunderstanding, build leadership skills, and work together on service projects to address community needs."[20] When I partnered with them, they were in need of a few energetic college mentors to serve as chaperones for an interfaith youth retreat weekend at a camp in northern Minnesota. The camp brings together three youth groups: one from a synagogue, one from a church, and one from an Islamic community. The opportunity was a truly a unique one, and it gained the attention of one of my students. Unfortunately, "when the gales of November come early"[21] to northern Minnesota, the result is subfreezing cold and snow. This shut the camp down early. Pivoting to another project with Interfaith Youth Connection, my student helped to plan their Interfaith Youth Day of Service, which joins "youth of many different religious and cultural backgrounds from across the Twin Cities every Presidents['] Day for the annual Interfaith Youth Day of Service."[22] Both activities fostered not only interreligious encounter but also leadership.

- Hands Across the World strives to "provide a first learning experience to newly arrived immigrants and refugees who do not have the language or living skills to thrive in our community." They achieve this through classroom teaching to "help both children and parents acquire the tools needed to become integrated citizens of Central Minnesota."[23] Students who volunteer with this organization spend their time tutoring recently arriving immigrants in English as well as spending time in recreation with the children. Recently, one of my students, an international student from China, spent her time at Hands Across the World helping children and adults to acquire English language skills. A non-native English speaker herself, she was able to quickly establish a rapport with those she served. Though interreligious encounter is not at the core of this organization's missions, it nonetheless can occur quite naturally. This Chinese student recounted a story of asking a young boy what music he was listening to on his earphones. He responded that he was listening to a song called "Mecca" by a Muslim rap duo named Deen Squad. Having some basic religious literacy, my student knew about making hajj to Mecca. However, she said she was surprised that a topic that seemed holy to her, religious pilgrimage, could be expressed in the form of popular rap music. She confessed that she perceived Muslims to have "conservative attitudes" that wouldn't allow for blending of religion with popular music genres. In her reflection she promptly acknowledged that this exposed her own ill-conceived stereotypes of Islam, and all it took was a young boy listening to rap music to counter it, something a standard textbook on Islam is less likely to do.

- Minnesota Interfaith Power and Light is a local chapter of the national Interfaith Power and Light organization that strives "to be faithful stewards of Creation by responding to global warming through the promotion of energy conservation, energy efficiency, and renewable energy."[24] The organization has affiliates in thirty-seven states and Washington, DC. They draw on rich wisdom of the various religious traditions to raise awareness around environmental stewardship and climate change. I had a small team of students work with the local affiliate in publicizing the organization in rural areas, and ultimately working with student groups on campus to bring an Interfaith Power and Light presentation to campus. The students helped design, lead, publicize, and implement a program tailored to their campus community in collaboration with the organization.

- By the Rivers: A Multi-Faith Life Cycle Learning Center is a newly established organization in my area that runs a variety of programs aimed at fostering understanding across lines of religious difference. Due to its funding challenges at the time, we were unable to run some of the innovative projects they had designed for my students, although we hope to in the future. One project involved training groups of students in pairs or threes to stage themselves outside their campus quad, equipped with their fancy cell phone video cameras, to engage fellow students in friendly, noninvasive, two-minute interviews around issues of religious diversity, identity, and dialogue. The students would receive training and then be given the opportunity to put it in to practice on their home campus. By the Rivers would then curate the various video clips into a professionally produced short film showcasing these themes on their campus.

- Interfaith at Cedar Commons represents an alternative to the traditional service-learning model by offering an opportunity that emphasizes engagement over service. Organized by Dar Al Hijrah Mosque, Trinity Lutheran Congregation, the local Baha'i community, the Campus Ministry Office, the Episcopal community, and Interfaith Scholars at Augsburg College (all located in the Cedar-Riverside neighborhood of Minneapolis), Cedar Commons organizes biweekly gatherings aimed at "building relationships across faith and non-faith traditions and learning from each other's experiences, stories, and convictions."[25] Should a student choose to attend these gatherings, he or she is required to become a regular participant over the course of the semester in order to develop relationships with those of various religious identities. Many neighborhoods in diverse areas have similar community programs that foster intercultural and interreligious understanding. Perhaps they present an opportunity for students to regularly engage and encounter these religious differences.

Custom Design. I often grant students freedom to design their own interreligious community engagement project. What they come up with often dovetails well with their current interests and studies. For instance, I had a group of students find a local Zen center and attend their morning mediation sessions followed by the social hour. Though initially they were drawn to the meditation session, they all acknowledge it was the social hour that drew them back. There they realized that the religious diversity of those attending was far greater than they anticipated. Engaging Jews, Christians, Buddhists, agnostics, atheists, and others wonderfully complicated the construct of religious identity for them.

Further, the presence of the Zen Buddhist priest helped to, in the students' eyes, authenticate the experience. I had another student who already served as a nanny for a Jewish family during the week. She worked it out with their Jewish elementary school to serve as a classroom volunteer to observe how the Jewish tradition influences childhood education. I had another student in the midst of his student teaching assignment at local charter high school. He was assigned to an eleventh grade history class. From our course readings, especially Stephen Prothero's *Religious Literacy*,[26] he became convinced that the teaching of religion had a primary role in history and social studies curriculum. He worked it out with the school, for his student teaching sessions, to incorporate how Christianity influenced the founding of the Americas and, in particular, early American attitudes toward Native American traditions. Students who design and implement their own projects that fit the learning objectives of the course often have very rich experiences. For this reason, I require that they give a ten- to fifteen-minute presentation on their engagement experience to the class at the end of the semester so their classmates can gain, at the very least, some of the lessons they did.

There are several other community partners I've worked with, and there are countless more possible. I've listed a few above to give the reader a sense of what might be possible in your area. Though many of these organizations are local to my area, they are not necessarily unique in their missions and the services they provide. Chances are that an instructor will find similar organizations in his or her area eager to collaborate.

Student Reflection and Assessment

Interreligious community engagement and service-learning without reflection and assessment misses the mark. These learning experiences are designed with student learning objectives in mind and, as such, lend themselves to some form of assessment, regardless of how low or high the stakes they might be for the students' overall grade in the course. I prefer to design assignments with these learning objectives in mind and invite students to reflect on them (as well as the course content) in light of their engagement experiences. The primary mode for doing this is through reflection, individually and in a group, as well as orally and in writing.

A straightforward way to do this is to give the students a direct, yet open-ended prompt that clearly relates their engagement to course content. It can be as simple as asking them to relate their engagement experience to a particular idea raised by a particular reading. It will depend on your course's focus, content, and learning objectives. For instance, I ask the students to reflect on Catherine Cornille's five conditions of interreligious dialogue and the four models of interreligious engagement proposed by the Vatican (both mentioned earlier in this chapter). I try to convince my students that they now have some experience from which they can make arguments. They are in positions to put their interreligious engagement experience into critical conversation with what they've read.

There are several ways to have the students complete these reflections. They might be required to complete short, half-page reflections after each engagement visit (this might be called an engagement reflection journal). They might be required to complete two or three two-page reflection papers throughout the semester. They might be required to complete a final reflection paper at the end of the semester. I have employed all of these methods, and sometimes concurrently. In addition, I hold small group reflection sessions where I meet with small groups of students (preferably all of whom are working with the same community partner) to discuss what is taking place in their projects: challenges, insights, ideas, and so on. Sometimes institutions will have an office for community engagement, and you might consider asking one of their trained staff to facilitate the reflection sessions. The instructor might also consider not being present for these sessions. Many students can be thrown off by the instructor's presence, since she is the one who holds the power of assigning grades to the reflection session. This can obviously inhibit students and change the dynamic of the session. Perhaps colleagues could facilitate the sessions, or the students might facilitate the sessions themselves.

Rules Are for Fools

I close this chapter with considerations and best practices for those thinking about incorporating interreligious community engagement or service-learning into their courses. There is no doubt that implementing such engagement projects takes significant time and effort, especially on the front end. Cultivating relationships with potential community partners and designing opportunities that meet both their needs and the student learning objectives of the course requires thoughtful work and often persistence. Some of the relationships I have been fortunate to establish have taken years, so one should not be put off if partnerships do not come quickly. On the other hand, once a strong relationship with a community partner is established, it requires very little time going forward in collaborating with them. It might be as easy as sending them a quick email asking if you are once again partnering next semester.

Significant challenges can arise during the semester, and they might be time-consuming and annoying. Sometimes students require constant "checking in" to gauge if/how they are getting along with their community partner. Likewise, sometimes community partners simply drop off and stop responding to students, and inevitably the students will come to the instructor, seeking help. It then becomes the instructor's responsibility to intervene and reach out to the community partner to determine what is going on. Sometimes community partners are unable to accommodate the students' service due to unforeseen challenges that come up in the middle of the semester. This leaves some of the students with only part of their service hours completed. What ought the instructor to do? It is useful to anticipate cases like these. Remain flexible and adaptable, and prepare your students at the outset to be as well. The world is big and complex, and things change often and sometimes quite rapidly. There is a lesson in this for us as instructors in the classroom, and for our students, who will be moving soon into the workforce, where they will often work on team-based projects in which people may retire, get sick, and drop out.

When a case arises in which a student is unable to complete his or her engagement experience with the community partner, remain calm and make it a learning experience (for everyone involved). It can be easy to panic, especially if we become too obsessed over sticking to all the assignment rules we laid out at the outset of the semester. Rules are for fools, especially if we become enslaved to them. Forget the rules and always keep the big picture in mind. There are probably countless ways to achieve your student learning objectives. With the SLOs in mind, work with the student to find a valuable way to achieve them with the time remaining in the semester. It may mean shifting to a new community partner or dreaming up a new assignment designed for that student alone. In short, build in such flexibility at the outset of your course design so that you are able to disregard any rigid rules and adapt on the fly.

There can be significant anxiety and uncertainty for the instructor in incorporating these experiences into their courses. It requires a certain amount of "letting go" and giving up control. It may be scary at first; however, I have found it always worth it in the end. Try to impress upon yourself and your students, "This is an experiment. We may have an idea of what it will look like and what we'll end up learning, but I suspect that it will turn out in a way we do not anticipate. We don't know exactly where this will go, but something worthwhile will come out of it, and it will be something you cannot get from your textbooks." With this communicated clearly to the students, they (and the instructor) are more likely to embrace the experimental nature of the project and rest more comfortably in its uncertainty. Finally, they too may be more open to letting go and allowing for a richer interreligious engagement experience.

Notes

1 Melanie Overton, "UMC's Interfaith Dialogue and Partnerships Can Appeal to Young," General Board of Higher Education and Ministry for The United Methodist Church, accessed March 3, 2017, https://www.gbhem.org/article/umc%E2%80%99s-interfaith -dialogue-and-partnerships-can-appeal-young.

2 Joint Educational Project, University of Southern California, in "What Is Service Learning?" on the website of Stanislaus State, Office of Service Learning, accessed November 8, 2017, https://www.csustan.edu/service-learning; also quoted in Eboo Patel, "Interfaith Service-Learning" (from Interfaith Youth Core's Spring 2003 Sacred Stories Performance), accessed November 9, 2017, http://www.isacs.org/misc_files/interfaithservice learningfinal.doc, p. 2.

3 Kimberly Vrudny, ed., Service-Learning Advisory Board, University of St. Thomas (St. Paul, MN: 2007). Website no longer accessible.

4 John C. Bean, *Engaging Ideas: The Professor's Guide to Integrating Writing, Critical Thinking, and Active Learning in the Classroom*, 2nd ed., The Jossey-Bass Higher and Adult Education Series (San Francisco: Jossey-Bass, 2011), 117.

5 See Patel, "Interfaith Service-Learning."

6 I recognize that many college and universities, given their location or religious affiliation, are unable to consistently gather classes made up of students with various religious identities. Therefore, I advocate for several ways to foster interreligious encounter in the community beyond the mode of cultivating a religiously diverse classroom.

7 Patel, "Interfaith Service-Learning," 7.

8 David Campbell and Robert Putnam, "America's Grace: How a Tolerant Nation Bridges Its Religious Divides," *Political Science Quarterly* 126, no. 4 (2011–12), 611–40.

9 Campbell and Putnam, 620.

10 Campbell and Putnam, 620.

11 Campbell and Putnam, 624.

12 Barbara Jacoby and Jeffrey Howard, *Service-Learning Essentials: Questions, Answers, and Lessons Learned* (San Francisco: Jossey-Bass, 2015).

13 Patel, "Interfaith Service-Learning."

14 Catherine Cornille, "Conditions for Inter-Religious Dialogue," *Wiley-Blackwell Companion to Inter-Religious Dialogue*, ed. Catherine Cornille (West Sussex: Wiley-Blackwell, 2013), 20–33.

15 Tanden Brekke, "Why Interfaith Engagement? A Civic Imperative," in *From Bubble to Bridge: Educating Christians for a Multifaith World*, ed. Marion Larson and Sara Shady (Downers Grove, IL: InterVarsity Press, 2017), 17–36.

16 Kate McCarthy, "When the Other Is Neighbor: Community-Based Interfaith Work" in her book *Interfaith Encounters in America* (New Brunswick, NJ: Rutgers University Press, 2007), 84–125.

17 Pontifical Council for Inter-Religious Dialogue, "Dialogue and Proclamation: Reflection and Orientations on Interreligious Dialogue and the Proclamation of the Gospel of Jesus Christ," Vatican.va, accessed November 8, 2017, http://www.vatican.va/roman_curia/pontifical_councils/interelg/documents/rc_pc_interelg_doc_19051991_dialogue-and-proclamatio_en.html, par. 42.

18 Interfaith Power and Light is a national organization with local affiliates in thirty-seven US states and Washington, DC. Their mission "is to be faithful stewards of Creation by responding to global warming through the promotion of energy conservation, energy efficiency, and renewable energy." "Mission & History," Interfaith Power & Light, accessed November 8, 2017, http://www.interfaithpowerandlight.org/about/mission-history/.

19 "Services," Sholom, accessed November 8, 2017, http://www.sholom.com/services.html.

20 "Interfaith Youth Connection," Interfaith Action of Greater Saint Paul, accessed November 8, 2017, http://www.interfaithaction.org/youthconnection.

21 Gordon Lightfoot, "The Wreck of the Edmund Fitzgerald," in *Summertime Dream*, Reprise Records, 1976, vinyl.

22 "Interfaith Youth Day of Service," Interfaith Action of Greater St. Paul, accessed November 8, 2017, http://www.interfaithaction.org/dayofservice.

23 "Mission," Hands Across the World, accessed November 8, https://www.handsacross theworldmn.org/.

24 "Mission & History," Interfaith Power & Light.

25 "What Happens Here," Cedar Commons, November 8, 2017, http://www.augsburg .edu/cedarcommons/activities/.

26 Stephen Prothero, *Religious Literacy: What Every American Needs to Know and Doesn't* (San Francisco: Harper, 2007).

Sources

Bean, John C. *Engaging Ideas: The Professor's Guide to Integrating Writing, Critical Thinking, and Active Learning in the Classroom.* 2nd ed. The Jossey-Bass Higher and Adult Education Series. San Francisco: Jossey-Bass, 2011.

Brekke, Tanden. "Why Interfaith Engagement? A Civic Imperative." In *From Bubble to Bridge: Educating Christians for a Multifaith World*, edited by Marion Larson and Sara Shady, 17–36. Downers Grove, IL: InterVarsity Press, 2017.

Campbell, David, and Robert Putnam. "America's Grace: How a Tolerant Nation Bridges Its Religious Divides." *Political Science Quarterly* 126, no. 4 (2011–12): 611–40.

Cornille, Catherine. "Conditions for Inter-Religious Dialogue." In *Wiley-Blackwell Companion to Inter-Religious Dialogue*, ed. Catherine Cornille, 20–33. Chichester, West Sussex: Wiley-Blackwell, 2013.

Jacoby, Barbara, and Jeffrey Howard. *Service-Learning Essentials: Questions, Answers, and Lessons Learned.* San Francisco: Jossey-Bass, 2015.

Lightfoot, Gordon. "The Wreck of the Edmund Fitzgerald." On *Summertime Dream*. Reprise Records, 1976, vinyl.

McCarthy, Kate. *Interfaith Encounters in America.* New Brunswick, NJ: Rutgers University Press, 2007.

Overton, Melanie. "UMC's Interfaith Dialogue and Partnerships Can Appeal to Young." General Board of Higher Education and Ministry for The United Methodist Church. Accessed November 8, 2017. https://www.gbhem.org/article/umc%E2%80%99s -interfaith-dialogue-and-partnerships-can-appeal-young.

Pontifical Council for Inter-Religious Dialogue. "Dialogue and Proclamation: Reflection and Orientations on Interreligious Dialogue and The Proclamation of the Gospel of Jesus Christ." Accessed January 18, 2018. http://www.vatican.va/roman_curia/pontifical _councils/interelg/documents/rc_pc_interelg_doc_19051991_dialogue-and-proclamatio _en.html.

Prothero, Stephen. *Religious Literacy: What Every American Needs to Know and Doesn't.* San Francisco: Harper, 2007.

Common and Diverse Ground

An Interfaith Dialogue Model for College Campuses

Diane R. Wiener and Jikyo Bonnie Shoultz

Telling Our Story

This chapter is a discussion of our unique model for presenting a successful Interfaith Dialogue Dinner Series at Syracuse University. Diane is the director of the Disability Cultural Center in the Division of Enrollment and the Student Experience, and Bonnie is the Buddhist chaplain affiliated with Hendricks Chapel. In this chapter, we will be using a combination of personal narratives, academic elements, and excerpts from informal conversations and interviews with participants, facilitators, and coordinators. Our goal is to reflect on the impact of the event series on people's lives; experiences of faith, secularism, and community; and relationships formed, both on and off-campus. As the series' current primary co-coordinators, we as coauthors will also reflect upon our own experiences, observations, and aspirations.

As is well-known and cited in Syracuse University's archival materials, in February 1870, at the Methodist State Convention in Syracuse,

New York, a resolution was passed to found a university in that city. Measures were taken to raise $500,000 to endow the university, with the city of Syracuse subscribing $100,000. Rev. Jesse T. Peck, who was elected president of the Syracuse University Board of Trustees, suggested purchasing fifty acres of farmland in southeastern Syracuse. The Board of Trustees of Syracuse University signed the university charter and certificate of incorporation on March 24, 1870.[1]

In order to describe our work, it is vital to underscore the role of Hendricks Chapel in our endeavors. As noted on the university's website, "Hendricks Chapel is the diverse religious, spiritual, ethical and cultural heart of Syracuse University that connects people of all faiths and no faith through active engagement, mutual dialogue, reflective spirituality, responsible leadership and a rigorous commitment to social justice."[2]

Although Syracuse University has been and remains affiliated with numerous bodies and entities, both religious and secular, its legacy in relationship to The United Methodist Church is a vibrant truth. In the recent past, and on an ongoing basis, Rev. Colleen Hallagan Preuninger (now director of the Shenandoah University Youth Theology Institute), formerly Syracuse University's United Methodist Ecumenical Campus Ministry (UMECM) chaplain, worked with fellow chaplains, students, faculty members, and a close cadre of administrative leadership to create a successful dialogue series at Syracuse University, open to the entire campus community and the general public.

During the spring 2014 semester, "Contentious Conversations" were hosted by the UMECM and the Lesbian, Gay, Bisexual, Transgender Resource Center (LGBTRC). This model for dialogic programs was, in many respects, an earlier incarnation of an approach toward "controversial" subjects that transformed later into the current model that we have formulated and that is described herein. In the fall of 2014, the Hendricks Chapel chaplaincies assumed sole coordinating responsibility for the programs; this remained the case during the spring of 2015.

Beginning in the fall of 2015, the Interfaith Dialogue Dinner series was created, sponsored, and coordinated by Hendricks Chapel in partnership with the Disability Cultural Center (DCC). Other cultural centers have been involved as collaborators throughout, and at times these administrative units have also acted as cosponsors (the three cultural centers other than the DCC are the Slutzker Center for International Services, the LGBT Resource Center, and the Office of Multicultural Affairs).

Our Model, Approach, and Philosophy

For the past two academic years (fall 2015–spring 2016 and fall 2016–spring 2017), we have utilized a consistent model for approaching each dialogue gathering. Every dialogue dinner has been hosted in the Noble Room in the historic Hendricks Chapel, built in 1930. The model is explained below. Note that accessibility, broadly defined, was and remains paramount in all our efforts.

Each session (two hours long) included a shared meal (described as "inclusive" and always involving vegetarian, gluten-free, kosher, and halal options, with ingredients and labels for all items), facilitated dialogue, and two times of mindful meditation (at the beginning and at the conclusion of each gathering). We used the following structure in our series, and projected this plan on a large screen located in the room, as well as read it aloud:

- Breaking bread: Gather for shared, inclusive meal
- Mindfulness from the beginning: Short meditation (led by Bonnie or a student Buddhist Association leader/member)
- Welcome and creating tonight's Community Agreements (led by Bonnie and Diane)
- Introductions and facilitated dialogue (led by co-facilitators—listed by name)
- Mindfulness in our closing: short meditation (led by Bonnie or a student Buddhist Association leader/member)

Our "Community Agreements," an egalitarian approach toward

the establishment of ground rules, became patterned, purposefully. We created the following language, for ease in understanding, to increase consistency (while being open to flexibility and transformation), and to save some time during each gathering: "During our Interfaith Dialogue Dinners in the past, we have 'traditionally' created a set of community agreements or ground rules, on-site, for our discussion. If you have others to add, let's do so together, now . . ."

The following agreements were then shared: (1) be present and respectful; (2) be mindful of different belief systems, values, and communication approaches and needs; (3) engage by joining in and by backing up ("share the floor"); and (4) what happens here is intended to be confidential (so please ask for direct permission from folks if you want to share anything someone said/shared beyond or outside of tonight's discussion and space). Again, all content was projected visually as well as read aloud. After reviewing, in turn, each of the agreements, Diane asked those gathered if there were questions, concerns, or amendments, and then verified that everyone consented to uphold the agreements. Additions and updates were made as requested and needed.

As noted, inclusion and accessibility, in the broadest possible understandings of these concepts, were (and will remain, always) at the forefront of our work. In addition to inclusive, free dinners, American Sign Language (ASL) interpretation was provided during each gathering. Deaf participants who are ASL users have been present during all but one of the 2015–2016 and 2016–2017 events. Each gathering announcement and all public relations content related to the dialogue dinners, included a message about ASL interpretation, as well as a clear and concise accommodations statement, directing all parties to the DCC's email address: "For any questions regarding accommodations or accessibility, email: sudcc@syr.edu."

On a volunteer basis, Rachael Zubal-Ruggieri designed the beautiful posters advertising our past two years of Interfaith Dialogue Dinners. Each semester-specific poster was screen-reader accessible, accompanied by an image-free, text-only version. Rachael is a long-standing employee at Syracuse University, as well as an undergraduate student. She is one of the cofounders of the Disability Student Union, an undergraduate organization dedicated to raising awareness of disability justice and disability cultures, for all campus constituents with and without disabilities. The posters' key image over the last two academic years has been an orange tree, recalling the vibrancy and symbolism of new growth and old rootedness, in combination with the orange that is so central to Syracuse University's identity and communication. The "fruits" on this tree have been consistent, iconic, and recognizable visual representations of religious and spiritual traditions, comingled with images of the topics for each semester, shown as highlighted "fruit." The alt-text descriptions on the digital versions of our posters thus also served to educate individuals who might have been unfamiliar with certain religious and spiritual images and symbols, regardless of whether they were using the digital version with a screen reader for accessible content.

Sessions were co-facilitated by chaplains, faculty, staff, and students, with two or three co-facilitators leading during each gathering. Undergraduate student attendance and participation have increased during each event we have hosted. During the fall 2016 term, we coordinated informal, thematic follow-up gatherings (during the same semester) to address questions and interests that arose during our planned dialogues.

Across campus, there has been increasing investment and interest on the part of students and other constituents in the Interfaith Dialogue Dinner Series. Our colleagues in the university's news, public relations, media, and communication leadership team have taken a great interest in and are deeply committed to assuring that everyone on campus is aware of the series; regular SU News stories have been featured and are clearly well received.

The series has been funded primarily by the Co-Curricular Departmental Initiatives Program within the Division of Enrollment and the Student Experience (and, prior, by the Division of Student Affairs), the administrative division within which the DCC is housed (Hendricks was housed within ESE, at the time of the writing of this chapter, but has since moved administrative location; its dean now reports directly to the chancellor). The funds are available via undergraduate student fees. Before approval, each cocurricular program initiative undergoes rigorous application evaluation, by committee, and likewise requires longitudinal follow-up and assessment of successes and opportunities for improvement.

As we have noted in our funding proposals, "at Hendricks Chapel [and at the Disability Cultural Center, our cohost and co-coordinator], we believe in encouraging peaceful discourse and creative engagement in the face of differences that can and do cause conflict, on the [Syracuse University] campus as well as in the larger society. The commitment of this ongoing dinner dialogue series continues to be to model and facilitate such discourse and engagement for and with our students."[3] Each interfaith dialogue dinner explores a major theme. Facilitators encourage intentional dialogue that navigates the issues raised by social movements that address perceived injustices, interfaith tensions, and timely issues of the day. It has been our experience that by gathering together on common ground over a shared meal, we can create a vibrant environment of peaceful and life-giving conversation around important and potentially divisive issues.

The most recent subtitle (and the inspiration for our chapter title) for the Interfaith Dialogue Dinner Series has been: "Common and Diverse Ground: Raising Consciousnesses by Acknowledging the 'Hidden' Things that Divide Us."

Here are the Interfaith Dialogue Dinner Series topics for the past two academic years.

Fall 2015:
White Privilege
Disability Culture, Faith, and Secularism
Sanctuary and Safer Spaces

Spring 2016:
Revisiting Privilege: The Intersections of Privileged and Marginalized Identities

Accommodations and Accessibility: Broadening Definitions,
    Changing Cultures
Racialized Campus Climates: Naming Racism and
    Healing Wounds
Stress and Wellness: What Is "Mental Health"?

Fall 2016:
#BlackLivesMatter
Islamophobia on Campus
Beyond Inclusion and Accessibility

Spring 2017:
Marginalization, Faith, and Secularism
Anti-Semitism Today
Remembering/Honoring/Responding to Pulse, Orlando
Reflections, Experiences, Observations

We asked participants, facilitators, and meditation leaders to
pause and reflect on their experiences by responding in any way they
chose to a series of five suggested prompts:

1. the impact of the event series on your life

2. the impact of the event series on your experiences of faith, secularism, and community

3. the impact of the event series on your relationships on and off campus

4. the relevance of the interfaith and secular "nature" and structure of
   the event series

5. the value of including a shared meal as well as mindfulness meditation in our gatherings

Some feedback was shared in person; other comments were
forwarded via email or discussed during one-on-one telephone conversations with one or both of the authors. Each party was advised,
"Please indicate if you wish to be rendered anonymous with only your
campus role noted, or if you prefer to be mentioned by name, as well

(if you do not comment along these lines, you will be rendered anonymous with your campus role mentioned, possibly)." Those who were contacted via email were also encouraged to forward the email "to anyone else who might be interested, as a prior participant, facilitator, meditation leader, visitor, etc." Below, we have included a sampling of excerpted feedback and other comments. All parties who were cited here agreed to be identified using their names, as well as by roles, in this chapter.

In response to the first prompt ("the impact of the event series on your life"), Rev. Colleen Hallagan Preuninger noted that, while the original dialogues ("Faith and Gender" and "Faith and Sexuality") occurred in the historic Hall of Languages, "as a central and 'neutral' location," it was important to the coordinators and participants to expand the format and to identify a broader base of support. The coordinators then decided to move the dialogues to Hendricks Chapel. Colleen remarked, "While those spaces had a measure of success, we sought to expand our series to all the chaplaincies . . . and eventually to expand to its current form beginning in the fall of 2015. With each expansion of the form and content and partnerships of the dinner dialogue space came additional complexity, nuance, and intention. The space bloomed, and the relationships between staff, faculty, and students bloomed with it."

She added:

> This space impacted my life (personally and vocationally) in many ways. It helped forge and strengthen personal and professional relationships, it made me increasingly aware of the importance of striving to create accessible spaces (food, space, content, language, etc.). It stretched my work as a chaplain and demonstrated the power of teaching skills of dialogue in an integrated curricular and cocurricular setting. I have brought my experience of cocreating this space with Diane and Bonnie (and others) to my new setting at Shenandoah University. In the spring of 2017, we piloted a dinner dialogue space at Shenandoah University (facilitated by faculty members, planned by a small team of faculty and staff)

heavily influenced by the Syracuse University interfaith dinner
dialogue series we created together.

In May 2017, Kate J. Corbett Pollack received her master's in
cultural foundations of education and a certificate of advanced
study in disability studies at Syracuse University. A regular participant in the interfaith dialogue dinner series, Kate has also acted as
a co-facilitator. She shared a lot of in-depth feedback with us, in
preparation for this chapter. Kate is also the coordinator at the Disability Cultural Center.

With respect to the first prompt, Kate had the following to say:
"The impact the series has had on my life is that I have learned ways
to facilitate conversation in a large group of people from diverse backgrounds. How to keep the conversation flowing, and how to potentially address when someone, perhaps inadvertently, says something
offensive. There are ways to keep the dialogue going smoothly while
still addressing that incident."

Continuing with her vibrant experiential description, Kate noted
the following regarding the second prompt ("the impact of the event
series on your experiences of faith, secularism, and community"):

> I feel that the diverse nature of the groups, and the guide-
> lines and boundaries established at the beginning of each di-
> alogue were helpful in facilitating an actual discussion, not
> just the espousing of judgmental or dogmatic opinions. The
> nature of the topics, themes such as homophobia, racism, Is-
> lamophobia, etc., could potentially turn into biased conversa-
> tions where people were hurt or offended by others. People
> involved in many of the dialogues have been [individuals with]
> marginalized identities, and those facilitating are, too. When
> facilitators are of diverse backgrounds and not from one dom-
> inant identity, that can set a standard for respect and listening
> that a dialogue organized otherwise might not manifest.

Kate further elaborated:

> But people will hopefully feel safe enough to really open up.
> And that is how a great dialogue becomes reality. Otherwise,

people will hold in their real opinions because they do not feel they are in a space where they can be honest without repercussion. If someone, for example, from the group said something racist or Islamophobic, perhaps without even realizing it, because that happens, the Muslim chaplain would address that and guide the conversation to another area. I have seen this done beautifully at the Interfaith Dialogues.

As a member of the Deaf community, Kate had many observations regarding that as well:

There is also always space for the Deaf community. Instead of asking if anyone Deaf might be coming, or expecting us to request interpreters, ASL interpreters are always there. And it is always the same two interpreters, or it has usually been the same two. That kind of precedent is comfortable for me as a Deaf person. I know which interpreters to expect, and I know that I can understand them. Having a different set of interpreters at every dialogue would feel jarring, because not all interpreters sign in the exact same style. It is easier for me to not have to adjust to a new person for each dialogue. Having ASL interpreters as a matter of course at every event means that the Deaf community is going to feel included. I have seen more and more Deaf and hard-of-hearing people come to the dialogues and participate using sign language, or, in some cases, voicing for ourselves. There is no pressure on us to arrange or cancel interpreting. And we know that if we want to sign, the interpreter will voice for us.

Kate added that she appreciated the fact that Diane "let people know about giving Deaf people time to respond and to be mindful of the interpreters." Importantly, Kate noted how conveying information about Deaf culture in a kind way makes everyone, hearing or not, feel more comfortable about how to proceed:

Sometimes, people in general feel like they just should know something, are embarrassed that they don't, and are afraid to ask. Well, everything is a learning experience. This also conveys to Deaf and hard-of-hearing members of the dialogue that they can join in the dialogue and not worry about their method of communicating not being understood. I have been left out of so many group discussions because the facilitator did not know how to manage having a Deaf person in the room. This means that [a] Deaf viewpoint is going to be missing from the conversation. And that viewpoint could potentially be very important. Diverse people have diverse experiences and opinions to offer.

In many respects echoing Kate's perspective, Colleen shared the following in response to the third prompt ("the impact of the event series on your relationships on and off campus"):

One of the greatest strengths of the evolution of these dialogue spaces was the possibility for relational bridging. This program provided opportunities to create and strengthen relationships between faculty, staff, and students across departments, divisions, graduate and undergraduate programs, and more. It offered an opportunity to explore the rich intersections of our communal life and lives. It was challenging and beautiful, and offered the opportunity for formation and growth on all levels (as organizers, facilitators, and participants).

Responding to the third prompt, Kate offered the following example "of how the series has helped in a friendship":

I am in a private, online women's group with friends from all over the country. In some areas of the U.S., things historically have not been diverse. However, more and more people are striving to make their spaces inclusive for an influx of more diverse community members, or just to be more friendly and inclusive in general. One of my friends was curious how her place of employment in Utah could serve diverse food and what that would look like. Drawing from the series [at Syracuse University], I was ready with an answer. My friend was very happy because she had not thought of many of those things, and she was able to take that information back to her place of employment and share that with her supervisor and colleagues.

Considering the fourth prompt ("the relevance of the interfaith and secular 'nature' and structure of the event series"), Colleen said:

> As a clergy person, chaplain, and spiritual leader, I value deeply opportunities to help others explore the intersection of faith/religion/spirituality/worldview/ideology/ethical framework and daily life (including specific timely issues or circumstances explored by the event series). I think this is an essential element of the series because it helps participants bring awareness to the assumptions/beliefs/worldview that informs how they engage in dialogue with others. It teaches skills of articulating their own position or thoughts, but also skills of active listening in dialogue with others. These are skills that are becoming increasingly necessary in our current political climate—yet are rarely taught or modeled. The interfaith dinner dialogue series is one small way that we are teaching and modeling dialogue.

Kate asserted, in response to the fourth prompt:

> Whether or not we realize it, religion can have a profound effect on our beliefs, values, ethics, and ideas. Even if someone is not practicing, somewhere along the line, their family likely was religious and from a particular religious culture or area which has somehow influenced them. Even a mainstream religion like Christianity in the United States is a culture. For those not raised in this dominant culture, ideas that are sometimes put forth as being typical and widely understood and accepted are not typical to everyone. I was having an online conversation with some friends in Texas yesterday about forgiveness. Forgiveness, as these friends knew it, is a very Christian culture idea to me. I was not raised being told anything about forgiveness, or expected to forgive anyone in the way that these friends were. They were both raised Christian, and although one is currently an atheist, she still is very aware of this concept of forgiveness and is able to recognize it within a conversation or topic very quickly, even it if is only subtly applied. I would not necessarily be able to pick that out.

Both Kate and Colleen articulated strong feelings about prompt five, "the value of including a shared meal as well as mindfulness meditation in our gatherings." Colleen said, "The elements of the shared meal and mindfulness meditation are essential to the success of the dialogue space. A shared meal holds sacred meaning in many faith traditions, offering an opportunity to engage with others who have gathered in a way that is nourishing and humanizing. The mindfulness aspect of the event offers those gathered an opportunity to engage with the dialogue content with grounded intention."

Kate noted:

Sharing a meal is great, especially when there is inclusive food. It is nice to be able to just relax and eat with everyone else and know that if you have a food allergy, or you are kosher, etc., you don't have to worry because there will be something hot for you to eat. Not just a couple pieces of lettuce. I think that discussing controversial or difficult subjects is best done on a full stomach. The meditation also is a great way to feel centered before the dialogue starts. Approaching a topic that way, I think, really is calming and better for everyone. The food also brings people to the event. One way to get people to show up to anything is to have food; good food, and plenty of it, if you can make that happen. And, when the food is consistently, every time, kosher, halal, gluten-free, vegan, etc., people will show up to all of your events, and you will also facilitate more diversity that way. Having a hot dinner is a great way to get students to come to an event. We all know students are very busy and often [very hungry] at the end of the day, and many are away from their families for the first time and also away from free, hot meals prepared by someone in the family for them. This can be an adjustment. It can make people feel homesick. I know that there have been undergraduate students who do not often get a free hot meal who come to the event for that experience. A lot of younger people at the university are on their own for the first time. Food is typically a very big deal to most people, and a lot of emotions can surround it. International students in particular have traveled very far from home to attend SU and are often not able to go home on breaks. I think that eating together and having food that you know you can eat is a very human experience, and can remind people of family and friends at home. It might not be [the case] for everyone, but I have seen so many times at the dialogue how this is true. It also is a way for you to get to know the people seated at your table before the dialogue even begins. Eating together is something that most cultures in this world participate in at some level, and inviting someone new to eat with a group is another way that humans connect.

Reflecting on the series as a whole, Rev. Gail Riina, Syracuse University's Lutheran Campus Ministry chaplain, considered her experiences both as an ongoing participant and in terms of her history as a co-facilitator:

I feel our Interfaith Dialogue Dinners are one of the most important things we do at Hendricks Chapel. Because of our long tradition of openness to people of all faiths and no faith, we are in a unique position to bring people together in a space that feels safe to them, to discuss important and sensitive questions, free of political consequences. In the past year, I felt privileged to co-facilitate with a student the dialogue on Black Lives Matter. I gained new insights into the complexity of our unconscious biases.

Dr. Susan D. Pasco, associate director of the Syracuse University Counseling Center, shared:

I attended two of the dialogues. The one on Black Lives Matter brought together students who had really diverse thoughts and levels of awareness and perspectives on race and racial tension. It was productive for students to hear each other and to realize that how we communicate across differences can be done in a safe and respectful way. Too often on our campus, groups of students discussing such topics already agree with each other. Those who might disagree with a dominant perspective remain silent or find another group to talk to. The value of these discussions is that they help people with diverse views to hear each other. The ground rules in this setting promote the idea that it's possible for people to discuss differing views in a respectful way.

Our Model Discussed, in Context

As we were composing this chapter, we received the announcement that the Interfaith Youth Core (IFYC) would again be hosting its Interfaith Leadership Institutes in the summer of 2017. This ongoing initiative is designed to support participants to "get equipped to create a movement for interfaith cooperation on [their] campus." The IFYC, with which Syracuse University has been affiliated for over a decade, upholds religious pluralism as a foundational principle. For IFYC, religious pluralism is part of how the "world" is "characterized," through: (1) respect for people's diverse religious and nonreligious identities; (2) mutually inspiring relationships between people of different backgrounds, and; (3) common action for the common good. Moreover, IFYC asserts that pluralism is "achieved" by two interacting conceptualizations, such that "American college students, supported by their campuses, can be the interfaith leaders needed to make religion a bridge and not a barrier." The two conceptualizations are "the science of interfaith cooperation" and "the art of interfaith leadership." More information about these outstanding and efficacious ideas, and, yes, beliefs, including the "interfaith triangle," can be found on the IFYC website (ifyc.org). In the Interfaith Triangle, "the science of interfaith" rests and thrives simultaneously at the heart of three Venn diagram–like variables: relationships, knowledge, and attitudes.[4]

In many interfaith dialogue spaces with which we have each been engaged historically, the emphasis has been, often, on relationship building, with participants' religious and secular identities as the necessary and understandable starting points to and for interaction. In contrast, our Interfaith Dialogue Dinner Series model at Syracuse University begins with the themes and topics for any given evening; while participants are asked and encouraged to identify or otherwise name their own faith and/or secular traditions, they are neither expected nor required to do so. Interestingly, what often seems to occur is that participants use their religious and secular identities as a means by which to respond to the topics of the evening, the topics thus being utilized as a set of lenses to perceive (not just visually!) the conversational world as it unfolds in the room, each time, but also temporally "across" these gatherings.

Participants as well as facilitators have reported to us anecdotally that our model seems to encourage folks to feel freer than might otherwise be the case to elaborate about the topics in ways that make their spiritual and secular lives become vibrant parts of the intersecting layers of identity formation—as well as the "life" of the discussions themselves—in part precisely because the interfaith dialogue dinner topics have primacy, not the participants' and facilitators' identities or (faith/no faith) self-identifications.

Thus, participants and facilitators from an array of identities and experiences, both privileged and marginalized (or, in some cases, both), inform the conversations about spiritual life and, in connection, the topics addressed, by starting with the topics and, in some sense, "coming to the table" regarding spirituality and secularism, in tandem, if not secondarily. Importantly, many of these identities and experiences often overlap and intersect—a truth that participants and facilitators typically emphasize strongly in our discussions each time. Pagans, Buddhists, Jains, atheists, agnostics, secular humanists, Muslims, Jews, and Christians, among others, gather together to talk about racism, homophobia, ableism, broad definitions of access and inclusion, belonging, and so on.

We also frequently received feedback that folks wished the conversations were longer, with more time and space to "go deep"; however, many have also commented that these dialogues satisfied a need to address topics and then return to them in conversations, not only during subsequent gatherings that we coordinated, but in individuals' professional, academic, and interpersonal lives. Friendships and alliances were formed synergistically during the dialogues, and we noticed many "regulars" who came frequently, if not always, and shared ideas related to spirituality, inclusion, and social justice, regardless of the evening's designated topic or theme.

The series and what we believe is its unique model reflect the values and further the work of the Contemplative Collaborative, an interdisciplinary and multifaceted Hendricks Chapel initiative of which we as authors are both members. As highlighted on our website:

> Syracuse University's Contemplative Collaborative supports students, faculty and staff who engage in contemplative practices, as well as teaching strategies, scholarly research, and discourse surrounding these practices, with the goal of cultivating focused attention in ways that foster insight and deepen understanding of complex issues. The Contemplative Collaborative bridges student life and academic life through a community of faculty, staff, administrators, and students with shared interests in mindfulness and contemplative practices that embody engaged learning, a mindful academy, and compassionate society. This community is comprised of more than 140 members, representing diverse disciplines and offices across the University.[5]

In conclusion, we feel it is important to highlight that the Interfaith Dialogue Dinner Series at Syracuse University has been one of many pragmatic approaches adopted to emphasize that mindfulness and contemplation play important and much-needed roles in campus life. We hope to continue to break bread together for a long time, with diverse participants, addressing difficult while necessary and potentially life changing subjects. And we hope that other campuses will consider adopting similar approaches in their own labors of love.

Notes

1 "Syracuse University History: History of the Founding of Syracuse University," Syracuse University Archives, accessed December 15, 2017, http://archives.syr.edu/history/founding_su.html.

2 Syracuse University Hendricks Chapel website, accessed November 8, 2017, http://hendricks.syr.edu/.

3 See Kelly Homan Rodoski, "Interfaith Dialogue Series Will Explore Issues Raised by Social Movements," Syracuse University News, *Campus & Community*, September 19,

2016, https://news.syr.edu/2016/09/interfaith-dialogue-series-will-explore-issues-raised-by-social-movements-93908/.

4   Interfaith Youth Core, https://www.ifyc.org/about.

5   "Contemplative Collaborative," Syracuse University Hendricks Chapel website, accessed November 8, 2017, http://hendricks.syr.edu/services-and-initiatives/contemplative-collaborative.html.

9

Spiritual Diversity and Mindfulness

A Pathway to Inclusion on a University Campus

Gladys Childs and Dennis Hall

This chapter focuses on the various aspects that come into play when considering the spiritual milieu on a university campus. We consider mindfulness to be a key component when designing initiatives, experiences, and extra or cocurricular activities. If the student experience is a patchwork, mindfulness can be the thread that sews it together into a quilt. We examine the challenges associated with the naiveté of other religious perspectives, the allotment of resources and space, the celebration of diverse holy days, and the multifaceted nature of student need. The interplay between student and spiritual life offices is crucial in identifying and meeting those needs and, as such, we also explore this dynamic.

Interfaith relations in campus ministry can be difficult to maneuver. Moreover, developing spiritual programming and activities that reach out to the entirety of the student body at a Christian university can be challenging when there is a need to address interfaith issues. Some of the questions heard from students, faculty, and staff are:

- How can I maintain my faith while reaching out to others?
- Are different faiths mutually exclusive?
- Do we need to have a Christian chapel service?
- Is it still okay to pray over a meal?
- If we want to have a prayer time, is it okay to pray aloud? What if something we pray offends others?
- Am I correct that all religions are saying basically the same thing?
- What about non-Christian holy days? How do we honor these?

With these questions and more in mind, university chaplains can have a difficult task of trying to meet the expectations of students from various faith or non-faith backgrounds.

Student affairs professionals, similarly, are charged with facilitating the holistic development of students. At a private, Christian institution, the role of spirituality is expected to be nurtured. Spiritual identity development applies to all students, not solely Christians. At our small and highly diversified campus, at Texas Wesleyan University in Fort Worth, such development applies to a wide swath of individuals, many of whom are, indeed, not Christian. The diversity of our student body heightens the need for interfaith collaborations and intentionality. By engaging with students with intentionality and mindfulness, communities such as ours can progress from a state of diversity into a state of inclusiveness.

To move from a state of diversity into a state of inclusiveness, it is important to identify what "interfaith" and "mindfulness" mean on our campus. Students on our campus routinely state that "interfaith" means all faiths are saying the same things, and one should not think their faith is better than another. Some students and faculty have shared that they have understood interfaith to mean supporting other religions while denying or downplaying their own. With these

past experiences, the exploration and development of interfaith programming on campus naturally leads to trepidation in many individuals. So how can leaders in higher education reconcile the need for
hospitality when the people coming to the table for discussion have
different ideas of how interfaith is defined and what religions are all
about? It behooves spiritual and student life offices on campuses to
define what interfaith means in their context. For our purposes, we
define interfaith cooperation as individuals of various faith traditions
fully standing in and living out their beliefs while seeking to learn from
religious perspectives different from their own.

Mindfulness has been defined as the ability to focus on one's
thoughts, feelings, and perceptions of moments in an emotionally
nonreactive manner.[1] This concept has framed the approach to providing an intentional, meaningful, and educational experience for students as it relates to diversity and inclusion. The ideas of mindfulness
have been shown to enhance the cognitive and social-emotional development of students, which is the cornerstone of higher education.[2]

Mindfulness in Designing Student Experience

The topic of student success continues to be a prominent one in
higher education research and literature. The successful student is
considered the output of colleges and universities, and as the market-
place of higher education becomes more competitive, accountability
for institutional outputs will only increase.[3] The field of higher education has seen the effect of this increase in accountability from the
Obama institutional report card to performance-based funding. This
leaves practitioners with the question of how best to structure a ho-
listically supportive and meaningful experience that facilitates student
success. Research conducted over the past decade by Angela Duckworth has indicated students are more successful when they display
grit in the forms of passion and perseverance.[4] This creates a natural
tie-in for approaches that include the tenets of mindfulness. Studies
have shown that mindfulness activities and behaviors are positively
associated with students' perseverance and resiliency.[5] This inferred

relationship then becomes a promising practice in the higher educational landscape that is ever evolving and increasingly competitive.

The inclusion of mindfulness into student-related initiatives, experiences, and cocurricular experiences, specifically as it relates to diversity and spirituality, does not require additional resources, funding, or time. Doing so requires prioritization of these concepts and the perception that value is added when they are utilized. The concept of mindfulness has been used in a number of different student experiences, including student leader trainings, service-learning, and various programs and events that have been hosted.

The first implementation of the tenets found within the concept of mindfulness occurred with a captive audience—student leaders. "Student leader" is a broad category with application to many students as well as one that possesses the potential to reach a much wider range of students across campus. The concepts of mindfulness were incorporated into resident assistant trainings, Greek life leadership symposiums, student life ambassador in-services, and orientation leader trainings. Mindfulness theory addresses awareness of context in the present moment. Mindfulness develops from comparing experiences that broaden the understanding of a situation by keeping an open mind to alternative perspectives.[6] Training is a way to develop competence in any given area, and as it relates to spiritual diversity on campus, one competency expected from our student leaders is the ability to contribute to a welcoming and inclusive community. Doing so requires individuals to engage in mindful behavior when presented with dissonant information. As such, mindfulness is foundational to inclusivity training and is evident in our approach.

As part of an institution founded in the Methodist tradition, social justice is critical to our mission and vision. Social justice, though, is not a unique attribute of Christianity or any one specific faith group. One strategy to engage students in a social justice arena has been the service-learning opportunities. Alternative spring break is one primary example of such service learning. The growth and development of participants is necessary to truly provide an experience that is service-learning. Similar to our efforts with student leader training, ASB participants had an experience that included facilitated reflection, diversity and inclusion training, and exposure to a myriad of differences among those served. Mindfulness, again, benefits the student experience within the vein of diversity including spiritual diversity.

To demonstrate open-mindedness, which is central to mindfulness, one must be exposed to experiences that fall outside one's comfort zone. In our previous examples, we have done so for targeted and somewhat captive audiences based on their roles on campus. General student activities and programs, however, can potentially posit learning outcomes associated with spiritual inclusivity.

As a chaplain and dean of students, we believe it is crucial for the student and spiritual life offices of campuses to work together to deal with issues of spiritual diversity and spiritual growth. With the myriad of student needs and the resources and knowledge available to each area, a combined effort will provide a better and more enriched environment.

As practitioners, we have discovered that the use of mindfulness plays a vital role when considering how best to serve the students and their interests. This practice has been demonstrated through numerous partnerships, including an interfaith prayer room, common meal, resident assistant training, student life ambassador trainings, service-learning opportunities, and numerous individual referrals in order to provide individualized support and guidance. The collaborative nature between the two functional areas of student and spiritual life adds to the inclusive culture on campus, but it has not been without its challenges.

Personal Challenges

In cowriting this chapter, it was important to include my (Gladys) own struggles of coming to an interfaith understanding as I have found colleagues to be wrestling with similar issues. In my tenure as the chaplain, I have struggled with all the needs, questions, and demands of our campus's interfaith strivings. It took me a year and a half of wrestling with these issues and attending interfaith conferences to find the place of balance between my own personal faith and the needs of a diverse student body. The big shift that finally focused me and put everything into place was while attending a recent Academy of Spiritual Formation where there was a major focus on hospitality.

On the first day, Amy Oden, a professor at Saint Paul School of Theology, discussed the idea of being a stranger and what that means. As part of a longer discussion, Dr. Oden said, "To be a stranger is a universal human experience and one in which there is vulnerability." In light of this idea, she asked us to reflect and consider the following questions, "What are the risks you are willing to take to welcome the other? What are the risks you want to be willing to take to welcome the stranger?"[7]

Participants then spent the next hour contemplating the question of what are the risks they would be willing to take. Near the end of this time, I realized that I did not want to be hospitable, as many of my prior interfaith experiences had been negative and often negated my own Christian faith. This thought then led me to the question of "How can I offer hospitality to others while maintaining my Christian faith?" Once our group reassembled, it was time for sharing, and I went up to the mike and told the whole room my struggles—that I did not want to be hospitable, but how can I do that and live out my Christianity fully and without guilt?

No matter what my feelings are, the reality is, I am in a climate that demands interfaith cooperation and promotion. So, how do I deal with the shifting sands of my environment without selling out? I am called to offer hospitality, but how? Upon further reflection and recalling the previous night's conversation with another participant in the spiritual formation retreat, I realized that I needed to pick my battles. As a professor and chaplain, I truly want students to feel welcome on campus; I want them to find a home. Part of that finding a home is to have their faith background welcomed and recognized. To be the chaplain is to offer interfaith programming; it is our university's culture. However, I can draw the line when people are trying to minimize our university's Christian heritage or when people are naively or purposefully maligning the truths of the Christian faith. With this, I can have balance, but I had to determine what the non-negotiables are.

Once I discovered this for myself, I felt open to being not only mindful of other faith perspectives but free to offer hospitality. It is because I am a Christian that I want to be considerate and engage other faith perspectives. It is because I am a Christian that I am willing to support a prayer/meditation room that is welcoming to all. It is because I am a Christian that I want to incorporate various faiths' religious holidays into our school calendar. However, because I am Christian and work at a United Methodist–affiliated university, we will continue to hold a weekly Christian worship service. Yet, I will seek opportunities to promote opportunities for other religious modes of worship and occasions for various faiths to come together and learn from one another.

With these realizations, I found a place of peace within myself. I am Christian; I am not going to apologize for it or for the priority we place, as a United Methodist–affiliated campus, on Christian-related events. However, there will be a weekly interfaith gathering and opportunities for different forms of religious expressions throughout the school year.

Celebration of Diverse Holy Days

In a country where Christianity is the dominant religion, it is natural that university calendars are organized around Christian holidays. However, considering the religiously diverse nature of many campuses, being mindful of holy days outside of the Christian tradition is important if we are to meet the needs of our student body. In an age when student retention is critical, this is another factor to consider when looking at the university calendar.

Abo-Zena states, "Religious minorities may alternately feel proud, unique, marginalized, unwelcomed, ashamed, or targeted."[8] On a higher education campus, it is our job to make students feel welcome and part of the campus community. One easy way to be mindful and welcoming is to recognize the major holy days of the various faith groups on campus. How one goes about recognizing these days can vary. Following are some options:

1. Including the major holy days on the campus calendar

2. Recognizing major holy days in internal institutional publications, such as weekly faculty/staff/student emails or newspaper publications

3. Allowing students to request permission to miss class on major holy days, with the expectation they make up work missed

4. Not scheduling homework or exams on all major holy days

An example of this change in policy comes from former Illinois governor Pat Quinn, who signed a bill that would permit college students to reschedule tests or assignments if they conflict with religious holiday observances.[9]

If educators and higher education administrators would think about the recognition of diverse holy days as the challenges faced by academia when they first began to address issues of race and gender, the transition could be made smoother. Imagine being the only Muslim on a Catholic university campus or the lone Sikh at a small Methodist college. We need to address religious diversity with the same zeal with which we tackle other aspects of multiculturalism on campus. A good way to begin is by integrating religious diversity discussions into other established diversity programming and classes dealing with this subject. Expanding the diversity dialogue to include religious differences adds depth to what being diverse means.

This does not mean that historically Christian universities must change everything they are doing or ignore or downplay their university's religious heritage. At Texas Wesleyan we only have two regularly scheduled weekly spiritual life programs: chapel and common meal. Chapel is a Christian worship service, and common meal is an interfaith gathering. As a United Methodist–affiliated institution, our

Christian heritage is important to us, and as such, we will continue to offer a Christian worship service and other Christian programming, such as Fellowship of Christian Athletes. Prayer will still occur before many of our activities. However, the spiritual life office does list, on the website, numerous faith communities in our area for students to get involved. We will stress healthy interfaith relationships, and we will support the prayer/meditation room and not put any specific faith symbol(s) on the walls so all will feel welcome. Moreover, we will continually challenge ourselves and the larger campus community to find ways we all can learn from faiths other than our own. Moreover, we will challenge religious naiveté on campus.

Naiveté of Religious Perspectives

Naiveté of religious perspectives is detrimental, as religions and religious beliefs have a prominent influence in all aspects of life. In today's global socioeconomic market, it is imperative to have some depth of understanding of the major world religions. Religious pluralism is here to stay, and no matter what faith background one comes from (or none), it is critical to develop an interfaith understanding. Madeleine Albright, in her book *The Mighty and the Almighty*, discusses her tenure as secretary of state for the Clinton administration. She notes the overwhelming nature of not understanding the major world religions, as religious issues are at the core of many conflicts internationally. This lack of interfaith information is a barrier to international relationships between countries. Naively, she and others in the State Department felt that democratic understanding of governance would unite countries, when culture and creed ever widen the divide.[10]

Numerous studies have been done on the lack of knowledge individuals have regarding religions.[11] Moreover, this does not improve when one investigates the followers of particular faiths. A general lack of basic knowledge regarding faith traditions and beliefs is rampant. Stephen Prothero, in his book *Religious Literacy*, discovered in relation to the Christian faith that most Americans cannot name one of the Gospels, only one-third identified Jesus as delivering the Sermon on the Mount, and 10 percent believe Noah's wife was Joan of Arc. Astoundingly, and most relevant to this research study, is Prothero's claim that devout Christians are, on average, at least as ignorant about the facts of Christianity as are other Americans. So, how do we inform ourselves and the students we serve?

On religiously affiliated campuses, the task is made somewhat easier, as most of these types of institutions require that one or more religion courses be taken. Encouraging students to take a course outside of their own understanding or a course that covers multiple religious perspectives should be encouraged. The tendency is for students to want to take a religion course they are familiar with or one for which they do not have any negative connotations attached. Advisors should be made aware of students' religious tendencies and help push them out of their comfort zones.

Other options are to take advantage of lecture series or annual university events to promote religious understanding. Having a panel discussion with religious leaders from different backgrounds, inviting speakers from diverse religious perspectives to campus on a rotating basis, or offering regular lunch-and-learn sessions where the campus community can come together and learn about various faiths can help promote a deeper understanding of differing religions. A final option would be to take advantage of the school's newspaper/media outlets to foster an awareness of why a basic understanding of various faiths is critical in being productive citizens and human beings.

Administrators, faculty, and staff also need to have specific training on how to relate with students from various faiths. As new employees are brought into an institution, this is a perfect time to provide faith sensitivity training. Offer lunch and learns to foster basic understandings of major religions. Perhaps the spiritual and student life offices could hold department-specific interfaith training. At Texas Wesleyan, our interfaith effort began with the president's office. A group of administrators, faculty, staff, and students were brought together to explore various ways to talk about interfaith and diversity issues and how to promote an upcoming visit from Eboo Patel, president and founder of the Interfaith Youth Core, and how we could encourage ongoing discussions.

The Challenge of Resources

Working at a small, private, enrollment-driven institution such as Texas Wesleyan University, the primary challenge to any functional area is resources. On our campus, those challenges include not only financial resources but space allocations as well. Developing a sustainable interfaith prayer room that is accessible and approachable to all students was not as simple as it may sound. In its first iteration, the prayer room was housed in a conference room in the campus's fitness center. The access to bathrooms was a plus; but in practice, providing access to all students was a barrier. The use of the prayer room caused a disruption in service to the students using the fitness center, as the locker rooms were overused. Moreover, the lack of privacy created an all-too-public prayer space. Quickly, it became evident a better solution was needed.

The second iteration of the interfaith prayer room was found in one of the residence halls. The space was private and had access to bathrooms, both very positive variables. However, issues mounted as access to a residential building was difficult for nonresidential students. As we found ways to provide open access, intangible barriers existed, preventing students from feeling comfortable when entering a residence hall. The desire of an interfaith prayer room to be welcoming and accessible was not met and, again, a better solution was needed.

Our university library then became home to the interfaith prayer room. Our colleagues in the library were accommodating and willing to provide space that could be cordoned off to create a welcome, open, private, and accessible space for students desiring a place to pray. This new location was in close proximity to restrooms, and we were given permission to provide towels and slippers in the restrooms to maintain cleanliness. However, the space allotment became temporary, as library renovations required the interfaith prayer room to be removed. This created a need for another solution.

The fourth, and hopefully final, iteration of the prayer room came in the form of a repurposed space in our campus center. Centrally located, accessible, and private, this newly renovated space is ideal for an interfaith prayer room. Landing on this long-term solution, though, included numerous lessons. Along the way, student and spiritual life relied heavily on student input and involvement to try and meet the multitude of desires and needs from our student body.

Another challenge involves financial resources. Within these collaborations, priorities must be set in order to know what resources are used for what purposes. This has led to the paradigm of approaching programmatic efforts as more meaningful as opposed to simply adding to the ever-growing list of requirements. In other words, we consistently try to add connections to spiritual diversity in the programs and events that we already coordinate. A primary example has been the alternative spring break program introduced to our campus in 2015. The cocurricular learning outcomes of alternative spring break include reflection and connection to one's spiritual development. While Texas Wesleyan University is steeped in the Methodist tradition, including the tenet of social justice, the framing of spiritual development and growth can apply to all interfaith students.

The final challenge of resources facing many institutions, including our own, is the time and energy of professional staff members. The staff in the areas of student and spiritual life have numerous and varied responsibilities. As with any other finite resource, any effort on one project or task means time and energy not spent on another. While this specific challenge cannot be called unique to our school, we have actively prioritized the work described here. That prioritization must be guided, or at least supported, by institutional leadership.

Challenges of Students' Needs

The higher education landscape commonly associates *need* with financial resources available to students. While this is certainly true at our institution, it is but one form of need that our students bring with them. Our small, private university boasts tremendous diversity within its student body, including spiritual, ethnic, nationality, socioeconomic status, age, and ability. Each affinity group can be presumed to have its own sets of needs based on the affiliation. However, when one examines the student body individual by individual as opposed to by classifications, student need grows exponentially.

Assessing students' developmental level, in order to provide appropriately structured experiences, is perhaps the biggest barrier. The metrics for these levels vary greatly and can include cognitive, emotional, social, identity, and academic development. At our institution, much of this assessment is qualitative in nature and largely based on the relationships already in place within our many communities.

Compounding the issue of these needs is the appropriate delivery. A seminal student development theory that persists more than sixty years after its initial publication is the Sanford Challenge and Support Theory.[12] A basic interpretation of this theory is that students grow when provided a balance of both challenge and support. That point of balance, and thus the avoidance of debilitation and complacency, varies for each individual just as their other developmental factors do. With this in mind, it is important to include spirituality and interfaith issues as part of a student's basic needs on campus.

Summary

In summary, spirituality and mindfulness on college and university campuses is foundational to offering students a thorough and well-balanced education. The global and multicultural nature of our world demands that graduates have at least a basic understanding of the need for religious literacy and interfaith cooperation.

While each campus is unique and has its own specific set of challenges and opportunities, it is imperative that the spiritual and student life offices join forces to work together to welcome all students and provide opportunities to support them as they inquire about their own faith and the faith of others. With limited resources, a joint front will provide a stronger network for student support and educational opportunities and programming that reach out to faculty, staff, and administrators. Moreover, if institutional presidents and cabinets would take the lead to encourage interfaith learning and cooperation, the educational benefits would be greater. Our students, and eventual graduates, will be better prepared to navigate and thrive in increasingly diversified communities and workplaces. Such preparation is integral to our institutional mission to produce competent global citizens.

No longer is it viable or sustainable to only focus on one specific faith group, even if a campus is faith affiliated. Programming and education for students, faculty, and staff regarding various faith traditions as well as interfaith understandings and opportunities are necessary to provide broad, meaningful, and relevant educational settings.

Notes

1 J. Kabat-Zinn, "Mindfulness-Based Interventions in Context: Past, Present, and Future," *Clinical Psychology: Science and Practice* 10 (2003): 144–56.

2 K. A. Schonert-Reichl et al. "Enhancing Cognitive and Social-Emotional Development through a Simple-to-Administer Mindfulness-Based School Program for Elementary School Children: A Randomized Controlled Trial," *Developmental Psychology* 51, no. 1 (2015): 52–66.

3 W. W. McMahon, *Higher Learning, Greater Good* (Baltimore: Johns Hopkins University Press, 2009).

4 A. Duckworth, *Grit: The Power of Passion and Perseverance* (New York: Scribner, 2016).

5 Schonert-Reichl, et al., "Enhancing Cognitive and Social-Emotional Development."

6 S. H. Carson and E. Langer, "Mindfulness and Self-Acceptance," *Journal of Rational -Emotive and Cognitive-Behavior Therapy* 24, no. 1 (2006): 29–43.

7 Amy Oden, lecture, Academy for Spiritual Formation, Fruitland Park, FL, March 6, 2017.

8 Mona M. Abo-Zena, "Faith from the Fringes," *Phi Delta Kappan* 93, no. 4 (December 2011): 15–19.

9 "Illinois Students Get Religious Liberty Protections," *Church & State* 65, no. 9 (2012): 22.

10 Madeleine Albright, *The Mighty and the Almighty: Reflections on America, God, and World Affairs* (New York: HarperCollins, 2007), 8–9.

11 S. D. Parks, *Big Questions, Worthy Dreams: Mentoring Young Adults in their Search for Meaning, Purpose, and Faith* (San Francisco: Jossey-Bass, 2000); S. Prothero, *Religious Literacy: What Every American Needs to Know—and Doesn't* (San Francisco: Harper, 2007); R. C. Spach, "Addressing the Identity-Relevance Dilemma: Religious Particularity and Pluralism at Presbyterian Church-Related Colleges," *Religion & Education* 34, no. 2 (2007): 55–76.

12 N. Sanford, *The American College* (New York: Wiley, 1962).

Sources

Abo-Zena, Mona M. Faith from the Fringes. *Phi Delta Kappan* 93, no. 4 (2011): 15–19.

Albright, Madeleine. *The Mighty and the Almighty: Reflections on America, God, and World Affairs*. New York: HarperCollins, 2007.

Carson, S. H., and E. Langer. "Mindfulness and Self-Acceptance." *Journal of Rational-Emotive and Cognitive-Behavior Therapy* 24, no. 1 (2006): 29–43.

Dalton, J., and P. Crosby. "Let's Talk about Religious Differences: The Neglected Topic in Diversity Discussions on Campus." *Journal of College & Character* 9, no. 2 (2007): 1–4.

Duckworth, A. *Grit: The Power of Passion and Perseverance*. New York: Scribner, 2016.

"Illinois Students Get Religious Liberty Protections." *Church & State* 65, no. 9 (2012): 22.

Kabat-Zinn, J. "Mindfulness-Based Interventions in Context: Past, Present, and Future." *Clinical Psychology: Science and Practice* 10 (2003): 144–56.

McMahon, W. W. *Higher Learning, Greater Good*. Baltimore: Johns Hopkins University Press, 2009.

Oden, Amy. Lecture presented at the Academy of Spiritual Formation, Fruitland Park, FL, March 6, 2017.

Parks, S. D. *Big Questions, Worthy Dreams: Mentoring Young Adults in Their Search for Meaning, Purpose, and Faith*. San Francisco: Jossey-Bass, 2000.

Prothero, Stephen. *Religious Literacy: What Every American Needs to Know—and Doesn't*. San Francisco: Harper, 2007.

Sanford, N. *The American College*. New York: Wiley, 1962.

Schonert-Reichl, K. A., E. Oberle, M. S. Lawlor, D. Abbott, K. Thomson, T. F. Oberlander, and A. Diamond. "Enhancing Cognitive and Social-Emotional Development through a Simple-to-Administer Mindfulness-Based School Program for Elementary School Children: A Randomized Controlled Trial." *Developmental Psychology* 51, no. 1 (2015): 52–66.

Spach, R. C. "Addressing the Identity-Relevance Dilemma: Religious Particularity and Pluralism at Presbyterian Church-Related Colleges." *Religion & Education* 34, no. 2 (2007): 55–76.

Striving for Mission Integration

Catholic Identity, Social Justice, and Interfaith Inclusivity

Nicholas Rademacher

M any faith-based institutions of higher education are confronted today with the challenge of preserving and enhancing their specific religious identity, while at the same time taking seriously the increasing religious diversity of the student body, staff, and faculty. There are many pressures that could lead a community to allow their mission to drift. For example, market-driven considerations could compel campus leaders to downplay the religious identity of the institution. Likewise, something as benign as forgetting or being ignorant of the religious identity of a faith-based institution could lead to its disappearance. Living the mission is essential, of course, while knowing and being the mission are fundamental to that living. Indeed, deliberate and careful reflection on and communication of the meaning and significance of the mission and identity of a college or university is necessary to carry forward, across succeeding generations, the most important reason for and purpose of the institution.

In this chapter, I share a response to this challenge undertaken by a Catholic, liberal arts institution of higher education located in the northeastern region of the United States, namely Cabrini University.[1] Specifically, I recount several university-wide initiatives as well as an approach I have implemented in the classroom to address the matter of mission integration noted previously. Of course, what is presented here is but one perspective, and there are many ways the university is tending to its mission other than what could possibly be shared in a short article such as this one. In any event, I write from my perspective as a faculty member in the Department of Religious Studies who has been immersed in university-level mission and identity questions for over a decade. This chapter represents a synthesis of a number of discrete projects that, when taken together, point to a more comprehensive illustration of mission integration work than any one of them alone might disclose.

The first section of this chapter introduces the journey of a particular student who was uneasy about the faith dimension of his religious studies course. The questions and concerns he raised in that class reflect tensions that exist among other students and even other members of the campus community beyond the student body. The second section of this chapter traces in broad strokes the ways the Cabrini University community has lived its mission with reference to its Catholic, interfaith, and social justice dimensions, leading up to the development of an interfaith course sequence. The subsequent two sections of the chapter address the foundational matter of deliberate and careful reflection on and communication of the meaning and significance of the mission and identity. Here, attention turns to Pope Francis's "culture of encounter" and the intersection of Catholic identity, social justice activism, and interfaith cooperation for the common good in the lives of Dorothy Day and Thomas Merton. Attention to exemplars of mission integration such as these two figures, who joined knowing, being, and doing their religious tradition in their own lives and in their public activities, helps to communicate what it might mean for a university community to integrate its mission in a way that takes seriously its religious identity, interfaith commitment, and contribution to the common good. The chapter concludes by pointing to the remaining work to be done with respect to engaging on a deeper level the intersection of essential components of an institution's mission and identity.

Recognizing the Challenge of Faith-Based Conversation

"Wayne" met with me privately during office hours at the midpoint of a course that explored the intersection of "faith" and "justice." He wanted to discuss his indecision over whether to remain in the class. He connected to the justice dimension of the course, which reflected his passion for pursuing the common good with all people of goodwill. He was devoted to a number of social justice causes, both in courses and through extracurricular activities. Yet he remained uncertain about how to address the faith dimension of the course, a topic that for him was profoundly personal. Even though we had been talking about faith from the broadest possible perspective, inclusive of people with religious commitments and those who eschewed such identification, he feared that he would be rejected by his peers if he openly expressed his identity as an atheist. The diverse band of students enrolled in that class, largely choosing this course to fulfill a core curriculum requirement, had been able to respectfully address many potentially divisive topics. Yet this young man did not feel comfortable openly identifying himself as an atheist before them. While Wayne knew there was no requirement for him to broach the subject in class, he felt that if he remained in the course, he would feel moved to address it at some point. He sought advice on how to proceed.

To what to attribute his misgivings? A tentative, unscientific analysis of the context in which Wayne and I attempted to sort out his dilemma highlights three challenges of teaching interfaith understanding. First, his reservations seemed to emerge, in part, from the generally low level of religious literacy among the student body. There was no working, shared vocabulary according to which we might be able to respectfully discuss religious/nonreligious difference. We had to start from scratch. Second, many of the students identified with a particular religious tradition, even if they admitted that they did not practice it. They seemed to expect that their peers would acknowledge the existence of some kind of higher power. Third, unlike Wayne, many of the students lacked practice in critical self-reflection on the values and commitments that guided their lives. An intelligent and sensitive young man, Wayne recognized himself as an exception to this norm.

While I did not have a simple answer for Wayne, we were able to find a way for him to proceed. I introduced him to resources from the Interfaith Youth Core and their alumni. Specifically, he found inspiration in the work of Chris Stedman, whose book *Faitheist: How an Atheist Found Common Ground with the Religious*, as well as his activity on social media.[2] Wayne became involved in the nascent interfaith club on campus where he became increasingly comfortable talking about his value system and his commitments without reference to a religious tradition. We continued to meet to discuss local and global events in light of our course content. Ultimately, before the semester was out, he chose to speak to his atheist identity in class. His position did raise questions from his peers who had not encountered a "serious" atheist, as one student described Wayne's commitments in an anonymous end-of-year reflection. Yet, ultimately, they were able to accept his convictions and to continue to welcome him into the classroom community.

While this situation had a fortunate ending, persistent questions arise each time I approach the class in which Wayne's journey transpired years earlier. How do we proceed with honest and meaningful conversation on/around/about interfaith understanding given widespread illiteracy on world religious traditions and frequent exclusion of atheism and secular humanism from this topic? How do we invite students into this conversation given their general inexperience in critical self-reflection on their own convictions and value systems?

Are there ways to ensure that students feel comfortable with these conversations about faith among their peers, especially those who adhere to traditions that are outside of the mainstream? How and in what ways can resources around Catholic identity, interfaith dialogue, and social justice be presented to demonstrate an integrated vision in line with the mission and identity of the university? While we can strive to create an inclusive classroom and campus community and reassure students that they are in a safe space, it is extremely difficult to know where they are with respect to their own comfort level in addressing these questions in themselves or among their peers. Many of the same questions extend beyond the classroom to other dimensions of students' experience across colleges campuses where questions of faith are live matters.

The Interfaith Movement at a Catholic Institution of Higher Education

The mission statement at Cabrini University has a title, "Education of the Heart." This expression emerges from the writings of St. Frances Xavier Cabrini (1850–1917), the founder of the Missionary Sisters of the Sacred Heart of Jesus (MSC). The MSCs are the sponsoring congregation of Cabrini University. The university revised its mission statement nearly ten years ago, to shorten it and simplify it. The mission statement emerged through a long process of conversation with numerous stakeholders, including students, staff, administrators, faculty, alumnae, and members of the board of trustees. The outcome affirms that Cabrini University is a Catholic institution where community members of all faiths, cultures, and backgrounds are welcome in the pursuit of academic excellence, leadership development, and social justice. In many respects, the essential elements of the distilled version of the university's mission are the same goals of many institutions of higher education, including academic excellence and leadership development. The university's Catholic identity, commitment to social justice, and welcome of learners of all faiths, cultures, and backgrounds points toward that which makes the mission of the institution unique. While the mission statement is simple, it is amplified in the university's Catholic identity statement, core values, core curriculum, and cocurricular activities.

Once revised, responses to the mission statement were mixed. For some, the social justice mission was a potential roadblock, viewed as unappealing to prospective students and their parents, whose first aim is to "get a job." They wondered what social justice might have to do with that objective. A similar question was raised with respect to the Catholic identity of the university. For some, matters pertaining to the religious dimension of the university are irrelevant to contemporary higher education and professional training. Major challenges remained: how to mediate these perspectives to the community in a holistic way, promoting Catholic identity, social justice, and the welcome of learners of all faiths, cultures, and backgrounds so that it infuses students' experience across campus?

The Cabrini University mission statement situates the campus community at the intersection of religious difference, cultural diversity, and the many ways that people understand social justice while unequivocally affirming its Catholic identity. In mission institutes for faculty, the university community has explored the relevance of the mission statement from an interfaith perspective. Diana Eck's writing on the shift from "diversity" to "pluralism" is one way that some members of the university community have informally articulated an understanding of interfaith studies, with its emphasis on constructive dialogue, developing knowledge of difference, striving to foster and facilitate common understanding, while sustaining and respecting the distinctiveness of one's own tradition.[3] Furthermore, some members of the university community have promoted a broad notion of faith that is inclusive of people with explicit religious commitments and those who do not identify with a particular religious tradition. In many ways, these perspectives reflect the university's "Charter of Core Values," which emphasizes respect for diversity; innovation and creativity; a community of dialogue and belonging; and dedication to excellence.

The Cabrini University community has become increasingly intentional about acknowledging its Catholic identity and exploring its interfaith commitments as part of its dedication to academic excellence, leadership development, and social justice education. Among other places, it has been integrated into the curriculum in the Religious Studies Department and through interdisciplinary initiatives, such as the social justice minor and the Voices of Justice living and learning community.[4] The university's partnership with Catholic Relief Services provides students an invaluable opportunity to learn alongside and collaborate with a faith-based agency that serves the world's most vulnerable populations on the basis of need, not creed, race, or nationality.[5] The university participated in President Obama's Interfaith and Community Service Campus Challenge. Students have taken initiative, too, by founding an interfaith club.

In the Justice Matters core curriculum at Cabrini University, as explained in official university material, faculty accompany students through a sequence of developmentally linked courses that involve students' reflection on their own values and commitments in relation to the communities to which they belong.[6] Over their four years, they contribute to community partnerships and address systemic change through community-based learning and advocacy. While they may encounter or engage interfaith dimensions of justice matters in these courses, the students most explicitly engage the topic of religion and faith through the "religious literacy" component of the core curriculum. Students are required to take one three-credit course that addresses the meaning and significance of lived religious traditions, with an emphasis on the Catholic intellectual tradition. This curriculum is undertaken in conversation with the student's own belief system. The core curriculum's emphasis on self-knowledge, community engagement, and advocacy has provided a rich context within which to grow the interfaith dimension of the university's mission.

The collaboration between Cabrini University and the Interfaith Youth Core (IFYC) points to this university's commitment to the interfaith movement. The collaboration between the university and IFYC dates back to 2010, when a small delegation of faculty and students attended and participated in the IFYC "Leadership for a Religiously

Diverse World" conference at Northwestern University in Evanston, Illinois. That same year, the university hosted an IFYC interfaith training session on campus to introduce faculty, staff, and student leaders to the practice of interfaith dialogue. Subsequently, the university participated in the President's Interfaith and Community Service Campus Challenge. The university conducted a Campus Religious and Spiritual Climate Survey in 2013. Faculty and students have attended IFYC Interfaith Leadership Institutes (ILI). An ILI alumna created an interfaith club on campus. In 2013, all first-year students read Eboo Patel's *Acts of Faith* as a prelude to Patel's visit to campus to address students, staff, and faculty on the meaning and significance of the interfaith movement. More recently, the university has worked closely with IFYC to develop an interfaith learning community and an interfaith course sequence.

This consistent collaboration has been facilitated by a shared vision. The IFYC is guided by three central ideas that profoundly resonate with Cabrini University's mission of an "education of the heart": respecting religious identity; fostering mutually inspiring relationships; and undertaking common action for the common good.[7] When Eboo Patel delivered the commencement address before the class of 2016, his message urged the graduating students to carry on the mission of the university in their future careers. His address was also an important reminder and call to action for the faculty and staff who live the education of the heart in their professional lives at the university.

During the 2016–2017 academic year, faculty from the liberal arts, including American Studies and Religious Studies, and preprofessional programs, including business, education, communication, and social work, undertook the revision of the university's long-standing social justice minor with the assistance of an IFYC and Teagle Foundation Interfaith and Pre-Professional Curricular Grant. This grant provided the necessary resources to shape already existing but disparate interfaith curricular and cocurricular learning initiatives into a coherent and comprehensive course sequence. Together, the faculty from within liberal arts and preprofessional programs shaped an interdisciplinary course sequence that aims to facilitate student learning around interfaith and social justice topics. Ultimately, this collaboration has assisted members of the Cabrini University community to examine its understanding of the interfaith movement, which largely finds expression through its mission and identity, in the curricular and cocurricular opportunities afforded to students and in the lives and work of individual students, staff, and faculty.

The work for this grant started on a firm foundation. Partnership between liberal arts and preprofessional faculty and programs has long been characteristic of the Cabrini University community. The core curriculum, Justice Matters, is but one area in which faculty work together. Courses in the social justice minor have been taught in collaboration with, among other individuals, faculty in the religious studies, communications, education, sociology, and American studies programs. Additional examples of partnership between liberal arts and preprofessional faculty or programs could be cited through living and learning communities, minors, certificate programs, and other initiatives on campus.

Faith Broadly Understood

The word "faith," let alone the matter of the institution's Catholic identity, can be a point of contention. The faith question is particularly acute for those who do not identify with a religious tradition and for those who equate faith and religion. To open up the conversation in the classroom, in faculty development around mission and identity, and as a backdrop to the conversation of developing an interfaith course sequence, it has been helpful to introduce a broader conception of faith, drawing on the work of scholars who have addressed this question in terms accessible to a wide audience. For example, Paul Tillich's emphasis on one's source of ultimate concern; James Fowler's emphasis on the relational components of faith between self, community, and shared centers of value and power; and Wilfred Cantwell Smith's work on belief, which is helpful in shifting the emphasis from creedal statements to asking deeper questions such as, "What is it that I set my heart upon?" Reflection on these resources serves as a heuristic technique to open up conversation around the broadest meanings of faith and religion without claiming to offer a definitive definition of the terms. The goal is to create a space within which people are welcome to join the conversation, that is, interfaith dialogue, regardless of how they identify with respect to religion.[8]

Set within this broader context of faith, interfaith dialogue is not as far afield as it may have seemed at first. Maria Hornung's *Encountering Other Faiths* draws upon this broader framework in her introduction to the practice of interfaith dialogue.[9] For her, the practice is connected with social justice as well. "The aim of interfaith dialogue," Hornung explains, "is to search together for what is true and good, convinced that none of us knows all truth and goodness and that interacting together we can reach a greater ability to live the truth and goodness we discover."[10] According to Hornung, "It enables a growth in maturity as a full human being" and imparts an appreciation for the challenge of finding common ground but also the possibility for doing so.[11] She explains that the practice of interfaith dialogue takes the participant into broader and broader circles of relationship and has an impact on the world itself. Interfaith dialogue, she explains, "generates belief in the possibility of a positive outcome without violence" and "enables the sacrifices that ensure that all the chances for justice and peace are taken."[12] Hornung's approach resonates with the interfaith and social justice dimensions of the university's mission statement, rooted as it is in social justice, inclusivity, and Catholic identity.

A Context So Old It Looks New Again

Clearly, the university has done a significant amount of work to foreground the interfaith dimension of the institution's mission. As this movement progresses, attention must turn to the ways the university's Catholic identity, the interfaith movement, and social justice intersect. The connection between these dimensions of the university's mission is in the school's DNA as a Catholic institution of higher education founded by the Missionary Sisters of the Sacred Heart of Jesus (MSC). St. Frances Xavier Cabrini, founder of the MSCs, was sent to the United States by Pope Leo XIII (1823–1829) who famously promulgated *Rerum Novarum* (1891), what is considered the first Catholic social teaching encyclical in the modern period. Successive popes and local bishops' committees have followed in his footsteps. Pope John XXIII (1958–1963) addressed his encyclical on peace, *Pacem in Terris* (1963), to all people of goodwill, the first encyclical directly addressed to an audience beyond the immediate Catholic community. *Nostra Aetate* (1965), the Second Vatican Council (1962–1965) document, affirmed the importance of engagement with world religions. Paul VI (1963–1978), John Paul II (1978–2005), Benedict XVI (2005–2013), and most recently Pope Francis (2013–present) have affirmed the importance of this insight.

Pope Francis has engaged the intersection of Catholic identity, interfaith cooperation, and a commitment to social justice in many different ways during his pontificate. In a moment of levity, Pope Francis invited soccer players from around the world to compete in an "interreligious match for peace" at the Olympic Stadium in Rome.[13] A number of religions were represented in the friendly competition, including the Buddhist, Christian, Hindu, Jewish, Muslim, and Shinto traditions. Before the match, Pope Francis invited the players "to bear witness to the feelings of brotherhood and friendship" that are characteristic of sport. The soccer match also served as a fund-raiser to support children who lack the necessary resources to complete their education. In this single, joyful event, by fostering interreligious cooperation and supporting economically and politically marginalized people, Pope Francis brought attention and took a definite step toward building what he calls a "culture of encounter."

This "culture of encounter" is more a verb than a noun. It is typified by action: building bridges across difference and reaching out to those who are marginalized. As a case in point, Pope Francis encouraged the soccer players to live out, in their everyday lives, the values inherent in their sport, to "render testimony to the ideals of peaceful civil and social coexistence, for the edification of a civilization founded on love, on solidarity and on peace." It might seem simple in the context of a friendly soccer match, but, he concluded, "This is the culture of encounter: working for this."[14]

As in sport, the pope calls each person to build the culture of encounter with respect to her or his own identity and to respect the identity of others. The values that characterize sport, he reiterated, "loyalty, sharing, acceptance, dialogue, trust in others" are "common to every person regardless of race, culture, and religious creed." While these values are held in common among all people, no one should be asked to set aside her or his specific religious identity while cooperating to build the common good. Here, Pope Francis articulated his central point: "Believers of different religions, while preserving their own identity, can coexist in harmony and mutual respect." The friendly soccer match served as a demonstration of this concept and an appeal to the millions of soccer fans worldwide to do the same.

Pope Francis locates the source of personal and social renewal in encounter with God. In his apostolic exhortation *Evangelii Gaudium* ("The Joy of the Gospel"), the pope explains, "Thanks solely to this encounter—or renewed encounter—with God's love, which blossoms into an enriching friendship, we are liberated from our narrowness and self-absorption."[15] The "culture of encounter" is an invitation to all people to listen to the cry of the poor and to provide them with elements necessary to be fully included in society, for example, with nourishment, education, health care, and dignified work. Pope Francis encourages dialogue to achieve these goals. He calls for dialogue among nations; dialogue between faith, reason, and science; and dialogue among people of different religious traditions.

The culture of encounter has become a central metaphor of the pope's teaching. He extends the idea to human encounter with all of creation. In his 2015 encyclical on the environment, *Laudato Si'* ("Praised be"), the pope evoked the "Canticle of the Sun," in which Saint Francis sings, "All praise be yours, My Lord, through all that you have made." He continues with an enchanting litany on the glory of

God reflected in creation through Brother Sun, Sister Moon and Stars, Brothers Wind and Air, Sister Water, Brother Fire, and Sister Earth, our mother.[16] In the encyclical, "Praised be," Pope Francis invites each person to recognize her or his kinship with the earth, to learn to live in greater harmony with the natural environment.

Interfaith dialogue is central to the pope's vision, including with respect to the environment. In the opening paragraphs he announced, "I would like to enter into dialogue with all people about our common home."[17] Significantly, individuals who represent diverse groups and organizations that share concern for the environment presented the document, including the ecumenical perspective, the role of professionals in the natural sciences, and the responsibility of those who work in the areas of economics, business, and politics, as well as of those who are in the field of education. Indeed, the pope invites all people of goodwill to examine their context and to become engaged in the culture of encounter. At the heart of the culture of encounter is a call for peace and justice through personal and social transformation that leads to action for the common good. As do all Catholic institutions of higher education, Cabrini University has a mandate to provide space for students to explore their relationship with God, including but not limited to liturgy, retreats, and prayer services. In pursuing academic excellence, the university has committed to promote interdisciplinary learning, research, and scholarship. In preparing social justice leaders, the university has committed to provide students with analytical and practical skills that move in the direction of the preferential option for the poor.

Models of a Culture of Encounter: Dorothy Day and Thomas Merton

In his address to the United States Congress in 2015, Pope Francis mentioned four Americans: Abraham Lincoln, Martin Luther King Jr., Dorothy Day, and Thomas Merton.[18] Among them, Dorothy Day and Thomas Merton—their stories recounted briefly below—illustrate particular ways that Catholic identity, interfaith cooperation, and social justice can be integrated. Day and Merton are exemplars of Francis's culture of encounter. What I present here in summary fashion is similar to what the students and I study, discuss, and practice in more depth in the classroom. Day's and Merton's stories can also be helpful in conversations around Catholic identity at the university more broadly.

Dorothy Day's early life was characterized by searching. Over a lifetime, she grew in her commitment to social justice through her wide-ranging reading practices and her expansive network of friends, colleagues, and allies in social justice work. Early in her life, she was influenced by Upton Sinclair and Jack London. She became a journalist to share her observations and insights on the working poor. She was a social activist who became involved in labor advocacy and the women's suffrage movement. She stood out from among her secular peers in her early social justice circuit because she responded to a persistent tug toward religion.[19] Long before formally entering the tradition, Day recalled that she would simply drop into churches. As Robert Coles put it, reflecting on his interview with her, "She would stop at a church, sit there, not necessarily say or think or do anything, simply *be*."[20] After several years of searching, she decided to become Catholic.

At first, Day was not sure how she would join her newly found Catholic identity with her lifelong commitment to social justice activism. She met Peter Maurin, who helped her to discover ways she might integrate her social justice commitment with her newly adopted religion. Maurin was an immigrant to the United States from France, an itinerant laborer who had adopted a life of voluntary poverty. He preached the gospel in word and deed. Together, Day and Maurin founded the Catholic Worker movement, which was built around a series of interlocking social justice components, including houses of hospitality, roundtable discussions for the clarification of thought, and farming communes where people from different walks of life would live, work, and study together. The houses of hospitality provided a context within which people could practice the corporal works of mercy: feeding the hungry, providing drink to the thirsty, sheltering the homeless, caring for the sick, clothing the naked, burying the dead, and ransoming the captive.[21]

Dorothy Day's conversion led to a rift between Day and many of her family and friends, who did not understand her decision to join the Catholic Church. Nevertheless, she did not cut off ties with those people in her life who did not share her passion and commitment to social justice. From a late-in-life perspective, Day told Coles that she did not make a distinction between secular idealism and religious idealism.[22] She regretted that when she was younger she did not notice how spiritual her nonreligious counterparts were. "I always knew how much I admired certain men and women (my 'radical friends') who were giving their lives to help others get a better break; but now I realize how spiritual some of them were, and I'm ashamed of myself for not realizing that long ago, when I was with them, talking and having supper and making our plans, as we did."[23] She acknowledged that religion can be a means of exclusion and a source of fear and hate.[24] She focused on religion as a source of love and service and strove to embody that dimension of the tradition.

Dorothy Day's inclusive approach welcomed people from different backgrounds. While she was clear about her own religious commitment, and certainly the name "Catholic Worker" made a statement about the movement's identity, all the while she was equally clear that she welcomed people of all backgrounds: "I say that we are not asking people to fill out membership cards here, and we're not interested in declarations of religious affiliation. I tell them that we are here to feed the hungry and offer any help we can to anyone who comes to us."[25] As Coles affirms, "By no means have all of them [people participating in the Catholic Worker] been professing Catholics or Christian or even religious in any conventional or explicit sense of the word. Agnostics and atheists in significant numbers have found their way to the hospitality houses and devoted time to them."[26] Dan McKanan attributes this approach to Day's "leadership through friendship," which she modeled by moving beyond the confines of the Catholic Worker and by providing an opportunity for all comers to participate by practicing the works of mercy.[27] The opportunity to "do concrete work on behalf of others" in an environment of open inquiry on matters of the mind and heart "is also of interest to students and others who are trying hard to connect the work of philosophers and novelists and historians to their own lives."[28]

Thomas Merton, too, is a role model for the culture of encounter, however unexpectedly, given that he was a monk who spent much of his adult life cloistered. Thomas Merton's journey to the monastery was indirect and unexpected. Early in his life, Merton's faith, broadly understood, centered on personal satisfaction. His conversion came as a surprise to him and to many of his friends. Even after his conversion and entrance into the monastery, Merton's outlook on life continued to shift. On his own admission, he entered the monastery in 1941 in a spirit of contempt for the world. His outlook gradually moved toward a feeling of compassion and ultimately love for the world. His famous experience at Fourth and Walnut in Louisville, Kentucky marks a significant turning point for him. He wrote, "I was suddenly overwhelmed by the realization that I loved all those people, that they were mine and I theirs, that we could not be alien to one another even though we were total strangers."[29] Merton felt a sense of solidarity with his neighbors, not a vague sense of obligation, but a real and abiding sense of love for those who were strangers and even unknown to him.

In spite of living within the boundaries of an enclosure, Merton learned about the events of his time through newspaper clippings sent to him by his friends. As Lawrence Cunningham recounts, he would have read about Buddhist monks who immolated themselves in Vietnam; Martin Luther King Jr.'s arrest and his composition of his "Letter from a Birmingham Jail"; the assassination of John F. Kennedy; and the death of Pope John XXIII.[30] He began to dedicate more and more of his writing to social justice topics, especially the civil rights movement and the peace movement. Cunningham explains that for Merton, "there had to be a complete overhaul of the existing social system in America that would allow civil rights to come to authentic fruition."[31] On the topic of peace, he wrote of his admiration for Gandhi and Martin Luther King Jr. He made plans, never fulfilled, to invite the latter to visit him in the monastery. Overall, Merton called for a transformation of values that led to violence in the first place.

While Merton's reflection on social justice emerged from his Catholic Christian perspective, he was in dialogue with all people of goodwill. At one point, he hosted an ecumenical retreat on the peace movement at the Abbey of Gethsemane, where he lived. "In fact," Cunningham explains, "the retreat of the peacemakers was a kind of model of the kind of dialogue for which Merton was inclined: small groups of like-minded persons who could speak on deep subjects from the integrity of their own positions."[32] Merton became famous for his participation in interreligious dialogue, which included his encounter with people from various traditions, including Judaism, Islam, and Buddhism.

He challenged those among his coreligionists who did not advance in building relationships with people outside of their limited experience and expectations of who was worthy. In his book *Conjectures of a Guilty Bystander*, Merton identified "a basic temptation: the flatly unchristian refusal to love those whom we consider, for some reason or other, unworthy of love." He invited those who held such views to "advance in the love which has redeemed and renewed us all in God's likeness" by encountering in love people of different races and those who believe in other religious traditions, people who do not claim religious affiliation, and those who reject religion altogether.[33] Speaking in the idiom of his Catholic identity, Merton crafted a vision of an inclusive community that welcomed people of all faiths, cultures, and backgrounds.

Conclusion

The presenting institution here, Cabrini University, operationalizes its Catholic identity in rich ways through its relationship with the Missionary Sisters of the Sacred Heart of Jesus, its partnership with Catholic Relief Services, its three-credit course requirement in religious studies, and various cocurricular opportunities for students to engage with the Catholic tradition. At the same time, the institution has committed tremendous resources to developing interfaith understanding among its faculty and in its curriculum. The institution's partnership with the Interfaith Youth Core has led to significant development in faculty training and enriched student learning in this area. An interfaith learning community and an interfaith course sequence will further enhance the ways the university operationalizes its mission to "welcome learners of all faiths cultures and backgrounds." In each of these areas and many more, most significantly its core curriculum, Justice Matters, the university advances its commitment to social justice. The community is living its mission.

These developments point to rich enactments of the university's mission and identity. Increasing religious diversity among students, staff, and faculty calls for a clear articulation of the university's identity while simultaneously demonstrating a commitment to the interfaith movement. No doubt a robust set of activities and programming helps to create a context within which all members of the community feel welcome and find ways to engage the mission, including nonreligious individuals, like the student Wayne noted above. Yet it remains incumbent on the institution to be able to provide, readily and easily, a comprehensive explanatory framework for how the various parts hold together rather than present them, intentionally or not, as disparate elements. Deliberate and careful reflection on and communication of the meaning and significance of the mission and identity is necessary.

Taken together, read through the lens of Pope Francis's "culture of encounter," Day and Merton model interfaith dialogue and social justice activism that is firmly rooted in their Christian identity. They did not privatize their religious identity but kept it at the fore in their private and public lives. At the same time, they respected their counterparts who hailed from different religious traditions or no religious tradition. They actively sought to dialogue and cooperate with all people of goodwill to build the common good. They exemplify what today Pope Francis calls the culture of encounter. In many ways, in conjunction with the words and example of Pope Francis, they help to illustrate the ways an institution like Cabrini University might strive for mission integration around its Catholic identity and social justice and interfaith commitments.

Faith-based institutions of higher education that are thinking through what it means for the religious identity of their institution to intersect with the interfaith movement and their contribution to the common good might consider the resources in their tradition that would help construct such an explanatory framework. Doing so, and sharing the stories widely in formal and informal ways, can help prevent the loss of the founding religious identity of the institution and help the community live its mission with greater understanding and, perhaps, a firmer sense of purpose. In this way, the community might move from strength to strength: living, knowing, and being the mission.

Notes

1 Cabrini University was founded in 1957 by the Missionary Sisters of the Sacred Heart of Jesus. The university continues to operate under their sponsorship. The residential campus is located approximately twenty minutes from Center City Philadelphia. There are 2,150 students, graduate and undergraduate combined. The majority of under-graduate students live on campus. See "About Cabrini University" (https://www.cabrini .edu/about).

2 Chris Stedman, *Faitheist: How an Atheist Found Common Ground with the Religious* (Boston: Beacon, 2012).

3 A brief overview of Eck's discussion of pluralism can be found on the Pluralism Project website, http://pluralism.org/what-is-pluralism/.

4 For a discussion of the Voices of Justice living and learning community that is relevant to this discussion, see Darryl Mace, Nancy Watterson, and Nicholas Rademacher, "Common Ground through Dialogue: Creating Civic Dispositions," in *The SAGE Sourcebook of Service-Learning and Civic Engagement*, ed. Omobolade Delano-Oriaran, Marguerite W. Penick-Parks, and Suzanne Fondrie (New York: SAGE, 2015), 93–98 and, by the same authors, "Foregrounding Relationships: Using Deliberative Dialogue and Engaged Justice in a Living and Learning Community," *Journal of College and Character* 13, no. 2 (2012): 1–8.

5 See Mary Laver, "Shared Mission: Catholic Higher Education in Partnership with Catholic NGOs," in *Journal of Catholic Higher Education* 27, no. 1 (2008): 159–70.

6 See the Cabrini University website for more information about the university's core curriculum (https://www.cabrini.edu/undergraduate/programs/justice-matters-core-curriculum). Jerome Zurek has written an article that addresses the dynamics of the core curriculum: "'Justice Matters': A Multifaceted Implementation of Catholic Social Teaching across the Curriculum," *Expositions* 10, no. 1 (2016): 17–31.

7 See the IFYC website, where these three guiding ideas are presented: https://www.ifyc.org/guiding-ideas.

8 See Nicholas Rademacher, "Religious Diversity, Civic Engagement, and Community-Engaged Pedagogy: Forging Bonds of Solidarity through Interfaith Dialogue," in *Teaching Civic Engagement*, ed. Forrest Clingerman and Reid B. Locklin (Oxford: Oxford University Press, 2016), 125–42, esp. 130–32. There I present in more detail how this approach works in the classroom by focusing on James Fowler's discussion of faith in his *Stages of Faith: The Psychology of Human Development and the Quest for Meaning* (New York: HarperCollins, 1981). Reference to this approach also appears in Mace, Watterson, and Rademacher, "Common Ground through Dialogue," 95–96 (see n. 4).

9 See Maria Hornung, *Encountering Other Faiths* (Mahwah, NJ: Paulist, 2007), esp. chap. 4, "Theoretical Underpinnings to Creative Exposure to Interreligious Dialogue," 45–69. See also Rademacher, "Religious Diversity, Civic Engagement, and Community-Engaged Pedagogy," 132–33, for a more detailed discussion of how this practice works in the classroom.

10 Maria Hornung, *Workbook for Encountering Other Faiths: An Introduction to the Art of Interreligious Engagement* (Philadelphia: Interfaith Center of Greater Philadelphia, 2007), 33.

11 Hornung, 33.

12 Hornung, 33.

13 What follows is drawn, in parts verbatim, from Nicholas Rademacher, "Pope Francis's Vision for the Common Good," *Cabrini Magazine*, fall 2015, 5–6.

14 Pope Francis, "Address of Pope Francis to Soccer Players and Promoters of the Interreligious Match for Peace," September 1, 2014 .

15 Pope Francis, *Evangelii Gaudium* (November 24, 2013), par. 8, https://w2.vatican.va/content/francesco/en/apost_exhortations/documents/papa-francesco_esortazione-ap_20131124_evangelii-gaudium.html.

16 See Pope Francis, *Laudato Si'* (May 24, 2015), par. 87, http://w2.vatican.va/content/francesco/en/encyclicals/documents/papa-francesco_20150524_enciclica-laudato-si.html.

17 Pope Francis, par. 3.

18 See Pope Francis, Address of the Holy Father to the Joint Session of the United States Congress (September 24, 2015), https://w2.vatican.va/content/francesco/en/speeches/2015/september/documents/papa-francesco_20150924_usa-us-congress.html.

19 Dorothy Day recounted her story many times in print and through interviews. There are many biographical treatments of Day. One of the best places to start is her *Long Loneliness* (1952; repr., San Francisco: HarperSanFrancisco, 1997).

20 Robert Coles, *Dorothy Day: A Radical Devotion* (Boston: Da Capo, 1987): 33–34.

21 See especially part 3, "Love Is the Measure," of Day's *The Long Loneliness*, in which she talks about Peter Maurin and the foundation of the Catholic Worker (see n. 19).

22 Coles, *Radical Devotion*, 25.

23 Coles, 29.

24 Coles, 28.

25 Coles, 31.

26 Coles, 17.

27 Dan McKanan, *The Catholic Worker After Dorothy: Practicing the Works of Mercy in a New Generation* (Collegeville, MN: Liturgical Press, 2008), 21.

28 Coles, *Radical Devotion*, 17.

29 Thomas Merton recounts his conversion experience in his journals. See *A Search for Solitude: Pursuing the Monk's True Life*, ed. Lawrence S. Cunningham (San Francisco: HarperSanFrancisco, 1996), 181. Merton's most famous memoir is *Seven Storey Mountain* (New York: Harcourt, Brace, 1948), though that text covers only his earliest reflections on the spiritual life, especially with respect to the intersection of his religious identity, social justice, and interfaith cooperation for the common good. Lawrence S. Cunningham provides an excellent introduction to Merton in his *Thomas Merton and the Monastic Vision* (Grand Rapids, MI: Eerdmans, 1999).

30 Cunningham, *Thomas Merton*, 105.

31 Cunningham, 107.

32 Cunningham, 114.

33 Thomas Merton, *Conjectures of a Guilty Bystander* (Garden City, NY: Doubleday, 1965), 156–57.

The Campus as a Clinical Setting

Reflections on School Chaplaincy and an Argument for Higher Standards

Aaron Twitchell

Over spring break, a group of students from my school traveled to Haiti. In an annual pilgrimage of service, our school travels to this country to support a local ministry focused on education and basic needs. Recently, one of those students asked to discuss her experience with me after school. For the rest of the day, I wondered which part of the trip was still stuck in her mind. Was it the poverty? Was it the underlying fear of being attacked or robbed, a fear punctuated by the constant presence of our armed escort? Did something about the group dynamic with classmates still bother her? As the chaplain of a Methodist–affiliated, independent day/boarding school, I serve a wide variety of students, and my interactions can be for any reason under the sun. When she first arrived, my student wasn't sure why she had come.

We spoke briefly about the medical clinics our students managed, the dangerous driving conditions, and how she felt guilty staying at a nice hotel. After a few minutes, she realized the profound poverty had bothered her on a very deep level but that, at the same time, the joy of the Haitian people had impacted her equally yet differently. This fifteen-year-old girl was having a difficult time facing the juxtaposition of pain and joy since both emotions were caused by the same set of circumstances. Our visit ended with "homework" for both of us (something to ponder), promises to check in again after a few days to review things we had learned about ourselves, and my showing her a couple of photos from my own experience in a Mexican border town.

Aside from explaining that my trips to Mexico were with a church group, there wasn't much religion going on in the twenty minutes my student spent in my office. Although I happen to know something about her religious background through other circumstances, she was not very interested in interpreting her experience in Haiti through the lens of any kind of theology. I did not ask her if she wanted me to pray for her in that moment. I did not stroke my beard, turn around and pull a Teen Study Bible from my shelf, and read to her Jesus's words about "the least of these." In fact, many pastors and people would wonder just what I would call the work I did that afternoon: Youth ministry? Mentoring? Counseling? None of these quite fits the bill, and yet all are an aspect of school chaplaincy and the pastoral care that a chaplain provides to students, faculty, parents, and even alumni.[1]

School chaplains are not there to shepherd congregations, and campuses are not their church, although chaplains may be called upon to provide theological consultation, represent the school's denominational heritage, or administer the sacraments and lead a Bible study. The chaplain is not there only to serve as a mentor, giving advice on how to choose a college or prom date, although a chaplain may be asked to walk with a student during her parents' divorce or to help face a disciplinary action or make sense of a breakup. A good school chaplain also knows that she is not the school counselor and that her role is not to provide mental health diagnoses, although she may be needed to assist with emotional support after the death of a parent, to recognize when a student might benefit from psychotherapy, or to serve as a confidential hearer to the faculty and staff. *Effective school chaplaincy is a specialized ministry demanding comprehensive and clinical training beyond what is normally required for ordination in order to meet the spiritual needs of and to provide appropriate emotional support to the school community.*

The Spiritual Needs of Adolescents

In her book *The Spiritual Child*, Lisa Miller discusses the importance of a child's spiritual health and the practical benefits of meeting spiritual needs.[2] Equal parts science and practical application, the book serves as a strong, broad starting point from which chaplains can conceptualize their role apart from institutional religion. Such a concept is necessary when working in an interfaith environment; Miller's research helps us understand the biology of adolescent spirituality, the data of which are true regardless of religious identity. Three conclusions are worth lifting up.

First, teenagers are biologically primed for spiritual growth and exploration. In much the same way that freshmen become fascinated with, for example, the Silk Road and basic physics, they are also eager to hear and think about transcendence, God, and the Four Noble Truths. Miller's use of magnetic resonance imaging (MRI) and other scientific and medical tests moves these ideas from conjecture to thesis.

Second, school-age adolescents *need* space to spiritually explore every aspect of their development. Even if students do not appear to need this space, ask for it, or seem to use it when and how it is offered, boys and girls are constantly interpreting everything that happens to them through the lens of their burgeoning spiritual quest: social lives, academic interest, successes and failures, hopes for the future, personal identity,[3] and even family histories. Thus, it is not enough to say that teenagers are interested in studying religion or spirituality; they are, in fact, studying *everything else* through the lens of spirituality.[4]

The third conclusion from Miller's research is two-pronged. Studies of older adolescents and young adults have found that those who could identify spiritual support during their teenage years were less likely to engage in risky behavior over the course of their emerging adulthood. In fact, having space and adults available to help a young person develop a personal sense of spirituality was the single greatest predictor of overall mental and emotional health.[5] The second aspect of this conclusion is that once a person reaches adolescence, the positive spiritual influence need not (and often does not) come from a parent. Put another way, spiritual leaders on school campuses have great potential to positively impact the lives of their students during school and into adulthood.

Questions of religion and spirituality are fine and fair game for most teachers. A school chaplain is not the only person on campus qualified to hear about a student's conversion to the religion of the Flying Spaghetti Monster, or another student's suspicion of being multireligious after reading *The Life of Pi*. English teachers, math teachers, coaches, just about anyone with whom a student has a good relationship should feel empowered to discuss topics of spirituality. Pastors and rabbis fill obvious roles for students journeying through the traditions of their respective religions.[6] School mental health counselors are there to ensure that students are mentally and emotionally stable and are able to cope with the demands of school and life. And therapists can play a role in providing spiritual care for students, especially when a student's depression or anxiety contributes to or stems from spiritual or emotional distress.

But when spiritual needs, religious faith, and emotional well-being collide in the face of tragedy or personal crisis, the clinically trained interfaith school chaplain is uniquely positioned to provide particular care for those in need. Clinical training allows the chaplain to provide interfaith pastoral care according to the high standards set by the certifying body who supervised their training. As a student is describing her crisis, pain, confusion, or fear, the clinical chaplain is listening not only as an agent of faith and spiritual leadership but also as someone who has gone through rigorous and supervised hours of training, self-discovery, psychotherapeutic skills acquisition, and crisis/ grief counseling. Pastors deal with tragedies and crises plenty of times throughout their careers as they serve their congregations. Clinical chaplains are trained *specifically* for them.

The Value of Clinical Chaplaincy and Its Role on the School Campus

Normally, seminary students are required to enroll in a variety of courses in practical theology, pastoral care, and cognate studies. The education that students receive also includes two field education internships, one at a church and one at a hospital. It is important to note that this is a *typical* seminary experience; many students, particularly those who, at the time, are not interested in ordained ministry, elect other kinds of internships resulting in a sizable number of graduates who have not had any experience in contextual ministry.

Assuming students desire to enter some kind of vocational ministry and ordination, they will use the seminary experience to test the waters of a wide range of interests, subfields, disciplines, experiences, and schools of thought according to the theology, traditions, and expectations of their denomination (or none, if they are nondenominational). Upon graduation, seminary students enter into or proceed to work though their respective denominational processes for ordained ministry, which can vary widely. Every May, hundreds of future ministers graduate with a basic, if useful, understanding of theology, history, pastoral care, biblical studies, ministry skills, and denominationally specific polity. The typical master of divinity degree sheds very little light on chaplaincy of any kind. It is a general ministry degree meant to provide some depth and a lot of breadth into various principles of theology and ministry. It makes sense, then, that specialized ministry would require further, specialized training.

Yet secondary schools do not expect such training of the chaplains they hire. A cursory search of openings reveals a wide array of job descriptions, expectations, roles, education and experience requirements, and titles. For example, an individual hired to serve as a "director of religious/spiritual life" often will be considered along very similar lines as other programming specialists, such as community service leaders or diversity practitioners. A bachelor's degree is all that is required of such a leader, with classroom or coaching experience "a plus." There is often little difference between schools' hiring preferences of school chaplains and those of religion teachers.

There are two primary roles served by school chaplains and their otherwise-titled counterparts that have varying degrees of relevance to actual spiritual care. The first is commonly referred to as "director of community service" or "service learning." In order for schools to avoid hiring an experienced leader capable of forming, nurturing, and growing a service-oriented culture, they will often slide this responsibility in with the chaplain's job on campus. While important, it is not difficult to see why leading the school-wide community service program not only takes away from a chaplain's project of spiritual work but also runs the risk of undermining his or her sense of vocation. People do not go to seminary and seek ordination in order to be in charge of fund-raising programs, important as those may be.

The second role is arguably closer to the vocation imagined by a school chaplain but nevertheless runs the risk of misunderstanding the aim and practice of interfaith pastoral care. Many school chaplains are employed by the institution for the primary reason—whether explicitly stated or implicitly communicated—of the existence of a chapel building on campus. In reading job descriptions, it is painfully easy to infer that since tearing down the chapel or church would be unimaginable, it makes sense to continue to employ somebody to warm the space. I once organized a gathering of school chaplains meant to foster camaraderie, idea sharing, and so forth. At one point in the day, the headmaster of the host school appeared to greet us and to spend a few minutes peering into the world of school chaplains. One seasoned chaplain in our group asked the headmaster why his school had a chaplain, evidently interested in the administrator's perspective on the role and purpose of a chaplain. The headmaster's response was diagnostic: "Well, we have this chapel here, so we've got to have someone to use it."

The problem with this scenario is twofold. First, students and other community members are perceptive of the ornamental nature of such a chaplain's presence and role on campus. Chaplains are given little to no other responsibilities; their offices are normally in the basement of the chapel, limiting their visibility; and since their presence in the community is so strongly attached to the building, which is itself often deeply rooted in the Christian tradition, it is difficult for these ministers to gain trust with and access to students of different faiths. As schools have become more interested in meeting as many needs as possible with available personnel, the definition and expectations of quality school chaplaincy at secondary schools have not kept pace with the high standards of other school leaders.[7] The results are chaplains who are educated but untrained.[8] They may reflect an open mind toward other faiths (though not always), but they are not truly rooted in interfaith contexts. Their skills may be born out of talent, but those skills are neither clinically derived nor capable of being objectively reviewed by anyone outside the chaplain's own perspective.

I am arguing, therefore, that expectations of school chaplains ought to be significantly raised. The benchmarks of a more effective school training might be: extensive training in a clinical setting; ongoing support, education, and training by clinical supervisors and colleagues; participation in a local community of clinical chaplains; and, ideally, board certification in clinical chaplaincy from a recognized and appropriate certifying body.[9] My assertion is based on the following factors: clinical training provides the experience school chaplains need beyond the seminary degree; the principles of clinical chaplaincy translate well into adolescent spiritual care; certification may be the *only* form of accountability for the work school chaplains; and, finally, participation in a professional community of clinical chaplains allows school spiritual leaders to maintain their expertise, share cases, receive feedback, and experience vocational growth beyond classroom pedagogy, coaching, and so on.

My experience as a school chaplain for six years has convinced me that school chaplaincy unquestionably deserves more attention from both denominations and independent schools. Improving hiring practices in this way and raising expectations for training and professional development will ensure that the person providing spiritual care and leadership is the best person for the role, flourishes within appropriate vocational boundaries, provides excellent care, and is valued among students, families, and school leadership. These benefits are on top of the personal satisfaction that a school chaplain might gain from knowing he or she provides *expertise* in the same way other officials do on campus.

I will elaborate on the value of clinical training and corresponding certification/board membership, explain why it is the best way to ensure best practices in school chaplaincy, and then describe the practical benefits using concrete language and examples. Finally, I will describe a case study that illustrates the skills and expertise gained through clinical training and its professional community.

Clinical Training: From One Required Unit to Board Certification

Since the 1930s, clinical pastoral education (CPE) has been the primary mode of training for pastoral care providers, including future parish ministers.[10] It was developed to explore spiritual and emotional roots of mental illness but has expanded to include other settings, such as hospitals and prisons.[11] Most seminaries offer CPE, but there is no telling which and how many graduates will have taken a unit, since it is almost never a graduation requirement.

While programs vary widely, a few things can be said about CPE and why the first unit is often also the last for many seminarians and pastors. First, CPE is normally done at a hospital, and hospitals are not pleasant places.[12] Second, interns are surprised to discover aspects of themselves of which they were not previously aware and how powerfully these hidden parts influence the care they provide. For example, an intern with a difficult childhood relationship to his father may discover that he either avoids middle-aged male patients or finds it difficult to maintain neutral feelings toward them. Even though they may have addressed these personal issues to the point of managing them well on a day-to-day basis, when asked to occupy an intimate space with a "fatherly" patient, interns often discover unturned stones of pain, anger, and sadness. Interns are asked to look deep within and examine their stories, experiences, and families in front of others in a group setting and privately with their clinical supervisor. The lessons learned, while difficult, are essential to forming the self-critical distance needed to provide objective care.

A third common feature of CPE that often makes it easy to stop at one unit is cost. A unit normally consists of four hundred hours spread over the course of either a summer or an academic year. In the case of the former, the unit is full-time: interns spend forty hours per week at the site, with thirty of those hours serving with patients, eight in group work, and two in one-on-one supervision. The academic year placement is often ten to fifteen hours per week, with those hours distributed similarly. Tuition can be expensive when one factors in loss of income, so people are hesitant to do more than is necessary.[13]

School chaplaincy is, perhaps uniquely in terms of contextual ministry, well positioned to respond to these otherwise reasonable objections to advanced training. Most chaplains are on a ten-month contract freeing up time over the summer for training and professional development. Alternatively, if schools recognize the value of CPE, they can work with the chaplain to structure the school year in such a way to allow for the training. The return on investment of CPE makes it a superb candidate for schools to utilize on behalf of their chaplain. Also, as much as I am advocating for ministers to embrace further CPE training and for schools to recognize its value by increasing hiring standards and covering all or part of the cost, I invite churches and denominations to consider setting aside funds to help support ministers who are interested in clinical ministry.

To illustrate my point, consider the following analogy: A minister without specialized clinical chaplaincy training who is expected to effectively serve an interfaith school community is like an oncology patient seeking care from a general practice physician. Family care doctors are, of course, highly trained and competent to provide excellent medicinal advice and care. They may even have completed a rotation in hematology/oncology. But they are not expected to treat cancer patients, and they would not expect to be hired as an oncologist. Neither form of medicine is to be lifted up over the other. Family care physicians train for their setting as oncologists train for their specialty. One is a general practitioner while the other is a specialist. Likewise, one unit of CPE opens an important door for ministers and clergy to provide good pastoral care to their congregations or certain other ministry settings. It is simply not sufficient for a school chaplain.

My assertion that school chaplaincy ought to be treated as a specialized context and, therefore, ought to require more training is supported by denominations' own responses to other forms of contextual ministry. The United Methodist Church, for example, offers certificates in "older adult ministry" and "youth ministry," to name a few. Other churches have developed whole other sets of standards for supporting military chaplains and, of course, hospital chaplains. Ministers and chaplains on school campuses ought to be held to the same standards as these forms of contextual ministry, each demanding its own, appropriate education and training.

Beyond One Unit: Some Examples of the Practical Value of More Training

Most certification bodies require a minimum of four units for board certification. It is this commitment to training and development that I believe ought to supplement the theological education and ministry training typically received during seminary. While one unit of CPE introduces the intern to important concepts, such as boundaries and overidentification, it is not enough to equip the school chaplain to negotiate the corresponding struggles with adolescents, fellow faculty, parents, administration, and most profoundly, the self.

For example, most seminary students learn that boundaries are meant to "protect the minister," and that the best way to practice good emotional boundaries is to "keep the door open" and "never be alone with a parishioner." This is the extent of boundary training. But it does not take long for a pastor, regardless of the setting, to learn that there is not always a door and that maintaining physical boundaries is different from resolving emotional ones. Regarding literal doors as boundaries, the setting of effective school chaplaincy and pastoral care can change often: on the athletic field, in the dorm lounge, the campus center, even the hospital room. Life happens increasingly beyond physical boundary markers such as door thresholds and offices, and chaplains must be emotionally prepared. Moreover, few teachers would agree to share private matters with an office door wide open to passing preteens, and teachers make up a sizable portion of the chaplain's community of care. Emotional boundaries must be identified and practiced *for all settings*, and while this work begins in the first unit of CPE, more time is needed to develop these skills.

An effective practitioner understands that the appropriate degree of clinical intimacy between caregiver and care recipient is determined by the caregiver, not necessarily the condition of the office door or the setting in which the visit takes place. Again, relying on physical barriers to make these choices for us is dangerous, as establishing appropriate boundaries is a sacred responsibility. With regard to emotional boundaries alone, the following areas should receive significant attention and supervision before becoming interested in school chaplaincy: sexual identity, including any complicated or unresolved trauma; the role of sexual energy in pastoral visits;[14] the intimacy of spiritual care;[15] dual relationships; the chaplain's relationship to gender; and, broadly speaking, the chaplain's emotional needs, both met and unmet. These are just a few psychosocial arenas for which advanced levels of clinical training are needed for the chaplain to address. Doing so not only protects the pastoral counselor but also ensures high-quality care for the students and community.

Boundaries of age, sexuality, gender, and intimacy is just one area of attention given to chaplaincy interns during CPE as they prepare to give spiritual care. The spiritual care *received* during advanced levels of CPE training is of equal benefit to the future school chaplain. One memorable encounter between a supervisor and an intern during a clinical unit went something like this (paraphrased):

Intern: I just can't help it; I feel a call to a special ministry toward girls who are struggling with abusive or absent fathers, broken families, etc., especially since I now have two daughters myself. It's a sign!

Supervisor: Are you prepared to walk every single one of those young ladies down the aisle at her wedding?

Intern: Of course not.

Supervisor: You need to recognize where this is coming from or you will never be able to build and maintain appropriate emotional boundaries.[16]

The biblical image of the wise and foolish men and their respective houses built on rock and sand comes to mind here (Matthew 7). Basic teachings on boundaries in seminary and first-unit CPE may be enough to hold up a pastoral leader under sunny skies and fair weather. But their ministries (and, unfortunately, personal lives) are in danger of severe damage and eventual destruction at the first sign of a storm.

Most future pastors learn early on that they must contend with an over-realized sense of care and helping; we don't need a textbook or study to recognize the danger of "falling in love" with those we serve and care for. Even seasoned parish clergy are susceptible to being overwhelmed by these feelings under the right circumstances or season of life. It is widely accepted that clergy need lifelong support and accountability to manage these very human experiences, and yet school chaplains often do not have dependable access to such benefits.[17] Why not? If anything, since they are working directly with minors, school chaplains need *more* support for maintaining their emotional health, especially those at boarding schools, where physical boundaries between self and community are even more blurred.

Translating Clinical Training and Certification into School Chaplaincy

There are many groups involved in clinical pastoral training. One is the decentralized, local chapter model of the College of Pastoral Supervision and Psychotherapy.[18] It is regular, mutual, clinical, pastoral, and *interfaith* accountability upon which school chaplains should be depending for vocational flourishing. In the CPSP, a local chapter is made up of no more than twelve fellow clinical chaplains, at least one of whom must already be board certified. A candidate must be a member of a local chapter for one year before he or she can seek board certification. In that year, a member must participate in the life of the chapter, submit and receive feedback on case studies, offer feedback on others, justify pastoral care methods and motivations, and demonstrate significant professional and clinical growth. Finally, the candidate submits a significant portfolio of materials in an application for certification, including: a brief sketch of one's life; a theory paper of pastoral care, counseling, and clinical chaplaincy; two case studies; and a supervisory evaluation.

One key aspect of the CPSP process is that it is the *local body* that oversees and approves certification, which is important since they are the ones who know the candidate best, including his or her history, skills, training, philosophies, and weaknesses. Once complete, a board-certified clinical chaplain continues to participate in "chapter life," receiving feedback, experiencing documented and demonstrable innovation in clinical skills, engaging in relevant professional growth, attending conferences, and most important, being held accountable to the high standards of pastoral psychotherapy and clinical chaplaincy. All of this work, practice, and growth takes place in an interfaith setting. As an example, my local chapter consists of a Pentecostal military veteran-turned prison guard–turned pastor; a United Methodist missionary caregiver; a born-Jewish, now-ordained Zen Buddhist;

an American Baptist minister; a nondenominational Christian, and a few Presbyterians. Our ten members are diverse with respect to race, sexual identity, gender, and religion, just like my school campus.

Throughout the training and certification process, a clinical chaplaincy student will learn basic and advanced theories of spiritual support, clinically informed emotional support, and the skills to effectively midwife a human being through the pangs of the life cycle. As my Zen Buddhist colleague beautifully describes her hospice chaplaincy: "It means to act as a light on a dark path until the path is once again illuminated by the person walking on it, then the chaplain's light fades away until it is *mostly forgotten*" (emphasis added). Clinical chaplaincy and good pastoral care are marked by the possession of enough self-awareness that in times of crisis the chaplain does not confuse the patient's light with his or her own.

And what is adolescence if not ten years or so of one crisis after another, broken up by periods of intense euphoria and self-discovery? Hopefully, therefore, the analogy between the hospital room and the ailment of the teenage experience has begun to emerge. The school chaplain ministers to adolescents who are suffering from very real emotional ills and who are living through significant spiritual struggle. These needs must be met at school as well as at home if students are to have the opportunity to live full lives.

The Role of Case Studies in Clinical Campus Chaplaincy

Chapter life in clinical chaplaincy is marked by case studies. In these reviews, the chaplain seeks feedback from colleagues on their pastoral care. A case study includes an assessment of the subject's needs, relevant biographical and medical information, a verbatim of what was said during the visit by all parties, major questions on which she desires consultation, and exploration into several psychosocial concerns for the subject according to the visit and the chaplain's understanding of the best psychotherapeutic approach to those concerns.

The group goes over the entire manuscript and follows a process in order to accomplish several goals: (a) draw reasonably certain conclusions regarding the subject's spiritual and emotional needs; (b) recognize what the chaplain did well during the encounter; (c) based on the group's intimate knowledge of the chaplain's life, experiences, education, training, and ministry, determine specific reasons for each pastoral movement and clinical decision; (d) scrutinize those movements and decisions; (e) offer ideas and suggestions, both general and specific to the presented scenario; and finally, (f) create an overall picture of the chaplain's methods and motivations of care, both at the time of the visit and in broader context of their chaplaincy.

Case studies begin with demographic data so that colleagues can have a picture of the care recipient. Next is a statement of what the chaplain hoped to accomplish during the visit. These objectives are what the chapter will evaluate. Were they met? Should other goals have been considered? For example,

> *Circumstances:* A sixteen-year-old boy enters the office and asks to have a talk. This case study is a composite of two separate visits over the course of three days.
>
> *Objectives:* (1) perform a spiritual assessment, (2) explore advanced chaplaincy techniques of indirect communication and the use of irony, and (3) determine how the student is coping. This last objective will be shared with the school counselor.

The next part of the case study is a verbatim account of the visit, reproduced to the chaplain's best ability, for the group to reenact. One person plays the role of each participant so that the experience of dialogue is replicated. Verbatims are the best tool for individual chaplains to receive feedback on their pastoral care and counseling techniques. They allow for colleagues to get a glimpse into how a chaplain functions in his or her context, offer pointed feedback to the caregiver, and allow for growth. Once the reenactment of the visit concludes, the group freely offers its feedback on the pastoral care provided by the chaplain.

Most case studies will also feature a "chaplain's experience" portion during which the subject is asked to summarize his or her state of mind. What feelings were brought up in you during the visit? What did you do with those feelings? Was the visit particularly difficult? Why?

Finally, case studies should feature one of the unofficial hallmarks of pastoral care and counseling: the spiritual assessment. Spiritual assessments are the chaplain's toolbox for establishing a baseline of vitals, and they can be highly contextual.[19] Possible steps in a spiritual assessment include the following:

- Conduct an appraisal of the subject's religious and spiritual beliefs and the role these beliefs play in his or her presenting conflict.[20]

- Discover how these beliefs are functioning in the person's life, both within the current set of circumstances and more broadly.[21]

- Assess how the person is actually coping with the presenting issue, both in light of the beliefs just discussed and also in light of anything else that comes up during the visit (spiritual assessments can and should be ongoing).[22]

- Determine if any action is appropriate beyond the current visit.[23]

Spiritual assessments are not checklists of questions or a series of interrogations, and the information does not need to be obtained interview-style. Good chaplains are able to perform the assessment as the dialogue naturally unfolds.

Spiritual assessments are valuable sources of data for the clinically trained school chaplain. They allow him or her to practice, improve, and develop methods of care that best suit his or her environment, they facilitate helpful cooperation between the chaplain and other care providers on campus (even when anonymity is appropriate), and they serve as important indicators of context when going through case studies with colleagues.

Advanced Clinical Techniques for School Chaplaincy

As the school chaplain grows in skill and technique, he or she becomes more comfortable using a variety of tools in order to provide excellent pastoral care. It is these tools that set apart clinical chaplaincy from other forms of contextual and parish ministries. Chapter life, case studies, professional development for clinicians, and ongoing education all help to sharpen a school chaplain's skills and allow for innovation. A brief discussion of a sample of these skills may help to illustrate the value of clinical training.

The use of humor is a difficult skill to master. However, it can also be one of the most effective techniques to communicate truth to and establish trust with young people (and adults, for that matter). One of the most common mistakes made by career youth pastors, parish ministers, and other non–clinically trained clergy is the assumption that a "good sense of humor" is the same as the effective use of humor in pastoral care. In reality, the use of humor ought to be purposeful, careful, and well refined.[24]

Indirect communication is one of the most effective methods of pastoral care. It is so successful because of its recognition that human nature can get in the way of emotional and spiritual growth. People often actively deny the truth when it is spoken directly to them, especially by figures of authority, real or perceived. So instead of making statements of fact to a teenager who is wondering why her parents are angry at her for lying, a chaplain might find a way to communicate ideas indirectly. For example, instead of saying, "Lying is wrong; that is why your parents are angry," a chaplain may want to avoid aligning himself with the student's parents in order to preserve the pastoral relationship. But to avoid implicitly condoning the young lady's habit of lying, and to invite her to consider its potential damaging effects, the chaplain might ask, "Have you ever been lied to? Did you ever think that someone's decision to lie to you was justified?" The first question asks the student to put herself in the converse role, which is a skill that she is capable of at her age but often not the natural first step. The second question would hopefully reveal to her situations in which lying *might be* acceptable, which would uncover the truth that *her decision* to lie does not fall into the same category.

The use of irony gently reveals the disconnect between what a person would expect from oneself and what he or she is actually

227

doing or saying. It is the productive older cousin of sarcasm, the latter being a language that adolescents speak fluently. Therefore, irony is highly effective because although the truth often feels out of reach or unrecognizable for teenagers, it becomes quickly apparent and acknowledged when revealed through the use of ironic statements or questions. Consider the following: "I think it is interesting that such a confident person would be so opposed to asking for help. What are you afraid of?" A movement like this turns the conception of confidence upside down. Instead of confidence being seen as antithetical to the idea of seeking support, the statement proposes that self-confidence not get in the way of asking for help. Using irony with teenagers is one of the most powerful and consistent ways to avoid defensiveness while pointing out flaws in reasoning or judgment.

Silence is vastly misunderstood in pastoral care. With the rise of "ministry of presence" has come myriad ways to "use silence." The danger is the *mis*use of silence and the substitution of purposeful pastoral care for simply being present. To be clear, being present and silent can be both powerful and sorely needed when it is done so decisively. But silence can also be contraindicated, especially when: it is reactive in response to emotional turmoil within the chaplain's mind; its use is not properly and regularly reflected upon by a chaplain with a group of peers; it is misunderstood by the recipient.

Finally, one of the most important skills and traits gained through clinical and interfaith training is the use of **prayer and other aspects of religion**. Prayer functions prominently in the vocation of parish ministers, as it also does in the lives of seminarians and other clergy in their young careers. But perhaps no practice is more widely misused in a clinical relationship than prayer. When should a chaplain pray? How? For what and for whom? As witnesses to God's presence and activity on earth, shouldn't chaplains be champions of prayer in the lives of our patients and students? And yet the timing, nature, content, and language of the prayer often reveal more about the person praying than about the person being prayed for. Training and supervision are the best ways to develop appropriate and effective uses of prayer because they not only allow the chaplain to explore and master the scenarios in which prayer is called for, but they also reveal the chaplain's own social and spiritual location, which are necessary data points to avoid projection and other clinical blunders. With regard to religion, the concern is similar. The chaplain must understand the role that his or her religious beliefs plays during visits and how to avoid using religion as a crutch or shield. For school chaplains, it is necessary to keep up with the latest studies and data on trends in adolescent religion and spirituality, identity, and practice.[25]

Conclusion: A Call for School Chaplaincy Standards of Care

Most denominations devote considerable resources toward the ministries of military and prison chaplaincies. Likewise, most schools are committed to maintaining high standards for their campus leaders. School chaplains have managed to be overlooked in both worlds. School chaplaincy is seen as a specialized ministry, on the one hand, but practitioners are not required or encouraged to receive any kind of training reflective of that specialization. Such training exists for fields such as youth ministry, older adult ministry, outdoor and wilderness ministries, military chaplaincy, and others. But it is my view that little attention is paid by denominations to developing skills and expertise focused on school chaplaincy. For schools' part, based on a cursory review of job descriptions posted to a wide variety of boards and search firms, schools have little to no concept of the actual purpose of a school chaplain. Most confuse such a leader with community service, chapel services, and parish ministry; to schools, they are all the same thing and require the same set of skills.

I want to argue that the established mode of pastoral care training, CPE, is the most effective way to train school chaplains. At a *minimum*, two units ought to be required for a school chaplain. Once hired, the school should support the chaplain in his or her continued training up until board certification in the appropriate chaplaincy organization. Such support recognizes the value of the specialized training needed to effectively serve students and adults of all faiths. It is no different from the training required in other specialized fields, sacred and secular. It is time for school and church communities to hold school chaplaincy to the high standard that its practitioners and recipients deserve.

Notes

1   In this essay, "school chaplaincy" and "school chaplain" refer to professionals on secondary school campuses, as opposed to college/university chaplaincy or primary school chaplaincy and ministry to young children.

2   Lisa Miller, *The Spiritual Child* (New York: St. Martin's Press, 2015).

3   Jane Kroger, *Identity in Adolescence* (New York: Routledge, 2004), 124.

4   Another way to put it is to say that at this stage of development, teenagers are beginning to significantly differentiate from their parents and to establish a self-perception in relationship to the world around them. Therefore, as they study any subject, they are studying it through the question of, "Where and how do I fit into this new information?"

5   Miller, *The Spiritual Child*, 204.

6   The roles of parish-based religious leaders are declining. In fact, anecdotal evidence suggests that families are increasingly looking to private schools to provide the kind of moral, character, and spiritual education once received at places of worship.

7   For example, deans of faculty, headmasters, and so on are still expected to possess advanced degrees, even though such expectations continue to drive up the cost of hiring and retaining them.

8   The required education of school chaplains varies widely. Some schools only require a bachelor's degree.

9   These certifying bodies include the Association for Clinical Pastoral Education (ACPE), the College of Pastoral Supervision and Psychotherapy (CPSP), the National Association of Jewish Chaplains (NAJC), and the National Association of Catholic Chaplains (NACC).

10   Some denominations require one unit of CPE for ordination, but not all.

11   Robert Leas, *ACPE: A brief history*, https://www.acpe.edu/pdf/History/ACPE%20Brief %20History.pdf.

12   I respectfully told my field education advisor at seminary that I did not want to "work in a hospital" because I was afraid of going into the rooms. She wisely responded, "Well, then it looks like that's where you need to be!" CPE is about facing such fears, since that is often what chaplains help their patients do themselves.

13   CPE tuition can vary widely from $400 to as much as $1,500 depending on location, program size, and other factors.

14 See Stephen Faller, *The Art of Spiritual Midwifery: DiaLogos and Dialectic in the Classical Tradition* (Eugene, OR: Wipf and Stock, 2015).

15 See, for example, Donald Capps, *Giving Counsel* (St. Louis: Chalice, 2001), 233–34.

16 Having one's thoughts and feelings toward one's pastoral purpose, calling, vocation, and even personality examined by a group and supervisor is an important part of what is meant by the term *clinical*, when it is used to refer to chaplaincy. In the case of this dialogue, an intern's sense of pastoral vocation and self-understanding is challenged by the supervisor, inviting the intern to question the "calling" and give it appropriate attention. Indeed, the feeling of being "called" toward a particular group of people based on gender, age, or a similar classification ought to be carefully considered, within oneself and within one's spiritual community.

17 During an exercise in which none of my school colleagues or administrators offered me feedback on my professional goals for the year, one education consultant offered me this: "The problem is, every person here can provide feedback on others' goals because they all know what it is like to be a teacher; nobody here knows anything about what you do." Indeed, though headmasters and other colleagues, including the directors of counseling, can be supportive of chaplaincy ministry, none of them are prepared to consult *specifically* on pastoral care. Their feedback can only center on secular and institutional questions and concerns, such as the public face of a chaplain's ministry, cooperation with and support of the mental health providers, teaching, and other aspects of campus and community life. When contemplating the moves made during a particular pastoral visit, say, with a young man who feels confusion surrounding his Jewish identity and his actual beliefs, to whom on campus shall the chaplain turn?

18 The CPSP is the organization to which I belong, so it is the one I am referencing here. Any legitimate certifying body is capable of accomplishing the goals of training and accountability according to the chaplain's ordaining tradition.

19 The spiritual assessment used by an ER chaplain should be different from one used by the prison chaplain.

20 What are your religious/spiritual beliefs? Where do you find the hope to go on? Are there any immediate religious needs that remain unmet?

21 Do your religious/spiritual beliefs usually help you or cause you anxiety? What about your religion remains unresolved given your current situation? Do you have a religious community with which you share life's ups and downs?

22 How are you coping with what is going on? Do you feel overwhelmed? Can you imagine what life will be like when [the situation] is resolved?

23 Would you like me to contact your pastor/rabbi/religious leader on your behalf? Have you considered a professional counselor or therapist? Are there any other needs you would like to discuss? For schools, the assessment should always include the chaplain's thoughts on whether or not other adults should be brought into the light regarding the student's situation. As mandatory reporters, chaplains may need to inform parents, counselors, medical professionals, other administrators (including the headmaster), or even the authorities depending on the nature of the visit. It is almost always the case that children are relieved when the appropriate reports are made following a disclosure.

The training I have described is a highly effective means to acquire the skills and knowledge needed to refer and/or report.

24 See, for example, Donald Capps, *Laughter Ever After: Ministry of Good Humor* (St. Louis: Chalice, 2008).

25 For the religion of teenagers, read Christian Smith, *Soul Searching: The Religious and Spiritual Lives of American Teenagers* (New York: Oxford, 2005).

PROSPECTIVE INTERSECTIONS

From Priority to Practice

Interfaith Cooperation and United Methodist Higher Education

Eboo Patel and Carolyn Roncolato

Pratheepa Ravikumar came to Hendrix College, a United Methodist school in Conway, Arkansas, from Rogers, Arkansas, where she grew up in an Indian family surrounded by a thriving Hindu community. The conclusion of her first-year orientation at Hendrix was a camping and canoeing trip with nineteen of her fellow first-year students. Over the course of the trip, Pratheepa became friends with Naomi, a Muslim student also from Arkansas, with whom she bonded over shared interests and friends. At the end of the first day, as everyone was heading to bed, Naomi stepped out of their tent to pray. Donning a white hijab, she chose a quiet spot behind the tent. Another student saw Naomi's vague outline in the dark and her white hijab moving up and down in the motions of prayer. Frightened by what she saw, she alerted one of the student trip leaders. He also found it suspicious, and together they approached Naomi and asked her who she was and what she was doing. Naomi, prostrate and in the midst of her prayer, was unable to stop and answer. Increasingly agitated, the student leader threated to get an authority figure.

Naomi quickly finished her prayer and calmly told them who she was and what she was doing. Though the students apologized profusely and the situation was resolved, it was a painful way for Naomi to start her college experience.

Pratheepa was shocked by the students' lack of awareness and their inability to recognize a Muslim person praying. This experience sparked in her a commitment to increase religious literacy and help people build relationships across lines of religious difference at Hendrix. Pratheepa went on to start a Friends of India group, and Naomi started a Muslim student association. Often working together, these groups increased the visibility of religious diversity on campus, offered support and community for religious minority students, and sparked growth in Hendrix's commitment to interfaith cooperation. Last year, Pratheepa, now a graduating senior, served as an orientation leader. Remembering her own experience, she worked to ensure that there was discussion about religious diversity during orientation and shared her own story with incoming students. Over the course of Pratheepa's time at Hendrix, interfaith cooperation and religious diversity awareness grew dramatically. Campus leadership responded to the need, experience, and interest of students like Pratheepa and made great strides toward offering more resources for their religiously diverse student body and increasing opportunities for interfaith cooperation.

Increasingly United Methodist campuses, like other institutions across the country, are religiously diverse. As Pratheepa's story suggests, campuses need to prepare for and respond to what this religious diversity means for community life. In their book *No Longer Invisible*, Douglas and Rhonda Jacobsen argue that higher education has reached a new era characterized by what they call "pluriform religion."[1] Religion is present to a new degree and in new ways on campuses. This new religiosity rarely fits into traditional doctrinal categories, is often blurred and blended with secularism, and is not always clearly recognizable as religion. Campuses have the opportunity to respond to this changing context with energy and intentionality. The Jacobsens wrote," Paying attention to religion in higher education today is not at all a matter of imposing faith or morality on anyone; it is a matter of responding intelligently to the questions of life that students find themselves necessarily asking as they try to make sense of themselves and the world in an era of ever-increasing social, intellectual and religious complexity."[2]

Attending to religion in its many forms presents opportunities for campus leaders to build stronger community, care for all students' religious needs, and prepare students for responsible global citizenry. The United Methodist Church has been forthright in its encouragement of and commitment to this very type of religious engagement. Issuing clear statements on interfaith cooperation and dialogue, the denomination has laid a foundation upon which United Methodist colleges and universities can build a commitment to religious diversity and interfaith engagement.

This chapter brings into conversation The United Methodist Church's teachings on interreligious engagement and the theories of interfaith cooperation that Interfaith Youth Core relies on in working within higher education. We begin the chapter with a reflection on the foundations within The United Methodist Church that have led to the denomination's commitment to both higher education and interfaith engagement. We proceed to look at the five recommendations for engaging interfaith relationships outlined in The United Methodist *Book of Resolutions*. We explore how each resolution relates to the theories of interfaith cooperation and then share an example from a United Methodist college or university that is an exemplar of each guideline. In the final section, we discuss nine practices that IFYC has found to be critical to advancing interfaith cooperation on campuses and ways that they can be and have been employed by United Methodist schools. In conclusion, we return to the social principles that guide The United Methodist Church as guidelines and signposts for this work.

The United Methodist Church and Higher Education

Since the early eighteenth century, education has been a core value in the Methodist tradition. John Wesley, the founder of Methodism,[3] championed education as foundational to living full and ethical lives. He argued that education gave people a better understanding of both themselves and others, allowing them to better engage and serve the world. In addition, Wesley believed deeply in and fought for all people's access to education. Early on, he opened a school in Bristol for the children of coal miners who were often overlooked and underserved. The commitment to education equality is deeply embedded in the United Methodist tradition, leading nineteenth-century church leaders to establish colleges that granted degrees to women and African Americans, and to its current commitment to quality public education for all children.[4]

Today, United Methodist colleges and universities are leading the way in welcoming religious diversity and cultivating interfaith cooperation on their campuses. Whereas United Methodist–associated colleges and universities make up 2 percent of the accredited schools in the United States, more than 10 percent of the US institutions that committed to President Obama's Interfaith and Community Service Challenge were related to The United Methodist Church.[5] This commitment to interfaith cooperation can be understood as an important continuation of Wesley's early commitment to education in two specific ways. First, Wesley and the Methodist leaders that followed recognized that education should prepare students for the changing world around them. Increasingly the United States is becoming religiously diverse, which means that in everyday life we regularly engage people from different religious traditions. Responsible citizenry in the current context requires religious literacy as well as skills to build relationships across lines of difference. If United Methodist education is going to prepare students to be responsible and engaged global citizens, then it needs to prepare them for this kind of religious diversity.

Second, the early Methodist movement did not fear that a diverse student body would be detrimental to students or to Methodism. Methodist institutions of higher education were never solely intended for Methodist students nor were they created to be homogenous spaces of learning. As Melanie B. Overton, writing for the United Methodist General Board of Higher Education and Ministry, has stated, "This commitment to interfaith partnership is merely one modern expression of an educational tradition that has endeavored to avoid narrow sectarianism since its origin at Cokesbury College. After all, when Cokesbury College was founded in 1784, the first two professors were not United Methodists, rather, they were a Quaker and a Catholic."[6]

Valuing diversity as a strength of education is a long tradition in The United Methodist Church and core to the denomination's identity. The question is, what are the best ways to uphold this commitment in United Methodist education today? In the following sections, we look at two sets of guidelines, one from the United Methodist *Book of Resolutions* and one from the Interfaith Youth Core, for critical insight on engaging religious diversity on today's campuses.

Interfaith Cooperation and The United Methodist Church

The 2016 United Methodist *Book of Resolutions,* which contains the most up-to-date and official positions of the denomination, includes a section dedicated to interreligious issues, with five guidelines for interfaith relationships.[7] These guidelines concretize the church's broad commitment to interfaith cooperation, offering a foundational framework for the development of interfaith programming and strategy at colleges and universities. In the following section, we unpack these recommendations, put each into conversation with theories of interfaith cooperation, and share an example from a United Methodist school that upholds the recommendation.

1. Identify the various faith communities and familiarize your congregation with them.[8]

Engaging religious diversity begins with seeing and knowing the people you are in community with. As this guideline suggests, this work is not just or primarily about discussion between religious leaders. Rather, the guideline calls for congregations to engage each other, indicating that interfaith cooperation involves and implicates the entire community.

Interfaith cooperation is a civic project. By this we mean that engagement across lines of religious difference happens in and has implications for local, national, and global communities. The civic spaces of our daily lives are increasingly religiously diverse, offering ever more opportunity for engaging difference. Sociologist Peter Berger describes this phenomenon as "pluralization," defined as the presence of ever-increasing diversity and therefore choices in modern society.[9] He claims that the hallmark quality of the modern experience is "the near-inconceivable expansion of the areas of human life open to choices."[10] Because of pluralization, religious diversity is growing in local communities and on campuses. This means ongoing opportunity to learn about and familiarize oneself with religious and nonreligious communities. It also means that engaging across lines of difference is a skill that we will continue to need as diversity continues to grow.

This guideline can be interpreted in two ways for colleges and universities. First, it calls campus leaders to learn about the religious communities in the local area. Familiarizing oneself with local faith communities strengthens campus-community partnerships and opens a realm of possibilities. Campus leaders may find education partners who are willing to host students, speak on campus, partner for service projects, or hire students for internships. Furthermore, many campuses are unable to meet all the religious needs of their student body. Connecting with local religious communities helps cultivate better resources for religiously diverse students who may not have their religious needs met on campus.

Second, campus leaders should identify and familiarize themselves with the religious and nonreligious communities represented by students, staff, administrators, and faculty at their institution. The first step is knowing what traditions are present, and the second step is learning enough about those traditions to know what their needs may be. For example, Shabbat-observant Jewish students may not be able to use electricity on Shabbat, which means they need nonelectric dorm keys. Muslim students may need to eat after sundown during Ramadan, which means they need dining halls to stay open late. Campus leaders need to know the communities represented on their campus, build relationships with and among the various groups, and learn about their religious needs.

Oklahoma City University offers a great example of how a school can "identify and familiarize" themselves with the religious communities in their area. One of their most popular courses is World Religions. During the course students visit local religious communities, including a synagogue, an Islamic cultural center, and a Buddhist temple. Students also organize a World Religions Exposition in which they, along with staff, faculty, and local community representatives of a wide diversity of religious traditions, gather on campus, share their traditions, and answer questions. This event gives students the opportunity to familiarize themselves with those in their community while also teaching them common beliefs and practices about a host of religious traditions.

2. Initiate dialogues with different faith communities, remaining sensitive to areas of historic tension. Be open to the possibilities for deepened understanding and new insights.[11]

This guideline suggests that it is not enough to learn who is in our communities, to know that there are Jewish and Sikh communities in your town, for example, or that the student body is 10 percent Muslim. Rather, The United Methodist Church calls for intentional engagement with the people in those communities in an effort to build real relationship. It even suggests reaching out with hospitality to initiate the relationship.

The importance of this guideline is well supported by sociological research. In his article "E Pluribus Unum," social scientist Robert Putnam shows that as diversity increases, so does social isolation and distrust of the rest of the community.[12] The simple presence of diversity does not lead to understanding or positive relationships. However, the research also shows that intentional networks of engagement across lines of difference have a tremendous impact, leading to meaningful positive relationships and a stronger civic society.

Social scientist Ashutosh Varshney studied communities throughout India that had equivalent percentages of Muslim and Hindu populations. He examined why some of these communities erupted into violent religious conflict while others remained peaceful in the face of national crises. He found that those communities that had preestablished formal and informal networks and relationships between Muslims and Hindus were able to weather relatively serious storms.[13] Varshney's research shows the power of intentionally building relationships across lines of religious difference before there is a crisis. Initiating dialogue in order to build a foundational relationship is a proactive step in creating strong and healthy communities.

The second part of this guideline recommends attention to historical tensions. At IFYC, we refer to this as having a radar screen for religious difference. Having a religious difference radar screen requires paying attention to current events locally, nationally, and globally. It also includes learning accurate and positive knowledge about traditions as well as developing literacy about the history of religious traditions, movements, and conflicts. Attending to these areas can help campus leaders curate and engage in productive and positive interfaith dialogue and events.

The last part of the recommendation suggests that engaging in dialogue across lines of religious difference is not intended for the purpose of winning people over to one's side, hashing out conflict, or proving who is right. The intention of the dialogue is better understanding, relationship building, and new learning. Entering dialogue with this type of intention sets the tone of the conversation, allowing for different kinds of learning and new depths of relationship.

Hendrix College in Conway, Arkansas is putting this guideline into practice. Hendrix College had a long-standing weekly "fellowship dinner" put on as a program for Christian vocational discernment. Dr. Robert Williamson, director of the new Interfaith Initiative at Hendrix, recognized that whereas the meal itself was open to all faith traditions, the program primarily served Christian students. Motivated by the interest and engagement of students involved in interfaith cooperation, Dr. Williamson, in cooperation with other staff, faculty, and students, changed the fellowship dinner to an Interfaith Community Meal. Each week, campus or community members design and host a dinner and program to which all Hendrix students are invited. The Interfaith Community Meals have been running for approximately a year and have included a program for Rosh Hashanah put on by Hillel, a program on Diwali hosted by the Friends of India, one by the Students for Black Culture on the role of the black church, a program by pagan students, and a program by a professor on feminism as a worldview. About the dinners, Dr. Williamson remarked, "There is a huge amount of energy around this program. There is a real sense of comradery. People feel validated and celebrated. This is one of the places where diversity is most obvious on campus."[14]

Building on their assets, Hendrix campus leadership saw these dinners as an opportunity to integrate interfaith cooperation into their campus culture. The Interfaith Community Meal now creates space for students to gain appreciative knowledge, develop relationships across lines of difference, and practice interfaith dialogue.

   3. Work with persons of other faith communities to resolve economic, social, cultural, and political problems in the community.[15]

As this guideline suggests, the value of interfaith cooperation extends beyond religious communities or spiritual enrichment. It is a powerful tool in working toward broadly impactful civic goals that are important for a healthy society. This guideline suggests looking for shared values across lines of religious difference and finding ways to act on those values together. For example, two communities may both be committed to fighting hunger and homelessness, while being motivated by different religious beliefs or worldviews. By working together on the issue, there is a greater chance of making progress toward the goal. Through the process of working together around a shared value, people develop relationships and potentially find other places of commonality.

In their study of religion in the United States, sociologists Robert Putnam and David Campbell found that people most often develop relationships with those who are religiously different than they are through shared interests.[16] They ask readers to imagine having a friend named Al, with whom they do beekeeping. "As you get to know Al, you learn that in addition to his regard for apiculture, he is also an evangelical Christian. Before learning that, you may have been suspicious of evangelicals. But if your pal Al is an avid beekeeper—just like you—and is also an evangelical, then perhaps evangelicals are not so bad after all. . . . Perhaps upon realizing that you can be friends with Al, a member of a religious group you once viewed with suspicion, you come to re-evaluate your perception of other religious groups too."[17] Evidence shows that as people build more religious bridges, they become warmer to many different religions, not just those from which they know someone.

The "My Pal Al" phenomenon demonstrates that connecting with people of other religious traditions around shared values and interests increases appreciation for other religious traditions. By working with different religious and nonreligious communities to resolve economic, social, cultural, and political problems, students have the opportunity to build relationships through common action, and in the process, increase their appreciative attitudes about other traditions and worldviews. As such, through this process, people are not only bettering the community but are also changing long-term perceptions of those who are different.

One of the ways this guideline can be implemented is through service-learning programs such as that at Wofford College. Recently named to the President's Higher Education Community Service Honor Roll, Wofford has developed a strong interfaith service-learning and civic engagement initiative. One of their courses, developed and taught by chaplain and professor of religion Dr. Ron Robinson, is an interfaith civil rights tour of the South. Dr. Robinson takes students to important civil rights sites in Atlanta, Birmingham, Montgomery, Little Rock, and Selma, where they study the history of the place, discuss local interfaith cooperation, and meet with community leaders. They conclude the trip with a civil rights activism training at the Highlander Center in Tennessee. The course brings together students from many different religious and nonreligious worldviews. Each brings his or her own perspective, values, and tradition to the initiative. Over the course of this trip, the students live, work, and study together, sharing experiences and perspectives. By engaging a shared topic and focusing on the issues they face together, they form deep bonds that enrich the learning experience and have long-lasting effects on their attitudes toward other religions.

4. Plan community celebrations with an interreligious perspective together with persons of other faith traditions.[18]

This recommendation builds upon the recognition that our civic spaces are increasingly diverse. Communities are themselves made up of multiple communities. In other words, a campus is a community that includes people who have multiple belongings to other communities. One important way to create an overarching culture of belonging is to be attentive to and inclusive of, and to make visible, the multiple communities that make up the campus community.

The inclusion of a multiplicity of voices and traditions in community celebrations is an important part of creating an inclusive narrative. In his piece "Why Stories Matter" Marshall Ganz argues that stories are key to leading, building, and changing communities.[19] Ganz claims that in order for the many communities within a community to bond as a cohesive whole, they need a unifying narrative, "a story of us" that anchors them in the "fierce urgency of now."[20] Community celebrations are places in which this narrative can be told and performed.

The recommendation to include the plurality of traditions in community celebrations is especially pertinent to college campuses. This includes inviting a diversity of voices to help celebrate a campus-wide event, such as graduation or the opening of a new building. It also includes the public celebration of different traditions—for example, a public celebration of the Hindu festival of Diwali, an Iftar dinner during Ramadan, or a campus-wide Passover Seder. Seeing a public celebration of one's own tradition encourages a feeling of welcome, of being at home and being part of the story. It is powerful to see that the broader community knows something about your tradition and is excited that you are there. This guideline presents an opportunity to reconsider campus identity and who sees themselves within it.

Lastly, this guideline recommends having "an interreligious perspective," which is different from having an eye to different religions. "Interreligious" refers to the relationship between different traditions, the ways they interact and engage. As compared to a siloed presentation of different religious or nonreligious traditions, the interreligious perspective encourages the encounter and engagement between them. Furthermore, religious studies scholar Hans Gustafson argues that an interreligious perspective "involves the examination of encounters that one is already a part of."[21] In other words, we have relationships and are in community with those who are religiously different. Having an interreligious perspective means reflecting on the life we already have together, the quality of relationships, and the ways our encounters have shaped and continue to shape us. It also means using events as opportunities to intentionally build and enrich relationships across lines of difference, to cultivate appreciative knowledge about each other's traditions, and to demonstrate ways that religious and nonreligious traditions have shared values and commitments.

A leader in embracing this guideline, Lebanon Valley College, recently renovated their Frederic K. Miller Chapel in order to be more representative and inclusive of multiple religious traditions. As part of the college's interfaith commitments, they started a series of religious holiday open houses to which they invite the entire campus and local community. The open houses include programming, time for questions, and celebratory food. Celebrations include the Muslim holiday of Isra and Mi'raj, led by the Muslim chaplain at Lebanon Valley; and the Hindu holiday of Diwali. Through these open houses, Lebanon

Valley publicly celebrates diverse religious traditions. Created with an interfaith perspective, these events invite the broader community into the celebration to increase religious literacy and cultivate relationships. This is a step beyond providing accommodations for religious communities on campus to active learning and engagement with traditions. Lebanon Valley is a majority Christian school. However, campus leadership recognizes that the number of students who adhere to a particular religious tradition does not determine whether the campus should put resources toward supporting those students and learning about their traditions. It's valuable for all religious and nonreligious people to learn about and engage with other religious and nonreligious people and traditions.

5. Develop new models of community building that strengthen relationships and allow people to dwell together in harmony while honoring the integrity of their differences.[22]

This guideline encourages forming community that does not depend on or require sameness, watering down one's tradition, or avoiding differences. It suggests looking for new ways to build communities that are made up of strong relationships in which differences are recognized and honored.

Harvard scholar of religion Diana Eck makes the critical differentiation between diversity and pluralism. She argues that diversity is simply the fact of different kinds of people living in close proximity. In and of itself diversity is neutral, neither good nor bad. Pluralism, on the other hand, is an achievement. She wrote, "The language of pluralism is the language not just of difference but of engagement, involvement, and participation. . . . Pluralism is the dynamic process through which we engage with one another in and through our very deepest differences."[23] Based on Eck's work, the vision of pluralism that we at IFYC are working toward is composed of three things. The first is mutual respect for identity. In a pluralistic society, people have a right to form their own identities and to express their identities, and those identities should be reasonably accommodated. Second, moving beyond respect to actual engagement of difference, pluralism requires relationships between communities. Last, pluralism requires common action for the common good. Our various identities and relationships can only exist and thrive if we have a collective interest to uphold the shared principles and structures that benefit all of us. This definition of pluralism does not depend on certain religious belief or theological commitment. It's a civic goal that depends on an open invitation to the table. This is a vision of community in which our differences are brought into the conversation and honored. This guideline is a reminder that we can engage with those across lines of religious difference without losing our particular identity or watering down our faith.

The diversity of the United States, let alone the world, means that we need ways to live together in the midst of profound difference. This is hard and requires practice. Colleges and universities give students the opportunity to practice living and working with those who are different from them. Practicing this work on campus will prepare them to continue to be leaders throughout their personal and professional lives.

Recognizing the importance of this kind of practice, University minister Eduardo Bousson started a "speed-faithing" program at Nebraska Wesleyan University. Although there is limited interfaith diversity on campus, there is significant intra-faith diversity. Reverend Bousson saw the diversity among the many practices of Christian students as a launching pad to engage difference. He hosts his well-attended speed-faithing events three times a semester. Students gather, write down their religious or nonreligious identities on note cards, and move around the room, discussing questions with one another without revealing their religious affiliations. Example questions include, "Who's your hero?" "When have you had an experience of awe?" and "When have you experienced love?" After they answer all the questions, Reverend Bousson announces the various religious identities in the room, highlighting that students have found commonality and shared deeply with people of religious and nonreligious worldviews different from their own. This experience of speed-faithing gives students practice that will later help them engage a much broader world of diversity outside of college.

The guidelines laid out in the *Book of Resolutions* call for intentional engagement across lines of religious difference in order to seek better understanding, work together for the common good, and strengthen communities and relationships. The United Methodist Church's rationale for interreligious engagement is not to only find and affirm what they share with other traditions, nor is it to convert others. United Methodists are invited to intentionally engage religious diversity because the relationships themselves are valuable, and religious difference is a good thing.

IFYC's Leadership Practices for Interfaith Excellence in Higher Education

Higher education is a unique context in which to engage religious diversity and prepare civic leaders for a number of reasons. First, campuses are a microcosm of broader society, allowing students to engage on a smaller scale—while being heavily supported—dynamics and issues that they may face throughout their lives. Increasing levels of religious diversity on campuses offers opportunities for both building relationships and navigating tensions and conflict. Second, colleges and universities are sites of knowledge production. Faculty, staff, and students study, research, discuss, practice, and publish new material that informs broader society. Third, colleges and universities have a history of setting civic priorities for the rest of society. Campuses start practices and vocalize concerns, such as environmentalism or LGBTQ rights, and eventually those priorities move from campuses to broader society. Lastly, campuses graduate a critical mass of leaders who have learned material, internalized values, and practiced skills, which they can transfer to broader society.

For these reasons among others, IFYC works with higher education in the United States. Through our experience working with more than five hundred college and universities, we have recognized consistently effective strategies and patterns for campus-wide interfaith efforts. We have identified nine "Leadership Practices for Interfaith Excellence."[24] These leadership practices should not be seen as sequential, and are most successful when pursued together, allowing them to support and strengthen each other. They are intended to be implemented both broadly, touching many areas of campus life, and deeply, with considerable time and attention to complexity. As we have discussed, The United Methodist Church has identified interreligious engagement as a priority and offers guidelines that anchor the work of promoting interreligious cooperation and relationship building within their faith tradition. Below, we demonstrate how IFYC's leadership practices offer specific examples of how to implement the United Methodist commitment to supporting interfaith efforts.

The first leadership practice for interfaith excellence is establishing a connection between interfaith cooperation and the institution's mission and identity. The United Methodist Church has made this easy for United Methodist schools by stating clearly and consistently the United Methodist commitment to interfaith cooperation. Anchoring interfaith cooperation in the campus's own story builds a strong foundation for the other leadership practices.

The second leadership practice is developing a campus-wide strategy for interfaith cooperation. The strategy should flow from the mission and identity connection and may include vision statements, strategic plans, or campus-wide learning goals. In order for interfaith cooperation to truly become a campus priority, it needs to be integrated into all levels of campus life. For example, McMurry University underwent a formal process of internationalization when they decided to intentionally recruit and admit a more diverse student body. This process included close attention to institutional commitments; administrative leadership, structure, and staffing; curriculum, co-curriculum, and learning outcomes; faculty policies and practices; student mobility; and collaboration and partnerships. Attention to both religious diversity and potential for interfaith cooperation is being addressed at each level of the institution.

The third practice is to incorporate interfaith cooperation in the school's public identity. Expressing interfaith cooperation as part of a school's public identity is the external complement to the internal campus-wide strategy. This recommendation suggests using marketing and communications to highlight interfaith as a campus priority. This simultaneously draws religiously diverse students, staff, and faculty to the school while modeling interfaith commitment to other schools and broader society. North Central College has the following statement on their campus ministry webpage: "For more than 150 years, North Central College students from different faith traditions have united as a campus community where mutual respect produces vibrant discussion and collective action. Affiliated with The United Methodist Church, North Central encourages students to ask questions and develop their personal faith during this spiritually pivotal time in their lives."[25] In this public statement, North Central proclaims both their United Methodist identity and their commitment to religious diversity.

The fourth leadership practice is respecting and accommodating diverse religious and nonreligious identities. Foundational to successful interfaith programming, this practice involves formal policies and practices that address issues of religious accommodations. This recommendation requires knowing who is in the community and knowing what their religious needs are. As we mentioned earlier, Lebanon Valley remodeled their chapel space to better meet the needs of non-Christian students. As part of the remodel, they created an additional prayer room, designed with Muslim students' religious experience in mind.

The fifth recommendation is to make interfaith cooperation an academic priority. The field of interfaith studies is growing quickly, with courses, minors, and certificates being created all over the country. This priority includes both content and pedagogical practices. Oklahoma City University created an interfaith studies minor intended to help students "gain a broad overview of the world's major religious traditions, learn how to interact with persons from a variety of religious backgrounds, and demonstrate leadership skills in religious communities or organizations."[26] The school stresses the value of these skills for people in all professions, encouraging students to pair the minor with nursing, business, political science, and sociology.

Sixth, impactful interfaith cooperation on campus requires building competence and capacity among faculty and staff. Campus professionals play a significant role in shaping students' experience of campus. If students are going to feel welcome and have their needs met, faculty, staff, and administrators must be attuned to religious identities. Recently, Hamline University decided to focus on religion and spirituality for their student affairs diversity trainings. They plan to bring experts from their area to train all student affairs staff to better understand, serve, and offer resources to their religiously diverse student body.

Seventh, campuses should encourage student leadership. In order for movements to be successful, they need student involvement and buy-in. Supporting student leadership contributes to student learning and the sustainability of interfaith programming. This means looking for ways to cultivate leadership, supporting students' ideas, and facilitating transitions of leadership as students graduate. For example, Hendrix College has revived the student interfaith group, which is now helping to organize and lead the Interfaith Community Meal. Staff and faculty are intentionally handing over leadership to students while continuing to offer ongoing support and resources that ensure long-term sustainability.

The eighth leadership practice is cultivating campus-community partnerships. Successful interfaith leadership requires experience in real communities with real people. By partnering with the local community, campuses not only gain educational partners but give their students more opportunities to engage in the real world. Interfaith learning is greatly strengthened by service-learning, internships, study abroad, and other experiential learning opportunities. As is the case with Wofford College's course on interfaith and civil rights, students gain a tremendous amount from learning outside the formal classroom.

The final recommendation is strong assessment of interfaith programs and campus climate. Interfaith cooperation remains a relatively new area of focus, and as such, schools need to continue to assess its impact to determine what is working and what could be improved. DePauw University has an interfaith internship program in which students spend a year learning to talk across lines of difference, visiting each other's places of worship, and engaging in ongoing dialogue. After participating in this internship, they are eligible to serve on the interfaith council. Rev. Kate Smanik, assistant dean of students for spirituality, service, and social justice, assesses all students involved in interfaith work at the end of every year to evaluate growth. Rev. Smanick and her colleagues created a rubric that asks student to evaluate where they were at the start of the year and where they are at the conclusion. This consistent assessment practice increases the effectiveness of their programming.

Conclusion: United Methodist Social Principles

The United Methodist Church has a social creed that serves as "a basic statement of [their] convictions about the fundamental relationships between God, God's creation and humanity."[27] The particulars of these convictions are detailed in a series of social principles. Two of these principles speak directly to religious diversity and the importance of interfaith cooperation. "The Social Community: The Rights of Religious Minorities," recognizes the long history of religious persecution and the frequency with which it continues to occur.[28] This principle condemns all forms of overt and covert religious intolerance. Additionally, it asserts "the right of all religions and their adherents to freedom from legal, economic, and social discrimination."[29] With this social principle, The United Methodist Church goes beyond denouncing discrimination to inviting its members to increase literacy about and awareness of other religious traditions, people, and communities. The Church calls its members to promote and defend the rights of all people to practice their religion as a way of living out their religious duty as United Methodists.

The second United Methodist social principle relevant for interfaith work is the "Social Principle on World Community."[30] This principle emphasizes that as a global community we are presented with immediate and pressing challenges—injustice, war, ecological crises, and so on. If we are going to survive as a human race, we must find ways to work together for the common good. Considering this global reality, The United Methodist Church commits itself "to the achievement of a world community that is a fellowship of persons who honestly love one another. We pledge ourselves to seek the meaning of the gospel in all issues that divide people and threaten the growth of world community."[31] As this principle declares, of top priority for The United Methodist Church is finding ways to understand and work across lines of difference. Recognizing that we need each other to survive, the Church proclaims that building global community is a religious concern.

With these explicit statements, The United Methodist Church situates itself as one among many religious traditions. It declares that engaging with and seeking understanding of those who are different is a strength that will make our world, our communities, and the individual's faith better. These statements make clear that it is a United Methodist responsibility to actively engage, build relationships with, and create community with those who are religiously different.

The United Methodist Church is an excellent example of a religious tradition that prioritizes interfaith cooperation as an innate value, a model that many would benefit from emulating. United Methodist colleges and universities have a unique opportunity to share this method of interfaith cooperation. At colleges and universities people from many different religious and nonreligious traditions gather, learn, and form community. Because people pass from the college context into many other settings, United Methodist campuses have a unique opportunity to share the United Methodist value of and method for interfaith cooperation with a diverse array of people.

The United Methodist *Book of Resolutions* states, "We United Methodist Christians, not just individually, but corporately, are called to be neighbors with other faith communities, and to work with them to create a community, a set of relationships between people at once interdependent and free, in which there is love, mutual respect and justice."[32] Situated at the core of United Methodist doctrine, this statement indicates that United Methodists engage in interfaith cooperation not in spite of their Methodism but because of it. Engagement across lines of religious difference is itself an act of faith that honors a deep and powerful tradition.

Notes

1 Douglas Jacobsen and Rhonda Hustedt Jacobsen, *No Longer Invisible: Religion in University Education* (New York: Oxford University Press, 2012).

2 Jacobsen and Jacobsen, 30.

3 The United Methodist Church is part of the Wesleyan family of churches, which regard John Wesley as their founder.

4 General Board of Higher Education and Ministry: The United Methodist Church, "Why Are United Methodists Committed to Education?," https://www.gbhem.org/education/scu, accessed November 9, 2017.

5 Melanie B. Overton, "UMC's Interfaith Dialogue and Partnerships Can Appeal to Young," General Board of Higher Education and Ministry: The United Methodist Church, February 29, 2012, https://www.gbhem.org/article/umc%E2%80%99s-interfaith-dialogue-and-partnerships-can-appeal-young.

6 Overton,"UMC's Interfaith Dialog."

7 The United Methodist Church, *The Book of Resolutions of The United Methodist Church* (Nashville: United Methodist Publishing House, 2016), 293–304.

8 The United Methodist Church, 296.

9 Peter Berger, *The Heretical Imperative: Contemporary Possibilities of Religious Affirmation* (New York: Doubleday, 1979).

10 Berger, 3.

11 The United Methodist Church, *The Book of Resolutions*, 296.

12 Robert D. Putnam, "E Pluribus Unum: Diversity and Community in the Twenty-First Century," the 2006 Johan Skytte Prize Lecture, *Scandinavian Political Studies* 30 (2007): 137–74.

13 Ashutosh Varshney, *Ethnic Conflict and Civic Life: Hindus and Muslims in India* (New Haven, CT: Yale University, 2002).

14 Dr. Williamson, in an interview by Carolyn at Hendrix College on March 13, 2017.

15 The United Methodist Church, *The Book of Resolutions, 296.*

16 Robert Putnam and David Campbell, *American Grace: How Religion Divides and Unites Us* (New York: Simon and Schuster, 2010).

17 Putnam and Campbell, 532.

18 The United Methodist Church, *The Book of Resolutions,* 296.

19 Marshall Ganz, "Why Stories Matter: The Art and Craft of Social Change," *Sojourners* magazine, 2009.

20 Ganz.

21 Hans Gustafson, "Interreligious and Interfaith Studies in Relation to Religious Studies and Theological Studies," *State of Formation*, January 6, 2015, http://www.stateofformation.org/2015/01/interreligious-and-interfaith-studies-in-relation-to-religious-studies-and-theological-studies/.

22 The United Methodist Church, *The Book of Resolutions,* 296.

23 Diana Eck, *A New Religious America: How a "Christian Country" Has Become the Most Religiously Diverse Nation* (San Francisco: HarperCollins, 2001), 70.

24 Eboo Patel, Katie Baxter, and Noah Silverman, "Leadership Practices for Interfaith Excellence in Higher Education," *Liberal Education* 101 (2015).

25 "Office of Ministry & Service," North Central College, accessed May 9, 2017, https://www.northcentralcollege.edu/ministry-service.

26 "Interfaith Studies Minor," Oklahoma City University, accessed May 9, 2017, http://www.okcu.edu/religion/minors-certificates/interfaith-studies.

27 "Social Principles and Social Creed," The United Methodist Church, accessed November 9, 2017, http://www.umc.org/what-we-believe/social-principles-social-creed.

28 "Social Principles: The Social Community," The United Methodist Church, accessed November 9, 2017, http://www.umc.org/what-we-believe/the-social-community.

29 "Social Principles: The Social Community."

30 "Social Principles: The World Community," The United Methodist Church, accessed November 9, 2017, http://www.umc.org/what-we-believe/the-world-community.

31 "Social Principles: The World Community."

32 The United Methodist Church, *The Book of Resolutions,* 294.

Is Religion
the Sinews of War?

Or Is It Just a Myth "Generally So Considered"?

John A. Tures

Introduction

"Money is not the sinews of war, although it is generally so considered." Thus, Machiavelli opens his tenth chapter of the second book from his *First Ten Books of Titus Livius*.[1] He established the lack of theoretical and empirical evidence between economics and conflict, while simultaneously recognizing how dominant the belief that such a connection exists. With religion, it is a similar story. We believe that the world is smothered by religious conflicts, without really scrutinizing whether or not such a connection between religion and conflict actually exists.

This article addresses not only the role myths play in society, but how faith and the church can team up with the academy and science to scrutinize such political conjectures. It's not just about evaluating a theory, but about how a church leader, a religious college, a political science class, an inquisitive instructor, and a journal dedicated to showing the relationship between all three came together to solve a mystery that people didn't even realize needed solving.

To examine the myth of religious conflicts perpetuated by the media and society, we test a hypothesis on the connection between the variables. It looks at Holsti's data on war issues between 1648 and 1989.[2] Results find that the myth of religious conflicts is vastly overstated.

Scrutinizing the Myth of Religious Conflict

A decade ago, the television show *Mythbusters* took cable TV by storm.[3] The program featured several special-effects experts who would test popularly held beliefs, which came from history, movies, other television shows, and commonly held phrases. For example, could one survive a nuclear blast by hiding in a refrigerator? Could a Greek city stop a naval invasion by using mirrors to burn the wooden ships? And is it really easy to "shoot fish in a barrel?"

After delighting my students by showing a few episodes, I shifted them from the explosions, elaborate tests, and host humor to the real value of the program: getting them to understand the scientific method (which the show would often adopt) and to challenge long-held myths. And that is exactly what our students did when we examined the relationship between faith and fighting.

Myths are "models that make sense," according to the editors of the volume *Rereading America*.[4] Or, as cowboy humorist Will Rogers once said, "It isn't what we don't know that gives us trouble, it's what we know that ain't so!"[5] They are the beliefs that we've held for a long time, without actually testing them. In fact, it could be dangerous to challenge those myths. In the times of the Greeks, one can remember Socrates's demise. Nowadays, one might expect ridicule, being shunned by journals and grant providers, and a fate worse than that of the ancient philosophers: being denied tenure.

Each semester, I have my students in their introductory classes work on a group project, saving individual projects for higher-level classes. And in my international politics class, a topic that my students and I chose to undertake was one of the most deeply held myths in society today: that religion causes conflict.

This is not just a theory advanced by secularists and atheists. You can hear such a myth echoed by devout members of the Christian faith, as well as practitioners of other belief systems. In fact, I pitched the idea of the research project to our students after one of our United Methodist Church bishops in Georgia gave a sermon decrying the actions of so many religions (including our own), claiming they were a source of conflict. He didn't believe my results, even when my findings put Christianity in a better light! But my results were not attributed to my faith. In fact, following the myth, I fully expected religion to dominate our study as a source of conflict.

Such a project was fraught with all kinds of risk. I was still working toward promotion. Teaming up with undergraduates is always very time-consuming, as you have to help students learn how to review the literature, gather data, and conduct the research, a process that takes significantly less time for the seasoned scholar. Moreover, teaching at a religious institution, either finding can be problematic. Finding a connection between the church and conflict could be attacked by that religion for being yet another case of a college finding fault with religious faith. And finding results that differed from what everyone else believed could upset those (of faith or without such beliefs) who realize they were wrong all along.

But it was The United Methodist Church itself, and our UMC-affiliated college in particular, that let me know that I had more than just a "safe space" with which to operate. I would be actively encouraged to evaluate such myths, which, like the television show, could be considered "confirmed," or "plausible," or "busted."

The National Association of Schools and Colleges of The United Methodist Church (NASCUMC) calls for us to "advance the work of education and scholarships."[6] It also involves partnering with the church to educate students. A key value is "academic freedom, where there is open and honest pursuit of knowledge and wisdom without restriction." Intellectual vigor is combined with moral integrity, as well as spiritual fulfillment.

Our research would therefore be conducted on a topic that could be of benefit to the faith, whether the results showed faith reduces fighting, or increases it. The former would show that religion should not be divorced from peacemaking efforts, while the latter could spur an honest effort to reform the faith. And our work would involve an honest test of the evidence, as well as an original work of scholarship.

LaGrange College, where I teach, has a similar mission. The oft-stated goal is to "challenge the mind" and "inspire the soul." The college claims a close tie with The United Methodist Church, combining the Wesleyan and liberal arts traditions "in the search for truth," utilizing our four pillars: civility, diversity, service, and excellence. LaGrange College "prepares students to be successful, responsible citizens . . . who aspire to lives of integrity and moral courage."[7]

Our students reviewed the literature, combining journalistic articles and books with those of academic scholarship, gathering data, coding cases based on the issue of conflict, and reporting on the results.

Students became excited by the project, spending hours outside of the class presenting the findings, learning how to use the project to conduct their own research in future classes. Several went on to graduate school, becoming teachers, coaches, and mentors at their places of work. But as hinted earlier, there is often a price to be paid for challenging myths. Time after time, our work was rejected, more for challenging the status quo than for having a flaw in the data, the literature, or the research design. One enthusiastic acceptance by the editor and several reviewers was withdrawn because of a recalcitrant reviewer. Despite skepticism from religious and nonreligious people, the students benefited more from the experience than having an additional line on the résumé. But interest generated by this edited volume will now help a wider audience learn what we found years ago, that the subject of the religious conflict is a myth that is not supported by the evidence, despite the fact that many believe such a connection exists. The following is our research and findings.

Clashes over Creed: A Review of the Literature

Why War and Worship?

Publications in the press and scholarly literature are replete with tales of religious wars, so frequent as to have us presume that nearly every conflict contains some element of faiths that fight. But our interest is not regaling the reader with such lurid tales. Our purpose here is to determine why scholars feel religions are compelled to engage in conflict.

Doctrinal Differences. When pinned down for a reason for a religious war, it is generally assumed that it is a difference in religious doctrine that produces the clash between different faiths. One creed contends one thing, while a different belief system has just that . . . something different. Given that yielding on one matter may cause the whole faith to be called into question, both groups are compelled to crush each other.

The most commonly cited work on the subject comes from Samuel Huntington's *Clash of Civilizations*.[8] In this argument Huntington argues that different religions produce different ideologies and differences in attitudes toward politics, which has the effect of turning religious disputes into political disputes.[9] Reychler also notes the belief that doctrinal differences come into play in the fighting between different faiths.[10] Fox finds that wars between religions are more likely to occur, as well as be deadlier, than other forms of conflict.[11] *Newsweek's* account of the fighting in Chechnya includes quotes from those wishing to impose sharia law on the country upon achieving independence, more harshly than even what the Taliban did in Afghanistan.[12] The story mentions Azha Ibragimov as saying, "This . . . was a religious war." And Horrelt argues that attitudes of the Muslim Brotherhood and Islamists in Iran are motivated by hostility toward Israel.[13]

Scared of Secularization. Though doctrinal differences may be the most obvious source of religious disagreement, other motives for such conflicts exist throughout the literature. We discovered that secularization may also play a contributing factor. Different dogmas have noted, with alarm, that the world may be headed in a distinctly

261

nonreligious direction. Fearing a loss in converts and membership due to this trend, religions feel compelled to "fight" to keep their numbers from continuing to decline, as well as their position in society as a source of both inspiration and policy making.

This may actually be an old concern. Shortly after returning from Mount Sinai with God's Ten Commandments, Moses observed his people worshipping a "golden calf" (Exodus 32). In his rage and retribution for straying from the path, roughly three thousand of his people were executed.[14] Ajami's critique of Huntington reveals that "modernity" (along with economics) might account for the real culprit for a "clash of civilizations."[15] Gopin and Dobbelaere also note the secularization trend as providing problems for the "religious conflict" argument.[16] And AjitSingh applies secularization to the religious conflict debate, making faith more of a "taboo" subject.[17] Even Fox found the number of conflicts between religion and nonreligion to increase slightly,[18] in his take on Dobbelaere's argument.[19]

It's All about Identity. In his research on the "Clash of Civilizations," Huntington uncovered another rationale for religious conflict: the politics of one's identity. In fact, one's religion determines one's culture, which (in turn), defines one's civilization.[20] Huntington poses the question of identity when dealing with such battles between different peoples. Since religions cannot be universally applied with so many faiths in existence, who you are determines your friends and enemies.[21]

For Feldman et al., the instability in Iraq is tied to identity politics, organized around religion.[22] In an uncertain world, or uncertain country, one's identity becomes one's form of security. "If you are a member of my ethnic, racial, or religious group, then we share at least some basic bond, which may be enough to ensure our loyalty to one another. I need some assurance that you will have my back, and identity is better than nothing," writes the author, a New York University professor and member of the Council of Foreign Relations. For Fox, the relationship between the politics of identity and religious conflict goes beyond the Iraqi case. He finds that most ethnic conflicts are actually religious conflicts, and that wars between different religions are on the increase, outstripping even conflicts between religious and nonreligious peoples.[23]

When identity politics are shoved to the forefront, conflicts can be about religion, even if there is a secular rationale for conflict. For Morrow, religious groups can clash for secular reasons, like jobs and income, because one group feels economic discrimination from another group.[24] This is what could spur conflict in Lebanon between Christians, Sunni Muslims, and their Shiite counterparts, between North Irish Protestants and Catholics, and even in Israel between Jews and Palestinian Muslims, according to Morrow.[25] And for Benson, "Northern Ireland degenerated into a place full of aggrieved people whose rage and humiliation found expression in feuds and retaliation and whose self-esteem was measured in terms of enviously depriving and begrudging others."[26]

Fraudulent Leaders of Faith. Another source of conflict involving religion is tied to the behavior of its leaders, or leaders of a country who would exploit the doctrine for political gain. "Leaders are adept at appealing to the deepest emotions of their groups for both positive and negative outcomes and are able to inflame as well as soothe anxious and suspicious followers," writes Benson.[27] In covering the Iraq War, Grossman documents how religious leaders wrap up patriotism with biblical justification for the battle.[28]

Powers finds a case where "a history textbook used by high school seniors throughout Serbia blames the outbreak of the current conflict in the former Yugoslavia on the Vatican, which 'launched a battle against Orthodoxy and Serbs through the Catholic Church and its allies.'"[29] The Serbs fought back, it goes on, "'to prevent a repeat of the genocide they suffered in World War II.'" This is the result of "manipulation of religion," according to Powers.[30] Even optimists like Gopin conclude that some radicals will still attempt to exploit religion for their own ends.[31]

Emotional Connections to The Creed. Not all sources of conflict between religions can be tied to doctrine, secularization, identity, or the behavior of leaders who hijack the faith for their own selfish purposes.

Sometimes, one's faith can produce such an attachment as to excite passions not normally associated with other possible issues of conflict. "There are a variety of possible explanations as to why people choose one religious response over another regarding conflict. Certainly one cannot dismiss the cognitive or emotional needs that may be met by a particular text, idea, or spiritual image," Gopin observes.[32] Bajekal documents how the battle over holy sites in Jerusalem is driving the recent conflict between Israel and Islam, given how central the city is to the religion of each.[33]

Based on this literature, we have generated a theory about the relationship between religion and conflict, which finds that the two are connected. The independent variable is the presence or absence of a religious issue, and the dependent variable is the presence or absence of conflict itself. In this theory the relationship is positive, indicating that the presence of a religious issue will increase the likelihood of conflict; when religious issues are less prevalent, so, too, will conflict be less present.

Why Prayer and Peace?

But not all of the research concludes that different belief systems are likely to battle each other. For each rationale given for religious conflict, there is corresponding argument undercutting that position. The result may be that, while religious conflicts are not necessarily absent, religion's role in war may turn out to be greatly exaggerated, especially when compared to others.

Do Doctrinal Differences Really Drive Disputes? Could differences in religious precepts really play that great a role in driving conflict? We may generally assume that because different religions exist, doctrine is at the heart of any disagreement between any two faiths. But as Morrow has observed, "a Belfast pub is not blown up to assert 'the Real Presence' or 'the Virgin Birth.'"[34] And it's not just the conflict in Northern Ireland where doctrine has been exaggerated. There are some in the *Newsweek* account of the Chechen conflict in the 1990s who assert that the war is not about establishing sharia law or that doing so would be a good idea.[35] And Gopin reveals that there may be more in the way of similarities among religions than differences. "There is an inordinate number of values among global religions, many yet to be analyzed, that may provide useful tools in conflict prevention, conflict management, compromise, negotiation, and reconciliation."[36]

Van Biema's account of Moses is one where doctrine could generate a pacific response.[37] One may be familiar with the notion that nearly every faith has some form of the Golden Rule from Luke 6:31— "Do to others as you would have them do to you." By highlighting a few marginal differences, one may overlook the overwhelming similarities between the teachings of each faith.

Should Religion Fear Secularization? Whether one fears or embraces secularization, all seem to believe that it is happening. But not all have concluded it has negative consequences, even for religion. Dobbelaere finds not only a secularization trend, but the likelihood that it would produce fewer religious conflicts and less bloody ones.[38] AjitSingh argues that younger people are more secular, as well as more tolerant of multiple faiths.[39] And Gopin has discovered that "among people of a secular, liberal religious, or cosmopolitan orientation, there is broad-based support for the notion that the best way to move society away from religious intolerance and toward pluralism is the development of a universal set of guidelines, such as those expressed in United Nations documents regarding political and civil institutions and individual rights."[40]

Isn't One's (Religious) Identity a Bit Inflated? As we saw in the previous set of arguments, some believe that human identity is intertwined with religion. For others, the role of religion is somewhat exaggerated in our lives. Tolson says that we tend to oversimplify people, lumping them together in groups, and blaming the actions of a few on the whole.[41] For example, many people feel all Muslims celebrated the attacks of 9/11, when very few did. It would be analogous to saying all Americans were violent people after the Los Angeles riots in 1965 or 1992. Tolson quotes Columbia professor of literature Edward Said, who said, "Islam is no 'monolithic whole,' but a divided body of competing 'interpretations.' In the same way, Christians are divided into Catholics, Orthodox, and a variety of Protestant sects, just as Judaism has its divisions. Said says religions should be treated "as vast complexities that are neither all-inclusive, nor completely deterministic in how they affect their adherents."[42] In other words, treating believers of one faith as the same may be a mistake.

Tolson and Said are hardly the only ones to reach such a conclusion. Grim and Frinke similarly feel that religion is also conflated with ideology.[43] For example, not all Arabs are Muslim, any more than all Chinese are Buddhist.[44]

Moreover, not all social behavior is reducible to religion.[45] By the same token, not all wars between people of a different religion can be attributed to that religion. Powers quotes the Reverend Peter Kuzmic, the president of the Protestant-Evangelical Council of Croatia and Bosnia, as saying, "The genesis of the war was ideological and territorial, not ethnic and religious."[46] Furthermore, Newsweek's coverage of the war in Chechnya reveals a less-than-clear role for religion.[47] A B. C. Davgladov was quoted in that article as saying that "this was not a religious war, but a war for independence."[48] Of course, there are those who feel as contemporary leaders like the president of France and the chancellor of Germany do, concluding "multiculturalism" is a bad idea. Huntington argues in "The Clash of Civilizations" that religious pluralism or even the presence of two religions sharing a border is a recipe for conflict.[49] But Grim and Frinke find scant empirical support for Huntington's thesis.[50] Rather, they conclude that religiously heterogeneous societies as well as dyads (pairs of states) on some "civilization fault line" (like "Catholic Spain" and "Muslim Morocco") are no more likely to war with each other than any other pair of contiguous states.

Some go even further, finding religious pluralism to be a prescription for peace. AjitSingh finds that people (especially the younger crowd) are less supportive of putting one faith on the spot or pedestal.[51] And Gopin feels that religious tolerance and pluralism are moving toward universalism.[52]

Are Religious Leaders Really So Revolting? Earlier, we documented how some religious leaders appear to be exploiting the connection with beliefs and battle for personal gain and glory. But we would be remiss in ignoring how some religious leaders also go the extra mile to push for peace. Morrow admits that Catholic and Protestant churches have appealed for an end to the violence (to no avail, at the time Morrow's piece was published).[53] But it was not lost on either side that the accord that finally ended the conflict is known as the "Good Friday Agreement," and was signed on that religious holiday. Reychler also concurs that religious leaders have attempted to halt the violence (even though he concludes that their role gets people to see the combat through a religious prism often by their mere attempts).[54]

Just as Grossman reports on those who waved the flag and carried the Bible during the Iraq War, she also takes time to show how religious leaders also appealed for an end to the fighting, including Pope John Paul II of the Catholic Church; Bishop Sharon Brown Christopher, president of The United Methodist Church's Council of Bishops; and other churches across America.[55] This open-minded behavior of leaders has also been shown to apply to the political arena as well. And as mentioned earlier, the rights of religious groups are making their way through the United Nations for special protection.[56]

Can't Religion Appeal to Reason Not Just Emotion? One may look with skepticism at world political leaders working through an international conference to protect religious groups, but there is a key historical precedence. Regardless of how scholars on both sides of the debate may feel about the present relationship between religion and conflict, agreement upon the past role of religion and conflict should receive more support. Throughout history, terrible conflicts were fought in the name of religion, for example, the Thirty Years' War, which ravaged much of Europe between 1618 and 1648.[57]

At the end of that war, the battered leaders gathered in Westphalia to try to ensure that nothing like that would ever happen again.[58] At this conference, the great powers of the time developed a policy known as sovereignty, allowing rulers to do within their borders as they saw fit, which included worship.[59] The question remains whether this "Peace of Westphalia" was able to inhibit the number of religious wars.

We propose an additional theory about the connection between religion and conflict. It is important to note that no one is claiming that the number of religious conflicts is zero, only that the numbers are exaggerated. Thus, the independent variable may be cast as a "type of conflict issue (religious or otherwise)," and the dependent variable is the frequency of conflict. In this theory, the relationship is more likely to be negative; the presence of a religious difference is less likely to generate conflict when compared to other issues.

Table 1 provides a summary of the arguments concerning the role of religion in international relations, for the reader's convenience. In the next section, we identify how a pair of hypotheses will be evaluated to contribute to our understanding of just what role religion might play, either as a source of conflict or conciliation.

THE DEBATE		
RELIGION = CONFLICT	*The Explanations*	**RELIGION = PEACE**
Conflicts result from religious incompatibility.	Doctrine	Religions have more in common than they have in differences.
Lack of religiosity puts pressure on faiths to keep members and make converts.	Secularization	Secularization leads to greater respect for religious diversity, making religious conflict less likely.
Identity provides security, and people are defined by their faith.	Identity	The role of identity in religion is exaggerated; religions are not "monolithic."
Religions can be exploited by leaders for power and personal gain.	Role of Leaders	Religious leaders are frequently the ones who call for violence to end.
Emotional attachments can be made to a text, idea, image, or holy site.	Emotion versus Reason	World leaders can be reasonable, establishing the end of religious wars

Table 1: Competing Ideas about the Role of Religion in International Relations

Are Different Faiths More Likely to Fight? Examining the Evidence

As noted earlier, for most people, the issue is settled: religion inevitably leads to war, and there is no need for empirical scrutiny on the subject. Thus, the notion of the "religious war" has entered into the mythical realm. But myths or untested assumptions must be evaluated rather than be implicitly believed without question.

To begin, we will use Holsti's dataset from his book *Peace and War: Armed Conflicts and International Order, 1648–1989.*[60] He breaks down each war by issue and time period. Of course, wars can be fought for single issues or multiple issues (a few can have as many as six rationales for conflict). Should a war have a single religious issue of contention, or one of several, it will be counted as a "religious" war for the purposes of our study, making a more difficult case for those who think religious wars are exaggerated. We will count these cases over the time periods that Holsti has provided: 1648–1713, 1715–1814, 1815–1914, 1918–1941, and 1945–1989.[61]

We can certainly observe whether religious wars are on the increase or decrease, compared to former years. But can we really say that the number of religious wars is "high" or "low" when isolated from other cases? In other words, if we find that there have been five religious wars in a given century, we cannot conclude whether that is "a lot" or "not very many," without something to compare it to. Therefore, we will look at three additional rationales for conflict between countries. One involves clashing over land, or real estate. A second involves battling for the gains from trade or control of a foreign country for the purposes of generating a market, or riches. A final type of war may be waged over who controls a given country, a regime issue. There is some precedent for the bundling of Holsti's data,[62] as Lake and O'Mahony have done.[63] The results can be found in table 2.

GENERAL ISSUE CATEGORIES

	Religion	Real Estate	Riches	Regime
Specific Issues	Protect Religious Confreres	Territory	Commerce/ Navigation	National Liberation/ State Creation
	Religious Unification	Strategic Territory	Commerce/ Resources	National Unification/ Consolidation
	Religious Irredenta	Boundary Territory	Colonial Competition	Secession/State Creation
				Government Composition
				Dynastic Succession
				State/Regime Survival
				Autonomy

Table 2: Bundling Holsti's War Issues into Four "General Issues" for Observation: Religion, Real Estate, Riches, and Regime[64]

It should be noted that the list of wars will not be exhaustive. The goal of this study is not to account for every issue that could be fought over, as Lake and O'Mahony attempt to do.[65] First, it is difficult to wedge every single issue into one of four categories. There would certainly be some cases where the reader would be justifiably wary about its inclusion in a general category and not another. We wanted to leave little doubt about the classification of the specific issues into the general issue categories. Second, it is not a goal of this study to provide an exhaustive overview of these issues; we simply want something to compare religious issues to other issues when evaluating why countries tend to go to war. That way, we can get a sense of how frequent such issues are as a source of fighting. While the issues will be coded in a mutually exclusive format, the wars themselves may not be. That is because, according to Holsti's classification system, an international dispute may be waged over all four issues, and some on other issues not analyzed in this chapter.[66]

Results of the Hypothesis Tests

From 1648–1989. To begin our analysis, we collected information on all religious wars for which Holsti provides information, using the issues of protecting religious confreres, religious unification, and/or religious irredenta.[67] These religious wars are summarized in table 3.

HOLSTI'S (1991) RELIGIOUS WARS			
Disputant(s)1	Disputant(s)2	Beginning Year	Ending Year
France*	Holland	1672	1679
Turkey	Poland*	1672	1676
Turkey	Holy Roman Empire*	1682	1697
Russia*	Poland	1764	1764
Turkey	Poland and Russia*	1768	1774
Russia* and Austria	Turkey	1787	1792
Turkey	Russia*	1806	1812
Russia,* Greece, Great Britain, France	Turkey	1828	1829
Turkey, Great Britain, France, Austria	Russia*	1853	1856
Russia*	Turkey	1877	1878
India	Pakistan	1947	1948
Israel	Arab League	1948	1949
India	Pakistan	1965	1965
Biafra	Nigeria	1967	1970
Israel	Egypt	1967	1967
Syria	Lebanon	1976	1991**

*Denotes country for which religion is a war issue
**Estimated conclusion to the conflict. Is listed as "Ongoing" by Holsti in 1991.

Table 3: *All Religious Wars as Classified by Holsti from 1648 to 1989*[68]

Several observations about these religious wars are worth noting in the debate about the role of faith in foreign policy. First, the numbers appear to be relatively constant for the first three centuries of our study: roughly three to four "religious wars" in the 1600s, 1700s, and 1800s. These conflicts disappeared throughout the first half of the 1900s, only to reappear in the latter half of the 1900s with the greatest frequency in the entire dataset.

Second, the vast majority of the disputes from the 1600s through the 1800s involved one of two countries: Russia and Turkey. These disputes frequently involved the issue of "protection of religious confreres." Only after World War I did disputes tend to go beyond this dyad. Third, though it is not evident in this table, religion was rarely the primary source of any dispute between countries in Holsti's calculations.[69] In many cases, it was one of several issues, and usually listed below many others in terms of salience. Fourth, many times the conflict was considered "religious" by only one of the two disputants in question.

Both sides could claim to some degree that the data support their view. After all, there are sixteen wars with some religious component, and they do appear to be increasing with greater frequency in more recent years. On the other hand, most religious conflicts are limited to a pair of countries and are more of a distraction in nearly every case studied.

The next step is to determine two factors. First, how dominant was religion as a source of conflict when compared to other relevant issues? Second, how does religion compare to three other sources of conflict in frequency? The results can be found in tables 4 and 5. As one can see, religion is rarely a frequent source of conflict during the five time periods Holsti analyzed, never being higher than 15 percent of all wars in any given time frame. Compare this to the other three issues of conflict, which *never amount to less than 15 percent inclusion* in war in any period analyzed, occurrences far greater than that of religious conflicts.

TIME PERIOD	RELIGION	REAL ESTATE	RICHES	REGIMES
1648–1713	13.60%	77.30%	31.80%	27.20%
1715–1814	11.10%	83.30%	47.20%	58.30%
1815–1914	9.70%	54.80%	19.40%	145.20%*
1918–1941	0.00%	76.70%	36.70%	93.30%
1945–1989	10.30%	51.70%	20.70%	134.50%*

* It is possible to have a number in excess of 100%, given that wars can be fought over multiple issues, including multiple regime issues of conflict over "who governs."

Table 4: *Comparing Religion to Other Issues of Conflict in How Frequently They Emerge in War, Using Holsti's Data, from 1648 to 1989*[70]

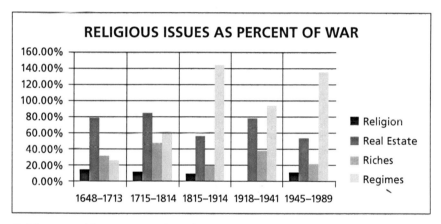

Table 5: *Graphic Representation of Results Comparing Religion to Other Issues of Conflict in How Frequently They Emerge in a War, using Holsti's Data, from 1648 to 1989*[71]

TIME PERIOD	RELIGION	REAL ESTATE	RICHES	REGIMES
1648–1713	5.88%	33.33%	13.73%	11.77%
1715–1814	4.40%	32.97%	18.68%	23.08%
1815–1914	3.26%	18.48%	6.52%	48.91%
1918–1941	0%	22.77%	10.89%	27.72%
1945–1989	3.28%	16.39%	6.56%	42.62%

Table 6: *Comparing Religion to Other Issues of Conflict as a Percentage of All Issues over Which a War Is Fought, Using Holsti's Data, from 1648 to 1989*[72]

As table 5 illustrates, religion is clearly a distant fourth of four issues when it comes to frequency of being included in a war. States are much more likely to battle when colonies or commerce, territory, and control of the government are at stake.

It may be confusing to follow tables 4 and 6, as a result, so we will explain the process by which Holsti classified his data.[73] From 1648 to 1713, 13.6 percent of all wars had a religious issue. When all issues that could be fought over are considered (and some war cases had at least five war issues), religion made up less than 6 percent of the total issues fought over between 1648 and 1713.

Table 6 shows that religion still remained the smallest rationale for a conflict when considering all of the issues. Religion never consisted of more than 6 percent of all the issues fought over by countries of any given period. By the same token, none of the other issues analyzed (real estate, riches, and regimes) made up less than 6 percent of all issues for which war was waged in a particular time frame. Clearly, wars are much more likely to be fought over issues of governance and land. Even when it comes to mercantilism, resources, and navigation rights, these concerns are more likely to appear in international conflict than religion.

Furthermore, results from table 6 refute the claim by those who feel that religious conflicts are on the rise. That is because religion is actually declining as a salient issue of conflict, falling from nearly 6 percent of all issues of conflict in the 1648–1713 time period to just more than 3 percent from 1945 to 1989. There may be more religious conflicts over the most recent forty-four years analyzed, but that is because there was also more conflict in general during that period, which means that religious issues actually fell as a rationale for fighting, and are therefore not increasing as a source of conflict relative to other issues.

Table 7 reinforces the data displayed in table 6. One sees that religion remains a very small factor over which countries might fight. While the latter half of the 1900s may have had more religious wars than the prior half of the century, they still pale in comparison to both other issues of conflict analyzed, as well as their numbers from the early years of the sample.

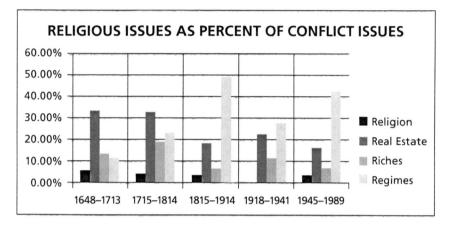

Table 7: *Graphic Representation of Results Comparing Religion to Other Issues of Conflict as a Percentage of All Issues over Which a War Is Fought, Using Holsti's Data, from 1648 to 1989*[74]

Battles and Different Belief Systems

In this conclusion, we wrap up the debate over the role of religion in international war and assess whether or not there is a connection between the two, based on the evidence from the hypothesis tests. Additionally, we speculate on additional forms of research that could be undertaken to further probe the relationship between the two.

What We've Learned

As Colombo, Cullen, and Lisle (2010) point out in their textbook *Re-reading America*, "myths are models that 'make sense'" of events. Wars may be complex in commencement, continuity, and conclusion. It is difficult for politicians and pundits, reporters and religious leaders, and even students and scholars of international relations and faith to sort them out. The myth of religious conflict offers a simple explanation for wars that are difficult to untangle in their origins. We assume that one's passion for a form of prayer would come into conflict with a different set of beliefs, and the zeal to which one devotes himself or herself to that faith would make an act as severe as war against another creed understandable. It actually becomes "comfortable" to think of the body bags as having some simple explanation, and (for some), an "acceptable" rationale for it.

As a result, a cottage industry has sprung up connecting religion to conflict, even before Samuel Huntington's landmark speech and publication *The Clash of Civilizations* in 1992.[75] But in our study, we found that the relationship between the two factors is overstated. Many wars considered religious in nature have other, stronger explanations for their origin and continuation. Religious wars have been few in number, especially compared to other sources of conflict. They have been decreasing, not increasing in number. Even many of the reasons given for those religious battles that do exist (doctrine, secularization, identity, and the behavior of leaders) have little support. Only the emotional connection to a word, an idea, an image, or especially a holy site seems to inflame religious adherents to clash with another.

Where We Go from Here

In our research, we have looked at all conflicts from the Thirty Years' War to the Cold War. But what does the world look like after the superpower confrontation that ended with the fall of the Berlin Wall in 1989? Continuing research will explore the decades after the United States and the USSR ended their competition peacefully, looking at cases involving conflicts in Third World countries that we often associate with religious wars. But as you can see from these results, such closer scrutiny is necessary to avoid having the same mistaken assumptions about religion and war in the Westphalian era.

Notes

An earlier version of this paper was presented at the Annual Meeting of the Alabama Political Science Association, Samford University, Birmingham, AL. The author would like to thank researchers Ashbi Alford, Ryan Bergman, Derecius Cheaves, J. Curt Ellison,

Andrew Gawler, Katie Hearn, Jatara King, Knox Robinson, Emmie Trull, and Isaiah Whitfield, LaGrange College undergraduates.

1 Niccolo Machiavelli, "Money Is Not the Sinews of War, Although It Is Generally So Considered," in *Conflict After the Cold War: Arguments on Causes of War and Peace*, 2nd ed., ed. Richard K. Betts (New York: Pearson/Longman, 2005).

2 Kalevi J. Holsti, *Peace and War: Armed Conflicts and International Order, 1648–1989* (Cambridge, MA: University Press, 1991).

3 *Mythbusters* cable television show, Discovery Channel (http://www.discovery.com/tv-shows/mythbusters/).

4 Gary Colombo, Robert Cullen, and Bonnie Lisle, *Rereading America: Cultural Contexts for Critical Thinking and Writing*, 8th ed. (Boston: Bedford/St. Martin's, 2010).

5 J. Dan Rothwell, *In Mixed Company: Communicating in Small Groups*, 9th ed. (Boston: Cengage Learning, 2016).

6 National Association of Schools & Colleges of The United Methodist Church (NASCUMC), "Mission Statement," accessed November 10, 2017, http://www.gbhem.org/education/nascumc.

7 "LaGrange College Mission," accessed November 10, 2017, http://www.lagrange.edu/about/history.html.

8 Samuel P. Huntington, *The Clash of Civilizations* (n.p.: American Enterprise Institute for Public Policy, 1992); Samuel P. Huntington, "The Clash of Civilizations?" *Foreign Affairs* 72, no. 3 (1993): 22–49.

9 Huntington; Huntington.

10 Luc Reychler, "Religion and Conflict," *International Journal of Peace Studies* 2, no. 1 (1997), accessed September 29, 2017, http://www.gmu.edu/programs/icar/ijps/vol2_1/Reyschler.htm.

11 Jonathan Fox, "Religion and State Failure: An Examination of the Extent and Magnitude of Religious Conflict from 1950 to 1996," *International Political Science Review* 25, no. 1 (2004): 55–76.

12 Bill Powell, "A Religious War?," *Newsweek*, October 13, 1996, 52, http://www.newsweek.com/religious-war-179300.

13 Nicole Horrell, "Revolution in the Middle East and Its Connection to Revelation," *Examiner*, 2011.

14 David Van Biema and Emily Mitchell, "In Search of Moses," *Time*, December 14, 1998, 80.

15 Fouad Ajami, "The Summoning," *Foreign Affairs* 72, no. 4 (1993): 2–9.

16 Marc Gopin, "Religion, Violence, and Conflict Resolution," *Peace & Change* 22, no. 1 (1997): 1–31; Karel Dobbelaere, "Towards an Integrated Perspective of the Processes Related to the Descriptive Concept of Secularization," *Sociology of Religion* 60, no. 3 (1999): 229–47

17 Charanjit AjitSingh, "Religion Fueling Conflict or Fostering Peace," *Current Dialogue* 33, no. 1 (July 1999), http://wcc-coe.org/wcc/what/interreligious/cd33-18.html.

18 Fox, "Religion and State Failure," 55.

19 Dobbelaere, "Towards an Integrated Perspective," 232.

20 Huntington, "The Clash of Civilizations," 23.

21 Huntington, 48.

22 Noah Feldman et.al., "Power Struggle, Tribal Conflict or Religious War?" *Time*, February 26, 2006.

23 Fox, "Religion and State Failure," 60.

24 Lance Morrow, "Religious Wars: A Bloody Zeal," *Time*, July 12, 1976, 46

25 Morrow, 46.

26 Jarlath F. Benson, "The Northern Ireland Conflict and Peace Process: The Role of Mutual Regulatory Symbiosis Between Leaders and Groups," in *Leadership in a Changing World: Dynamic Perspectives on Groups and Their Leaders,* eds. Robert H. Klein, Cecil A. Rice, and Victor L. Schermer (Lanham, MD: Lexington Books, 2009), 181.

27 Benson, 181.

28 Cathy Lynn Grossman, "No Rest on the Sabbath for Iraq War Debate," *USA Today*, March 3, 2003, 8.

29 Gerard Powers, "Religion, Conflict and Prospects for Reconciliation in Bosnia, Croatia, and Yugoslavia," *Journal of International Affairs* 50 (1996): 221–52.

30 Powers, 222.

31 Gopin, "Religion, Violence, and Conflict Resolution," 8–9.

32 Gopin, 9.

33 Naina Bajekal, "6 Reasons Why Jerusalem's Old City Has Once Again Enflamed the Region," *Time*, October 13 2015, http://time.com/3595090/jerusalem-old-city-conflict/.

34 Morrow, "Religious Wars," 46.

35 Powell, "A Religious War?," 52.

36 Gopin, "Religion, Violence, and Conflict Resolution," 6.

37 Van Biema and Mitchell, "In Search of Moses," 80.

38 Dobbelaere, "Towards an Integrated Perspective," 242.

39 AjitSingh, "Religion Fueling Conflict or Fostering Peace."

40 Gopin, "Religion, Violence, and Conflict Resolution," 11.

41 Jay Tolson, "Why Did So Many Muslims Seem to Celebrate 9/11?" *U.S. News & World Report*, April 7, 2008, https://www.usnews.com/news/religion/articles/2008/04/07/why-did-so-many-muslims-seem-to-celebrate-911.

42 Tolson.

43 Brian J. Grim and Roger Finke, "Religious Persecution in Cross-National Context: Clashing Civilizations or Regulated Religious Economies?" *American Sociological Review* 72, no. 4 (2007): 633.

44 Grim and Finke, 636.

45 Grim and Finke.

46 Powers, "Religion, Conflict and Prospects for Reconciliation in Bosnia, Croatia, and Yu-goslavia," 221.

47 Powell, "A Religious War?," 52.

48 Powell, 52.

49 Huntington, "The Clash of Civilizations," 22–49, esp. 33–35.

50 Grim and Frinke, "Religious Persecution in Cross-National Context," 654.

51 AjitSingh, "Religion Fueling Conflict or Fostering Peace."

52 Gopin, "Religion, Violence, and Conflict Resolution," 11.

53 Morrow, "Religious Wars," 46.

54 Reychler, "Religion and Conflict."

55 Grossman, "No Rest on the Sabbath for Iraq War Debate," 8.

56 Gopin, "Religion, Violence, and Conflict Resolution," 11.

57 Holsti, *Peace and War*, 26.

58 Holsti, 25.

59 Holsti, 39.

60 Holsti, 307.

61 Holsti, 307–8.

62 Holsti.

63 David A. Lake and Angela O'Mahony, "The Incredible Shrinking State: Explaining Change in the Territorial Size of Countries" *Journal of Conflict Resolution* 48, no. 5 (October 2004): 699–722.

64 Holsti, 48–49.

65 Lake and O'Mahony, 700.

66 Holsti, *Peace and War*, 48–49.

67 Holsti, 48–49, 85, 87, 140–42, 214–16, 274–78.

68 Holsti.

69 Holsti, 58–59.

70 Holsti, 48–49, 85, 87, 140–42, 214–16, 274–78.

71 Holsti.

72 Holsti.

73 Holsti.

74 Holsti.

75 Huntington, *The Clash of Civilizations*, 22.

14

The Business of Interfaith

Could Interreligious Engagement Change the Workplace Environment?

Mark E. Hanshaw

We have inherited a big house, a great "world house," in which we all live together—a family unduly separated in ideas, culture, and interests. [A family] who . . . must learn . . . to live with each other.

—Martin Luther King Jr.

My quick glance at a recent front page of the *New York Times* served as an apt reminder of the continued depth of influence that spiritual belief systems have upon our modern, shrinking world. Though anecdotal, the content on this single front page was striking. Of the multiple news articles scattered across the page, all but one had a religious dimension. Of course, this was but a single news page among the thousands that are produced across the globe each and every day. Yet, while this page may or may not be representative of the typical daily content covered across the news media spectrum, it does point to a pervasive reality. That reality, which has been a focus of scholarly research for more than a century, is that the world created and occupied by humans, in its breadth, can never be fully understood absent a sincere focus on the many ways religion has affected its shape. As the opening lines of the classic work *The Sacred Canopy* so profoundly attested, decades ago: "Every human society is an enterprise of world-building. Religion occupies a distinctive place in this enterprise."[1]

There are, of course, countless theories, and a good deal of disagreement by scholars and theorists, both old and new, regarding the precise role that religious systems actually play in defining our social environment. Indeed, some, such as the late founder of the subfield of the psychological study of religion, Sigmund Freud, even anticipated that individuals as a collective might eventually outgrow what he perceived to be an "infantile" need to lean on organized spirituality, and that faith systems would likely disappear from the landscape of human society.[2] Still, one glance at the *Times* headlines of the day might well serve to eliminate any doubt that, at least at present, religion still does play a quite important role in shaping our collective realm, regardless of the extent to which we may be inclined to recognize it.

The purpose of this article, meanwhile, is not to rehearse theories related to the precise role that religion does play in influencing our world but rather to consider how various institutions may best respond to the continued potency of religion, as a social and cultural force, especially within a world that is increasing in religious diversity. One potential response explored here involves the establishment of new educational opportunities aimed at the cultivation of practical experience in interfaith engagement and the enhancement of religious literacy, through novel programs designed specifically to support business, nonprofit, and service sector managers and employees. Increased interfaith awareness could potentially benefit organizations within a variety of social settings, ranging from public education classrooms to business boardrooms. Yet, what would such a strategic educational focus on interfaith engagement look like, and how and where should it be cultivated? Moreover, to what extent do the individuals who lead community and business organizations perceive a need for such training?

These are all important questions, and in an effort to cultivate an informed response to them, this essay examines the results of a survey of business and nonprofit leaders conducted within the region of North Texas during late 2016 and early 2017[3] in which participants were asked to consider the relevancy of interfaith engagement to their particular workplace settings. As is detailed below, that survey was administered to a diverse grouping of community leaders representing varying economic sectors. The survey results provided some important insights in terms of both the frequency that faith-related controversies are arising within workplace settings within a single geographical region and the present perceived need for an expansion of interfaith literacy programs aimed at supporting employees and the business community.

The Emergence of Interfaith Studies

In recent years, there has been a remarkable emergence of and growth in university-based educational programs focused on interfaith engagement.[4] These are not programs concentrating specifically on the historical study of religious systems or communities per se, although such topics certainly are relevant. Instead, these programs focus more particularly on the cultivation of skills and strategies that help recipients effectively inspire engagement and understanding between followers of differing faith traditions. Such programs, which take a variety of shapes, are typically interdisciplinary in scope and professional in orientation. They seek to encourage the development of a group of core analytical and leadership proficiencies and help students gain experience in applying these skills within settings where multi-faith encounters or conflicts are possible or likely.

In a 2016 report, the educational nonprofit organization Interfaith Youth Core outlined a grouping of specific unique traits that appeared to be characteristic of or common to programs in interfaith studies, as they have emerged across the country.[5] In arguing for the distinctness of interfaith studies as a defined academic discipline, the report identified three core elements as being significant. The first trait the report identified as being common among university-based curricular programs in interfaith studies was the adoption and utilization of an applied methodology. In other words, such programs focus attention on the specific and practical ways that faith perspectives and religious affiliation may affect and color interactions between individuals of differing backgrounds within shared social and workplace environments. Second, according to the report, interfaith studies programs place a reduced focus on the examination of the historic structures of religious systems and greater emphasis on the ways faith perspectives influence relationships and shape engagements between individuals and within social groups. Third, as the report notes, the practical nature of the types of inquiries undertaken within the field of interfaith studies demands insight drawn from varying disciplines, potentially ranging from sociology and psychology to business and health care administration.[6] Thus, instead of being a "siloed" discipline, interfaith studies necessarily function to bridge and draw from diverse fields of knowledge. Such programs, then, are inherently interdisciplinary.

While interfaith studies programs may draw upon the experience of faculty from a wide range of academic areas, they are argued to represent an emerging new coherent academic field that is distinct in its priorities from religious studies and other existing disciplines. The function of such programs is to train students to be prepared to act as "interfaith leaders" within the business and professional environments that they serve. The precise role of such "interfaith leaders," as summed up by one of the most noted proponents of interfaith education in the United States, Eboo Patel, is to encourage constructive engagement among individuals who might otherwise be reluctant to relate to one another due to perceptions of religious difference. As he observed in a recent text, "An important part of what interfaith leaders do is construct environments that highlight similarities in faiths across diverse people and groups, therefore making cooperation more likely."[7]

In other words, Patel believes that, when equipped with the right skill set, individuals can act as catalysts within their given realms of service to encourage both meaningful engagement and broader collaboration. In accord with the theory underlying these new programs, one needs more than historical knowledge about religious systems to function as an interfaith leader. It is also important that such individuals understand how to respectfully engage topics related to issues of faith, to assess specific needs of individuals rooted in the embrace of a religious perspective, and to facilitate conciliation. Thus, interfaith leaders should have the necessary skills to help move individuals and groups confronting religious tension away from conflict and toward collaboration.

As Patel and others observe, the precise skill set needed by interfaith leaders is broad. Yet it includes certain key proficiencies that are essential for one to be able to act effectively within the community to prompt heightened engagement across social divisions. These proficiencies include the possession of at least a foundational awareness of the distinctive characteristic traits of individual religious systems that differentiate one faith community from another, in terms of perspective and practice. Such fundamental awareness of the traits that differentiate social groups from one another is essential if an individual is to be able to anticipate potential disputes or problems that might arise as individuals interact with one another. As well, one should be able to articulate a narrative of the importance of interfaith cooperation, which may include specific personal examples of interreligious engagements. In other words, it is important for individuals to be able to reference examples of successful cooperation across religious and cultural divides, in order to encourage others to imagine the benefits that might flow from their own efforts. At the same time, one must possess the skills necessary to establish relationships of trust with individuals and groups representing diverse religious perspectives. Further, one must be able to facilitate opportunities for individuals of diverse backgrounds to gather and work collaboratively toward meeting common goals. Finally, one must possess the skills to be able to facilitate direct engagement between individuals and groups who see and understand the world differently, based on their own unique religious and cultural lenses.[8]

Based on the existence of at least anecdotal evidence, such as a review of the *New York Times* front page on a given day, many have argued that the skills possessed by those with a background in interfaith studies are in increasing demand across the domestic and global social spectrums. Given ongoing tensions surrounding topics of religion and religious difference, it is argued that interfaith leaders are increasingly needed within a variety of settings, ranging from schools and nonprofit service organizations to business, health care, and other professional environments. Individuals with training in the field of interfaith studies could play an important role, not just in the resolution of workplace and community conflict, but also in establishing environments that are designed to anticipate and minimize the instance of potential conflict.

While a theoretical argument can certainly be made for the potential need for the increased availability of interfaith training, is this need borne out in experience or recognized by business and community leaders? It was this question that served as the impetus for the survey cited here.

Assessing the Workplace Climate

In an attempt to better understand the perspectives of business and nonprofit leaders in the region of North Texas related to issues concerning interfaith awareness, a survey was conducted between late 2016 and early 2017. The survey instrument utilized in this investigation was disseminated to more than six hundred individuals identified as area business and community leaders by regional chamber of commerce organizations. Of that initial target group, more than a hundred individuals responded to the survey, representing a diverse array of industries and employment sectors.[9] Further, the respondents were associated with companies or employers of a wide range of varying sizes, in terms of numbers of employees.[10]

Through the survey, business leaders broadly indicated both an appreciation for the importance of specialized training in the area of interfaith engagement and an interest in the increased availability of more specialized training. At the same time, the survey reflected mixed responses regarding the optimal design for the delivery of training and, perhaps, differing perceptions about how such knowledge might be applied within given workplace settings.

Initially, the survey sought to assess perceptions regarding the level of religious diversity that exists within the radius of engagement of the businesses and service agencies included in the response group. While North Texas has been frequently cited in recent years as one of the most diverse metropolitan areas in the nation, this survey reinforced the perception that such diversity is broadly present across varied workplace environments. When respondents were asked to describe the diversity existing within their given workplace, more than 66 percent defined these spheres as either "very diverse" or "somewhat diverse."[11] Further, when asked to describe the diversity among the clients or consumers with whom their employer serves, 89 percent of respondents identified this group as being either "very diverse" or "somewhat diverse."[12]

While respondents did not specify the precise categories of diverse backgrounds present within their given workplace environments, the relatively high percentage of individuals reporting the existence of significant diversity among both coworkers and clients appears to suggest an environment wherein cultural conflict is at least possible, if not probable. The survey sought further to determine the extent to which miscommunication or conflict rooted in religious or cultural misunderstanding had actually taken place with the varied workplace environments represented through the respondent group.

Respondents were asked to identify whether the company or organization they represented had experienced issues or disputes arising between employees that were rooted in "religious or cultural difference or misunderstanding." In response, 23.1 percent reported that there had been such disputes; 42.1 percent reported that there had not been such disputes; and 34.6 percent reported being uncertain.

Respondents were additionally asked whether their employing organization had experienced issues or disputes arising between its employees and customers or clients, rooted in "religious or cultural difference or misunderstanding." In response, 40.4 percent reported being aware of such disputes within their organization; 28.8 percent reported that there had not been such disputes; and 30.8 percent reported being unsure.

While the responses to this category of questions lack the sort of specificity that would permit a detailed analysis of the specific types of disputes that have arisen within the workplaces captured through this survey, the results are still significant. With almost a quarter of respondents being aware of instances of religious and cultural conflict taking place among coworkers and more than 40 percent being aware of such disputes arising between employing organizations and those being served by them, the need for sophisticated interfaith workplace leadership may well be broader than many would have presumed. The very existence of such instances of conflict on such a broad scale may well offer the most compelling evidence to support the need for training aimed at addressing such challenges.

Meanwhile, even among survey respondents, there appeared to be a strong expectation that such issues were not ebbing, but quite likely to increase going forward. When respondents were asked whether they expected the prevalence of workplace conflicts stemming from "religious or cultural difference" to increase or decrease, the results were telling. Of the respondents, almost 82 percent indicated that they believed that instances of such workplace conflicts were likely to "increase substantially" or "increase somewhat" in coming years. Less than 7 percent expected to see a decrease in such instances of dispute.[13]

Assessing the Desirability of Interfaith Training

While this survey sought to assess the perceptions of business and community leaders regarding the prevailing workplace climate, its major purpose was to gain further insight into the perceived desirability of educational programs aimed at addressing the sorts of disputes and conflicts that may stem from religious bias or misinformation. Based on survey results, it does appear that the majority of respondents are engaged with organizations that are offering some type of diversity training at present. As to the effectiveness of existing training regimens, responses were somewhat mixed. However, the survey reflected significant interest in additional training, along with differing preferences as to the shape such programs might take.

When asked whether "official or unofficial diversity training was currently being offered within given workplaces, 56.7 percent of respondents said that it was, while 39.4 indicated that no such training was being offered. When further questioned about the effectiveness of such current training, 25.8 percent described the training they had encountered as "highly effective." A total of 59.7 percent of respondents described their training as "somewhat effective," and 14.5 percent described training as ineffective. Still further, for those who had themselves received some sort of diversity training, when asked if such programs prepared them to be able to "negotiate situations within the workplace" rooted in "religious difference," a significant number were hesitant. Of the respondents, 38.6 percent said that they did feel prepared to negotiate such workplace situations, while 21.8 percent said that they did not, and 39.8 percent indicated that they were unsure.

Taken in totality, these responses appear to display a clear awareness among business leaders of the need for training with regard to issues of religious and cultural diversity. They further indicate that attempts have been undertaken by many organizations to address these issues in some way. At the same time, there appears to be some significant uncertainty as to the effectiveness or the adequacy of current training offerings and strategies.

The conclusion that survey respondents desire to have access to more interfaith training options for employees was further reinforced through additional responses. When asked generally about whether a program designed to "provide skills and tools to help employees analyze and resolve situations involving conflict or challenge rooted in religious and cultural difference" would be of interest, an overwhelming 73.1 percent of respondents indicated that it would. Only 7.7 percent of respondents indicated that they would have no interest in such a program. More specifically, when asked whether a university-based program in interfaith leadership would be of interest and applicable to their workplace setting, a significant majority of 71.2 percent indicated that such a program would be appealing. Again, only 9.6 percent of respondents indicated no interest in such a program.

Taken together, these results appear to indicate a relatively broad-based perception among community and business leaders that some form of interfaith training is desirous and viewed as being of benefit. Responses to additional questions were consistent with these results. When asked whether an individual familiarity with various religious traditions and practices is a "competency that would benefit employees" in the present workplace, 71.2 percent of respondents indicated a belief that such a background would be "extremely helpful," while an additional 21.2 percent indicated that such knowledge would be "somewhat helpful." Less than 3 percent of those surveyed indicated a belief that such a competency would be either "minimally helpful" or "not helpful at all."[14]

When asked whether they might use or recommend a program in interfaith training, should it be available, respondents voiced significant willingness. Of the respondents, 49 percent stated that they would "certainly" use or recommend such a program, while an additional 27.9 percent indicated that they would be "likely" to access such a program. Meanwhile, 16.3 percent indicated that they would "possibly" use or recommend such a program, and only 6.8 percent indicated that they were "unlikely or would not access or recommend such a program, if it were offered.

While these results appear to indicate a very strong interest among business and community leaders in some sort of formal interfaith training, there does appear to be slightly greater disunity in terms of views on the optimal structure for such a program. When specific program format options were presented, respondents voiced the greatest interest in "short-term skills trainings" or "one-year post-graduate certificate programs."[15] At the same time, respondents were asked how universities could better prepare graduates to navigate and find success within religiously diverse workplaces, and the responses were varied. Among the suggestions offered by respondents were the following:

- Require all students to take a "global citizenship course."
- Require at least one course focused on "diversity training."
- Have students engage projects with a "multicultural emphasis."
- Hold "interreligious dialogue" sessions on campus.
- Promote global travel and exchange experiences.

Beyond these highlighted examples culled from the more than one hundred different suggestions offered, a further comment proved interesting. As one respondent observed, students frequently fail to recognize the importance of such training until they graduate and are in the workforce. Accordingly, this individual recommended that some form of religious diversity training be made mandatory for all undergraduate university students, regardless of their major.

Conclusions and Observations

Based on this data, what specific conclusions may be drawn relative to the potential utility and attractiveness of university-based interfaith studies programming? It is first important to recognize the limitations of the data cited here. While the individuals included in this study can safely be categorized as business and community leaders, the number included is relatively small and, perhaps, given that each of them was identified through a chamber of commerce organization, the sample may not be fully representative of the breadth of the community. It is also important to recognize that this sampling of business and community leaders is peculiar to the North Texas region and, therefore, may not well represent the views of similar leaders located in other geographic regions. Finally, it is worth observing that this study is preliminary, with the desire being that it will inspire additional studies of similar focus to be undertaken in other regions. Yet, despite these varied limitations, this study does appear to offer preliminary insights that are useful.

Among the principal lessons that might be drawn from this study is the recognition that business and community leaders are aware of the increased commonality of instances of interreligious tension and conflict arising within social and community spaces. While the precise levels of awareness indicated by results in this survey may not necessarily mirror opinions in other regions, this survey may be at least sufficiently instructive to establish some general baseline expectations. At least for the region represented in this survey, the levels of awareness of the existence of interreligious tensions appears quite high. Further, the survey results appear to underscore the broadly held belief among business and community leaders that steps should be taken to increase educational opportunities focused on issues related to interfaith engagement and conflict. Already, many of those included in this survey are either making available or participating in workplace trainings that address religious and cultural diversity in some way. Still, the survey appears to clearly indicate a strong interest by respondents in having access to more and better educational resources than currently exist.

What is not as clear from this survey is precisely what sorts of educational opportunities focused on issues of interfaith engagement would be most widely embraced by those surveyed. Certainly, respondents appeared to reflect some heightened interest in graduate certificate programs and short-term trainings, as preferred formats. Perhaps such inclinations are not surprising when addressing needs of existing employees. Employers, one could presume, are much more likely to prefer educational options that are least disruptive to ongoing business operations and the work schedules of existing employees. Thus, this survey may be read to indicate that a university's willingness to employ a strategy of offering some shorter-term educational programs focused on interfaith engagement skills could prove particularly useful for supporting regional businesses. Further, short-term and focused offerings may serve to expand awareness of and interest in longer-term programs. What is not clear from this survey is how the utilization of alternate delivery modalities may affect employer impressions. Thus, perhaps, perspectives regarding the preferred program format would shift if courses could be delivered in weekend, hybrid, or online formats, which might reduce any intrusion upon the work schedules of employees.

At the same time, this survey appears to suggest that employers are interested not just in retraining opportunities for existing employees, but also in having the assurance that new graduates, which represent a potential flow of prospective future employees, will possess skills in the area of interfaith engagement. Again, the survey does not reflect strong preferences for the form that programs in interfaith engagement directed at existing students may take. However, the general preference that students receive some detailed training in this area is strongly echoed through survey results.

Ultimately, based on this survey, it appears that a clear demand exists for the continued growth and expansion of interfaith studies programming. Questions may still continue to be debated about the most effective structure for such programs and whether the establishment of a specific field of "interfaith studies" is optimal. Yet, the need for expanded educational opportunities appears to be clearly evidenced through this survey. As this field continues to develop, it will be important that additional research be conducted in order to further clarify preliminary findings made here and to expand the scope of the analysis to include other geographic regions.

Notes

Martin Luther King Jr., "The Quest for Peace and Justice," in *Nobel Lectures: Peace 1951–1970*, ed. Frederick Haberman (New York: World Scientific Press, 1999).

1   Peter Berger, *The Sacred Canopy: Elements of a Sociological Theory of Religion* (New York: Anchor Books, 1967), 3.

2 Sigmund Freud, *The Future of an Illusion* (New York: W. W. Norton, 1961).

3 This survey was conducted by Texas Wesleyan University, Fort Worth, Texas, through grant support provided by the Teagle Foundation.

4 Existing interfaith programs across North America have taken a variety of shapes, including both graduate and undergraduate opportunities. Examples of undergraduate programs include a bachelor's degree in interfaith leadership at Elizabethtown College, Elizabethtown, Pennsylvania; minor programs at Loyola University, Chicago, Illinois; Nazareth College, Rochester, New York; and Merrimack College, Andover, Massachusetts; and a certificate program in interfaith studies at Benedictine College, Oakbrook, Illinois. Graduate programs have been created at Andover Newton Theological School, Auburn Seminary, Claremont Lincoln University, the Graduate Theological Union, and Georgetown University, among others.

5 California Lutheran University, *Interfaith Studies: Curricular Programs and Core Competencies*, IFYC, March 13–15, 2016, available at: https://www.ifyc.org/sites/default/files/Interfaith%20Studies%202016%20Conference%20Full%20Report.pdf.

6 California Lutheran University, 4.

7 Eboo Patel, *Interfaith Leadership: A Primer* (Boston: Beacon, 2016), 75.

8 Patel, 135–52.

9 Survey respondents reported being associated with the following industrial fields: education, 24.3 percent; nonprofits and NGOs, 17.5 percent; health care, 14.6 percent; legal and accounting, 6.8 percent; manufacturing, 4.9 percent; government supply and contracting, 4.9 percent; transportation, 3.9 percent; oil and gas, 2 percent; and other, 21.4 percent.

10 Of the respondents, 32.7 percent reported being associated with a "small employer" (defined as fewer than 50 employees); 18.3 percent reported being associated with a "medium-sized employer" (defined as having between 50 and 200 employees); 19.2 percent reported being associated with a "large employer" (defined as having between 201 and 1,000 employees); and 29.8 percent reported being associated with a "very large employer" (defined as having more than 1,000 employees).

11 In describing the level of diversity in their given workplaces, 32.7 percent described their workplace as "very diverse"; 33.7 percent described their workplace as "somewhat diverse"; 22.1 percent described their workplace as "slightly diverse"; and 11.5 percent described their workplace as "not diverse."

12 In describing clients, customers, and those served by employers, 58.7 percent described this group as being "very diverse"; 29.8 described the group as "somewhat diverse"; 10.6 percent described this group as being "slightly diverse"; and 0.9 percent described this group as being "not diverse."

13 In response to the question of whether instances of workplace disputes rooted in "religious or cultural difference" were likely to increase or decrease, 34.6 percent of respondents indicated their belief that such conflict would "increase substantially"; 47.1 percent indicated that such conflict would "increase somewhat"; 11.5 percent indicated that such conflict would "remain about the same"; 4.8 percent indicated that such con-

flict would "decrease somewhat"; and 1.9 percent indicated that such conflict would "decrease substantially."

14 An additional 4.8 percent of respondents to this question observed that a competency in understanding various religious systems would be "occasionally helpful."

15 When asked about the preferred format for a program aimed at providing existing employees with greater understanding of issues associated with "cultural and religious differences," 70.2 percent of respondents identified a preference for "short-term skills training"; 20.7 percent indicated a preference for a "one-year post-graduate certificate program"; 4.8 percent indicated a preference for a master's degree program; 3.8 percent indicated a preference for a traditional four-year undergraduate program; and less than 1 percent desired a two-year associate degree program.

About the Contributors

Kent Andersen, EdD, is the director of the Hess Center for Leadership and Service and the chair of engaged programs at Birmingham-Southern College in Birmingham, Alabama. He has written and presented on faculty professional development and the implementation of effective educational and learning design.

S. Wesley Ariarajah, PhD, a Methodist minister from Sri Lanka, served the WCC for sixteen years, first as the director of the Interfaith Dialogue Program and then as deputy general secretary. After teaching for seventeen years, he is currently professor emeritus of ecumenical theology at the Drew University School of Theology, Madison, New Jersey. He is the author of *Your God, My God, Our God: Rethinking Christian Theology for Religious Plurality.*

Eva Semien Baham, PhD, is assistant professor of history at Dillard University, New Orleans, Louisiana. She is the author of *African Americans in Covington* (Louisiana) and concentrates her work on the history of African Americans in south Louisiana.

Gladys Childs, PhD, serves as chair of the Religion, Humanities and Interdisciplinary Studies Department and as chaplain at Texas Wesleyan University in Fort Worth, Texas. She has been at Texas Wesleyan for sixteen years. Gladys is an ordained elder in the Central Texas Conference of The United Methodist Church, and she is the children's and women's group minister at LifePoint United Methodist Church in Haslet, Texas. She is also a speaker and consultant and works with many organizations, leading retreats and educational seminars.

Nathan Eric Dickman, PhD, is an associate professor of philosophy and religious studies at Young Harris College. He researches in hermeneutic phenomenology, philosophy of language, and comparative questions in philosophy of religions. He teaches a wide range of courses, on topics such as existentialism, Islam, ethics, and the historical Jesus.

Hans Gustafson, PhD, is director of the Jay Phillips Center for Interfaith Learning and adjunct faculty teaching in the area of (inter)religious studies in the College of Arts and Sciences at the University of St. Thomas, Minnesota.

Dennis Hall, PhD, serves as the vice president for student affairs/dean of students at Texas Wesleyan University in Fort Worth, Texas. He has been at Texas Wesleyan for just over three years and during that time has been part of a deepening collaboration with the university chaplain and faculty member, Gladys Childs, PhD. Dennis has a doctorate in higher education administration, and his studies have focused on student development theory, including spiritual development among students while in college.

Mark E. Hanshaw, JD, PhD, is associate general secretary for the United Methodist Board of Higher Education & Ministry. He formerly served as dean of the School of Arts & Letters and an associate professor of comparative religious studies at Texas Wesleyan University, Fort Worth, Texas. He is the coauthor of the text *From East to West: A Comparative Study of the World's Great Religions*.

Timothy S. Moore, DMin, MLitt, is director of donor development for Union Presbyterian Seminary in Charlotte, North Carolina. He is the coeditor of this book and of *Displaced Persons: Migration, Immigration, and Personal and Spiritual Displacement*.

Eboo Patel, PhD, the founder and president of Interfaith Youth Core, is the author of *Acts of Faith, Sacred Ground* and *Interfaith Leadership: A Primer.*

Chad J. Pevateaux, PhD, is an assistant professor of philosophy and religion, and director of liberal studies, at Texas Wesleyan University, Fort Worth, Texas. He specializes in comparative mystics.

Nicholas Rademacher, PhD, chairs the department of religious studies at Cabrini University in Radnor, Pennsylvania. He also serves as the coordinator of the social justice minor program and has published various articles on Catholic social thought.

Carolyn Roncolato is the campus engagement manager at Interfaith Youth Core and has her doctorate in theology, ethics, and human culture from Chicago Theological Seminary.

Jikyo Bonnie Shoultz, Buddhist chaplain at Syracuse University, head monastic at Zen Center of Syracuse, retired in 2006 from a disability research center at Syracuse University.

John A. Tures, PhD, is the chair of the political science program and a professor of political science at LaGrange College in LaGrange, Georgia.

Aaron Twitchell is a teacher and school chaplain at the Pennington School, a United Methodist–affiliated, day/boarding school in central New Jersey founded in 1838. A graduate of Seattle University and Princeton Seminary, he is an ordained teaching elder in the Presbyterian Church (USA) and a board-certified clinical chaplain with the College of Pastoral Supervision and Psychotherapy. He has led several national workshops on the spiritual care of adolescents in independent schools.

Diane R. Wiener, PhD, MSW, director of the Syracuse University Disability Cultural Center, teaches and publishes on social justice, inclusion, pedagogy, and empowerment.